PARABLES AND CONFLICT IN THE HEBREW BIBLE

This book examines the intimate relationship between parables and conflict in the Hebrew Bible. Challenging the scholarly consensus, Jeremy Schipper argues that parables do not function as appeals to change their audience's behavior. Nor do they serve to diffuse tensions in regard to the various conflicts in which their audiences are involved. Rather, the parables help create, intensify, and justify judgments and hostile actions against their audiences. To examine how the parables accomplish these functions, this book pays particular attention to issues of genre and recent developments in genre theory, shifting the central issues in the interpretation of Hebrew Bible parables.

Jeremy Schipper is Assistant Professor of Religion (Hebrew Bible) at Temple University. He is the author of *Disability Studies and the Hebrew Bible* (2006) and co-editor of *This Abled Body: Rethinking Disabilities in Biblical Studies* (2007). Schipper has published articles in a number of scholarly journals, including *Journal of Biblical Literature*, *Journal for the Study of the Old Testament*, *Vetus Testamentum*, *Catholic Biblical Quarterly*, and *Biblical Interpretation*.

Parables and Conflict in the Hebrew Bible

JEREMY SCHIPPER
Temple University

CAMBRIDGE UNIVERSITY PRESS
Cambridge, New York, Melbourne, Madrid, Cape Town, Singapore, São Paulo, Delhi

Cambridge University Press
32 Avenue of the Americas, New York, NY 10013-2473, USA

www.cambridge.org
Information on this title: www.cambridge.org/9780521764629

© Jeremy Schipper 2009

This publication is in copyright. Subject to statutory exception
and to the provisions of relevant collective licensing agreements,
no reproduction of any part may take place without the written
permission of Cambridge University Press.

First published 2009

Printed in the United States of America

A catalog record for this publication is available from the British Library.

Library of Congress Cataloging in Publication Data

Schipper, Jeremy.
Parables and Conflict in the Hebrew Bible / Jeremy Schipper.
p. cm.
Includes bibliographical references and indexes.
ISBN 978-0-521-76462-9 (hardback : alk. paper)
1. Bible. O.T. – Parables.   2. Bible. O.T. – Criticism, interpretation, etc.   I. Title.
BS1199.P3S35   2009
221.6'6 – dc22   2009000350

ISBN 978-0-521-76462-9 hardback

Cambridge University Press has no responsibility for the persistence or
accuracy of URLs for external or third-party Internet Web sites referred to in
this publication and does not guarantee that any content on such Web sites is,
or will remain, accurate or appropriate. Information regarding prices, travel
timetables, and other factual information given in this work are correct at
the time of first printing, but Cambridge University Press does not guarantee
the accuracy of such information thereafter.

Contents

Preface		*page* ix
Abbreviations		xiii
1.	**Breaking Down Parables: Introductory Issues**	1
	The Definition of Parables and Other *Meshalim*	5
	Use of the Term Genre in This Book	7
	Did the Parables Ever Exist as Independent Narratives?	10
	The Term "Parables" and Related Terms	12
	Parables and Taunts	12
	Parables and Fables	14
	Parables and Allegories	14
	Parables and Riddles	16
	The Intensifying Function of Parables and Other *Meshalim*	18
	Overview of the Essays in Upcoming Chapters	19
2.	**Devouring Parables: Jotham's Parabolic Curse in Judges 9**	23
	Matters of Background and Genre for Jotham's Parable	24
	The Content and Objects of Jotham's Curse	30
	The Growing Conflict as the Realization of a Curse (Judges 9:23–57)	32
	Conclusions and Implications	37
3.	**Overallegorizing and Other Davidic Misinterpretations in 2 Samuel 11–12**	41
	The Genre of Nathan's Speech in 2 Samuel 12:1–4	42
	How David Overallegorizes the Parable	46
	David's Reaction Based on His Overallegorization (vv. 5–6)	49
	Nathan's Response (vv. 7–15)	52

	The Parable's Aftermath: Judgment Versus Repentance	54
	Conclusions	55
4.	**Changing Face and Saving Face: Parabolic Petitions in 2 Samuel 14**	57
	What Do Joab and the Wise Woman of Tekoa Hope to Accomplish?	58
	2 Samuel 14 and the "Petitionary Narrative" Genre	61
	The Narrative Report as the First Method of Appeal: 2 Samuel 14:5–8	63
	Additional Methods of Appeal: 2 Samuel 14:9–17	66
	Turning Faces and Saving Face: 2 Samuel 14:18–23	70
	Conclusions	72
5.	**Grasping the Conflict: Ahab's Negotiation of Conflicts and Parables in 1 Kings 20**	74
	Problems in Discerning the Function of the Petition as the Basis of the Parable	76
	The Petitionary Narrative and Issues of Mercy	79
	Ahab as Interpreter of the Conflict	83
	Ahab's Actions in Light of Syrian and Israelite Battle Plans	87
	Conclusions	91
6.	**Intellectual Weapons: The Parable's Function in 2 Kings 14 and 2 Chronicles 25**	93
	Who Provoked the Conflict in 2 Kings 14?	96
	Problems of Correspondence between the Parable and the Royal Encounter	97
	Jehoash's Parable and Ancient Near Eastern Disputation Texts	100
	The Function of the Parable in 2 Chronicles 25	105
	Conclusions and Implications: Reading Parables within the Deuteronomistic History	107
7.	**Conclusions and Implications for the Study of Hebrew Bible Parables**	111
	Isaiah 5:1–7	111

CONTENTS

Ezekiel 17:1–24	117
Conclusions	122
Notes	125
Works Cited	149
Scriptural and Extra-Biblical Texts Index	159
General Index	166

Preface

The ideas for this book began during a class discussion in an undergraduate introduction to the Bible course at Siena College in the fall of 2005. As I introduced my class to the notion of 2 Sam 12:1–4 as a juridical parable, one student asked about Joab's place in Nathan's parable. I responded by using the multivalent interpretation of the parable as I remembered it from a class I took with Larry L. Lyke at Yale Divinity School in the fall of 1997. Lyke's wonderful book on parabolic narrative, titled *King David and the Wise Woman of Tekoa*, has influenced my thinking on Hebrew Bible parables a great deal, as evidenced by the number of times I cite it in this book. Yet, when I consulted his book after that particular class, I realized that I had not remembered his interpretation correctly and that he did not actually address the place of Joab in Nathan's parable. My student's question and my misreading of Lyke got me thinking about how parables operate in the Hebrew Bible. Soon I saw the need for a serious re-evaluation of some influential scholarly notions and assumptions about genre and function in relation to Hebrew Bible parables.

My first attempt to articulate the need for re-evaluation came in a paper on 2 Sam 12:1–6 that I presented at the Society of Biblical Literature's 2006 Mid-Atlantic Regional Meeting. Further research along these lines found encouragement and support when Stephen L. Cook, F. W. "Chip" Dobbs-Allsopp, Tod Linafelt, and the rest of the region's executive board nominated the paper for the Society's 2007 Regional Scholar's Award. I would like to thank them all for their role in this project's development. I continued to work out of my understandings of individual parables in two articles: "Did David Overinterpret Nathan's Parable in 2 Samuel 12:1–6?" *JBL* 126 (2007): 383–91, and "From Petition to Parable: The Prophet's Use of Genre in 1 Kings 20:38–42," *CBQ* 71 (2009): 264–74. Portions of these articles appear respectively in chapters 3 and 5 of this book. I would like to thank the editors of *JBL* and *CBQ* for granting permission to reuse these articles in this volume.

Although I suspect my work on Nathan's parable represents the creative highpoint of this book, the book as a whole aims to reinvigorate the scholarly study of Hebrew Bible parables by providing innovative readings of selected texts and by framing these readings within established scholarly conversation. Of course, any attempt at reorienting a scholarly conversation involves interpretative risk. At points where readers do not find my specific exegetical proposals compelling, I hope that they place their concerns with such details within the larger framework of the project's overall goals. This would allow for a more robust scholarly conversation about Hebrew Bible parables than currently exists. Ultimately, my goal for this book is not simply to convince readers of isolated exegetical points. Rather, I hope this book is a catalyst for livelier scholarship on Hebrew Bible parables.

As most readers know, a very lively scholarly conversation already exists in regard to the parables of Jesus and their function. I have tried as much as possible not to let this impressive body of scholarship guide my approach to parables in the Hebrew Bible. Thus, I have kept the references to scholarship on the parables of Jesus and to those in rabbinic literature to a minimum. This does not mean that I find such scholarship unimportant or that I am unaware of it; it means that introducing it as a primary conversation partner may distract from a clear articulation of how parables function in the Hebrew Bible. Nevertheless, after I finished writing nearly the entire manuscript, C. Clifton Black suggested to me that my conclusions fit well with Jesus' parables because when Jesus addresses his parables to a specific named audience, the parables tend to accelerate tensions between him and his addressees rather than resolve conflict or change his addressees' minds on a particular matter. Along these lines, I suspect that Jesus' reference to Isa 6:9–10 when explaining why he speaks in parables (Mark 4:10–12) fits into the arguments in the book better than I first realized. Nonetheless, this disclaimer does not hurt the conclusions I reach in this book. If my conclusions find support in the Hebrew Bible, how well they resonate with the parables of Jesus or the rabbis should not invalidate them.

Unless noted otherwise, I am responsible for all biblical translations in this book. My translations follow the versification in *BHS*. To make this book more accessible to readers without knowledge of Hebrew, I employ a simplified system of Hebrew transliteration that usually follows the "general-purpose style" transliteration system in *The SBL Handbook of Style*.

Before I conclude this preface, several other scholars deserve acknowledgment for helping refine and improve my thinking about parables through conversations, emails, readings, and bibliographic recommendations. I would like to thank Hector Avalos, David Downs, Jeremy Hutton, Mark Leuchter, Patrick D. Miller, and Dennis T. Olson for their various roles in the book's production. I would also like to thank my students in my special topics course on parables at Siena College in the spring of 2007. I appreciate that in his capacity as chair of Siena's Religious Studies Department, Peter Zaas allowed me to teach this course as a visiting assistant professor. My new colleagues in Temple University's Department of Religion, chaired by Rebecca T. Alpert when I arrived and currently by Terry Rey, have provided a wonderfully supportive environment in which to complete this project. The department arranged for me to work with a superb graduate research assistant, Elizabeth V. Lawson. Beth's careful editing greatly improved the quality of the manuscript as we prepared it for publication. Of course, this book would not have come about without the enthusiastic and much-appreciated support of my editor at Cambridge University Press, Andy Beck.

I am pleased to recognize and thank two scholars who proved especially helpful throughout this project's development. My friend since graduate school, J. Blake Couey, has discussed this project with me over meals, at conferences, in phone calls, and in emails. As far as scholarly conversation partners go, the only thing better than the sharpness of Blake's input is his unfailing generosity with his time and energy.

Each page in this book, if not each sentence, shows the influence of Nyasha Junior. She helped me clarify my writing and my arguments and, most importantly, finish the book. No one has endured and supported this project as she has. She is always involved in the best of my scholarship, my thinking, and my life. As my partner in everything, academic and otherwise, Nyasha improves it all. Every day.

Finally, I would like to dedicate this book to my father, Paul Howard Schipper. This book assumes that the best way to understand how a text operates is to read it slowly and closely. As a lifelong student of the Bible, my father helped teach me the value of digging into a text. To a certain extent, this book is a product of that lesson.

Jeremy Schipper
Philadelphia
Fall 2008

Abbreviations

AB	Anchor Bible
ABD	Anchor Bible Dictionary
AJSL	*American Journal of Semitic Languages and Literature*
AnBib	Analecta biblica
ANET	*Ancient Near Eastern Texts Related to the Old Testament.* Edited by J. B. Pritchard. 3rd ed. Princeton, 1969
BASOR	*Bulletin of the American Schools of Oriental Research*
BDB	Brown, F., S. R. Driver, and C. A. Briggs. *A Hebrew and English Lexicon of the Old Testament.* Oxford, 1907
BHS	*Biblica Hebraica Stuttgartensia*
Bib	*Biblica*
BibOr	Biblica et orientalia
BRev	*Bible Review*
BT	*The Bible Translator*
BZ	*Biblische Zeitschrift*
CAD	*The Assyrian Dictionary of the Oriental Institute of the University of Chicago.* Chicago: Oriental Institute of the University of Chicago, 1956–2006.
CBQ	*Catholic Biblical Quarterly*
COS	*The Context of Scripture.* Edited by W. W. Hallo. 3 vols. Leiden: E. J. Brill, 1997–2002.
EvQ	*Evangelical Quarterly*
FOTL	Forms of the Old Testament Literature
HAR	*Hebrew Annual Review*
HSM	Harvard Semitic Monographs
HTS	Harvard Theological Studies

IBC	Interpretation: A Bible Commentary for Teaching and Preaching
ICC	International Critical Commentary
Int	*Interpretation*
JBL	*Journal of Biblical Literature*
JSOT	*Journal for the Study of the Old Testament*
JSOTSup	Journal for the Study of the Old Testament Supplement Series
KAI	*Kanaanäische und aramäische Inschriften.* H. Donner and W. Röllig. 2d ed. Wiesbaden, 1966–1969
KJV	King James Version
LHBOTS	Library of Hebrew Bible/Old Testament Studies
LXX	Septuagint
MT	Masoretic Text
NIB	*The New Interpreter's Bible.* Edited by Leander E. Keck. 12 vols. Nashville: Abingdon, 1994–2002.
NRSV	New Revised Standard Version
NT	*Novum Testamentum*
NTS	*New Testament Studies*
OBO	Orbis biblicus et orientalis
OTL	Old Testament Library
RevQ	*Revue de Qumran*
RSR	*Recherches de science religieuse*
SBLDS	Society of Biblical Literature Dissertation Series
SBLMS	Society of Biblical Literature Monograph Series
SJOT	*Scandinavian Journal of the Old Testament*
SJT	*Scottish Journal of Theology*
STDJ	*Studies on the Texts of the Desert of Judah*
Syr.	Syraic
TZ	*Theologische Zeitschrift*
Vulg.	Vulgate
VT	*Vetus Testamentum*
WBC	World Biblical Commentary
ZAW	*Zeitschrift für die alttestamentliche Wissenschaft*

1

∾

Breaking Down Parables: Introductory Issues

"[Parables in the Hebrew Bible] are not, even indirectly, appeals to be righteous. What is done is done, and now must be seen to have been done; and God's hostile action can be confidently pronounced."
  –M.D. Goulder, *Midrash and Lection in Matthew*

"[A] first step when we fail with parables would be to structure the defeat, and to chart the contours of our ignorance."
  –John J. Bonsignore, "In Parables: Teaching through Parables"

Nearly 40 years ago, if you asked a Hebrew Bible scholar to define the word "parable," he or she would have most likely replied that it is a genre designation for a type of short story and that it comes from the biblical Hebrew word *mashal* (plural form: *meshalim*). He or she would have cited the story Nathan tells to David in 2 Sam 12:1–4 or Isaiah's song of the vineyard in Isa 5:1–7 as typical examples of this parable genre. For instance, in his influential 1967 article on the so-called juridical parable genre, Uriel Simon includes these texts among his examples (he also cites 2 Sam 14:5–7; 1 Kgs 20:39–42; Jer 3:1–5).[1] Yet, in 1981, George W. Coats responds to Simon by correctly asking, "How can the story in II Samuel 12:1–4 and the song in Isaiah 5:1–7 belong to the same genre?"[2] Coats' question suggests that between the late 1960s and the early 1980s, a number of scholars had begun reconsidering how we should use the term parable (*mashal*).

In the late 1970s and early 1980s, a cluster of articles contended that we should not define a parable as designating a particular genre of narrative with its own particular generic properties. Although we may translate the Hebrew word *mashal* as parable, this same Hebrew word is also translated as song, saying, and proverb, depending on its context. This raises a problem for understanding *mashal* as a genre designation since, as Coats observes, songs, proverbs, and parables cannot all belong to the same literary genre. Thus, scholars began to question whether *mashal* serves as a genre designation because it covers such a wide variety of forms of speech.

They noted that *mashal* comes from the root *mshl*, which means similarity or comparison. Throughout the Hebrew Bible, proverbs, sayings, songs, and even statements about specific peoples and cities may all function as different types of comparisons. Scholars began to speak of *meshalim*, or comparisons, in their various forms as proverbial *meshalim*, song *meshalim*, short story *meshalim* (i.e., parables) and so forth.[3] In other words, by the early 1980s, the term parable came to describe a *function* of a short story rather than a genre of a short story. A story from any narrative genre may become a parable if a biblical character uses it to draw a comparison. Thus, nearly 30 years ago, the general scholarly consensus shifted to suggest that we should not define a *mashal* by its type or form, be it a proverb, a parable (i.e., short story), or a song. Rather, we should concentrate on its content and function.[4]

This book reflects the influence of this approach. We define parables in the Hebrew Bible as short stories from any narrative genre that function as explicit comparisons created by a biblical character rather than the reader. Biblical characters create parables by comparing a story with another situation within their immediate context. Parables are speech acts requiring both a speaker and an addressee within the biblical text.

Nonetheless, although this shift from a formal to a functional understanding of parables serves as an important methodological corrective, it does not explain fully what function(s) the parables actually serve in the Hebrew Bible. Within the prose sections of the Hebrew Bible, parables appear exclusively within stories of severe conflict, in which at least one person dies (Judges 9; 2 Samuel 12, 14; 1 Kings 20; 2 Kings 14). In its poetic sections, figures such as First Isaiah and Ezekiel employ parables when announcing a divine judgment against their addressees. Each parable in the Hebrew Bible seems to address a severe conflict in some fashion, but exactly how it does so remains open to debate among scholars.

comparisons, if they used them at all. Thus, the fact that parables do not result in a significant change of behavior among their biblical addressees requires a serious reexamination of how they function within Hebrew Bible conflicts.

In order to reexamine the function of parables, we contend that Hebrew Bible scholars must reconsider the relationship of genre and parable. For reasons explained earlier, scholarship has not focused seriously on issues of genre in the study of Hebrew Bible parables over the last few decades. This book recasts the question of how parables address conflicts in the Hebrew Bible by reconsidering the role of genre in parabolic interpretation. We argue later that the recent preference for understanding the term parable as a function instead of a genre comes partly from a recent similarly understandings of the term genre. Further attention to recent developments in genre theory may lead to a more rigorous examination of how parables function in the Hebrew Bible.

By attending to issues of genre, this book moves the study of parables in the Hebrew Bible beyond the widely held notion that they function primarily to change their addressees' ways. Instead, the parables help create, intensify, and justify judgments and hostile actions against their addressees. Speakers do this by comparing a curse, a petition, a taunt, and so on, with the addressees' current situation. This book's essays demonstrate this thesis mainly through close readings of the parables appearing in the Former Prophets as well as the conflicts that surround these parables.

In preparing for the studies of specific parables in the following chapters, this chapter addresses the definition and function of parables in the Hebrew Bible. We examine the following issues: (1) the relationship between parables (short story comparisons) and other types of comparisons in the Hebrew Bible (song comparisons, proverbial comparisons, and so on); (2) the relationship between genre and the rhetorical use(s) of parables in the context of Hebrew Bible conflicts; (3) whether the parables embedded in prose originally existed independent of their larger narrative surroundings; (4) the label parable in connection to related labels such as fables, allegories, riddles, and taunts; and (5) the rhetorical function of parables within Hebrew Bible prose. Finally, we give brief overviews of essays in the upcoming chapters.

THE DEFINITION OF PARABLES AND OTHER *MESHALIM*

Although *meshalim* may appear in a variety of forms (e.g., songs, proverbs, parables), they all evoke some type of comparison. A problem is that few biblical comparisons outside the book of Proverbs (titled *meshalim* in Hebrew) include the specific label *mashal* (only 1 Sam 10:12; 19:24; 24:14; Jer 31:39; Ezek 12:22; 17:2; 18:2; 24:3). Thus, we have difficulty trying to identify *meshalim* based on their form or label alone. Instead, we must examine the way that they function as comparisons to determine whether they qualify as *meshalim*.

Some *meshalim* contain internal comparisons. Terms such as "like" or "just as" appear within the *mashal* itself. For example, Gen 10:9 contains the saying, "Just like Nimrod who was a mighty hunter before YHWH." In this case, the saying establishes Nimrod as the model or exemplar of a great hunter. One may praise a given hunter by using this proverbial *mashal* to evoke a comparison to Nimrod.[8] We find these types of comparisons throughout the book of Proverbs, as well as in other biblical poetic literature.[9]

At other points, the *mashal* becomes the basis of a comparison that the speaker or addressee creates. In other words, instead of containing a comparison, the *mashal* brings about one.[10] For example, in 1 Sam 10:12b, the narrator notes that the question, "Is Saul also among the prophets?" became a *mashal* in Israel. For this question to function as a *mashal*, one must create a comparison between Saul's activity among the prophets and another person's activity in another circumstance. Along these lines, the short stories that serve as parabolic *meshalim* (parables) do not contain explicit comparisons. Rather, as with 1 Sam 10:12b, they become comparisons when a character relates them to what he or she understands as a corresponding situation.

Following our definition of Hebrew Bible parables based on their function as comparisons rather than their particular form of speech, a number of texts in prophetic and wisdom literature may qualify as parables depending on how broadly we define the term short story (e.g., Isa 5:1–7; 28:23–9; Ezek 15:1–28; 16:1–58; 17:1–10; 19:2–14; 23:1–29; 24:3–14; Amos 5:18; Prov 9:1–6; 24:30–32; Job 33:15–33). In addition, some texts from the Former Prophets, such as Judg 14:14 or 1 Kgs 20:11, may imply a larger narrative or a short story to function as a riddle *mashal* (Judg 14:14) or a proverbial *mashal* (1 Kgs 20:11). Nonetheless, the Hebrew Bible labels a small number of these texts as *meshalim* (only Ezek 17:1–10; 24:3–14), even though they all may function as comparisons.[11] This fact suggests that a short story does not need to carry a specific label to qualify as a parable.

Nonetheless, the problem remains that no short stories within the prose portions of the Hebrew Bible receive the label of *mashal*, although many nonbiblical stories receive this label in later rabbinic writings.[12] In fact, the sages discuss whether entire biblical books or characters, such as Job, are parables (*b. B. Bat.* 15a). Similarly, some contemporary scholars argue that we should understand the entire book of Jonah as a *mashal* even though the book does not contain this label.[13] Although it remains possible that Job or Jonah functioned to evoke a comparison in some ancient circles, one biblical character (a speaker) does not tell these stories to another biblical character (an addressee) within a larger narrative. In other words, although they contain short stories, these books do not function as parables embedded within an ongoing narrative.

To be sure, through the repetition, contrast, or juxtaposition of words and motifs, a particular text or character within a biblical book may invite the reader to draw a comparison with another text or character or even with a situation external to the biblical text. This may allow an individual text to participate in the Bible's larger discourse, or reflection, on particular matters. For example, Jotham's parable in Judges 9 may participate in the book of Judges' discourse on kingship (we will return to Judges 9 in chapter 2). In this sense, every narrative may function as a parable (cf. *Song. Rab.* 1:8).[14] Yet, only the readers of the narrative have access to this type of parabolic discourse. The biblical characters who speak or hear parables do not show an awareness that they function as characters within the Bible. Thus, they do not have the same access to the narrative comparisons that the reader may create. For purposes of the current project, not every biblical narrative qualifies as a parable. Only those narratives in which the characters may access the comparison qualify as parables. The object of the comparison remains something within the particular narrative and not something within a different text or biblical book.

In at least five cases, a character in the Hebrew Bible tells a story that a character then compares to a situation in the surrounding narrative

(Judges 9; 2 Samuel 12, 14; 1 Kings 20; 2 Kings 14 [cf. 2 Chronicles 25]). These cases form the basis for the studies in this book. These parables provide the best examples of a story told by a character that becomes a comparison created by a character within the ongoing narrative.[15] That these parables all appear within the Former Prophets is a coincidence. At the same time, their function to intensify messages of hostile divine actions fits well with certain themes emphasized throughout the Former Prophets and other popular locations for parables, such as First Isaiah and Ezekiel.

USE OF THE TERM GENRE IN THIS BOOK

In the Hebrew Bible, characters create parables by comparing narratives that invoke a variety of genres to corresponding conflicts. Throughout this book, we pay close attention to the specific genre(s) invoked by the narrative in order to understand better how the parable relates to the surrounding conflict. Thus, we should explain how we use the term genre throughout this book in more detail.

Thirty years ago, many biblical scholars approached genre as a means of classifying texts. According to this approach, a text or speech act belongs to a given genre when it exhibits some minimally required number of properties or features that make up that genre in its hypothetically pure or ideal form. The notion that genres have pure or ideal forms, which can become impure when altered, has been popular in Hebrew Bible form criticism since at least the time of Hermann Gunkel near the turn of the last century.[16] If we understand the term parable as a genre, then we would investigate whether a particular text possesses enough requisite features of the parable genre in its pure form to qualify as belonging to this genre. This type of approach influenced the study of New Testament parables in the 1970s and 1980s, whereas Hebrew Bible scholars at that time began to emphasize function over form in the study of *meshalim*. Although distinctions among some form(s) of *meshalim* remained part of the discussion (e.g., wisdom sayings from admonitions), Hebrew Bible scholars focused more on how *meshalim* "performed" within the context in which they arose.[17]

Yet, since the early 1980s, biblical scholarship has witnessed major developments in its approach to genre theory. Whereas traditional approaches to genre focus on how it classifies a text for its readers, more recent approaches focus on how it provides a rhetorical orientation for its speakers. Writing in the early part of the 21st century, Carol A. Newsom observes, "Over the past quarter century, however, genre theorists [such as Alastair Fowler or Jacques Derrida] have become increasingly dissatisfied with an approach that defines genres by means of lists of features."[18] Such theorists suggest that although the term genre may refer to various modes of speech (including curses, taunts, wisdom sayings, and so on), we should not think of the term only as a means of classifying types of speech or texts. Rather, the term genre also relates to the rhetorical orientation of a text or speech act.[19] It is a manner of speaking as much as a manner of classifying. A text or speaker within a text may employ a particular mode or genre of speech to help structure a message or convey meaning.

In long similar lines, Marvin Sweeney and Ehud Ben Zvi suggest that "[the 21st century] form-critical scholars will no longer presume that genres are static or ideal entities that never change. Rather... they will study the means by which genres are transformed to meet the needs of the particular communicative situation of the text."[20] A text or speech does not belong to a given genre simply because it exhibits some minimal requirement of elements that make up that reconstructed genre in its ideal form. Instead, as Newsom explains, "rather than referring to texts as belonging to genres one might think of texts as participating in them, invoking them, gesturing to them, playing in and out of them, and in so doing, continually changing them."[21]

Newsom's observation fits well with the way speakers in the Hebrew Bible employ various narrative genres when creating parables. Speakers of parables do not attempt to duplicate some ideal form of a narrative genre. Instead, they invoke elements that recall and use particular modes of speech to provide their parable with a particular rhetorical orientation. Thus, in comparing their addressees' situation to a narrative invested with a certain rhetorical orientation, a speaker supplies additional rhetorical intensity to his or her point(s) regarding a corresponding situation. For example, we will find that Jehoash does not duplicate an idealized form of an ancient Near Eastern disputation text in his story of the plants and animals of Lebanon. Nonetheless, he invokes or plays with elements of this genre or mode of speech to emphasize the insulting nature of his reply to Amaziah (2 Kings 14). We may appreciate more precisely the rhetorical function of the comparison by paying greater attention to the particular narrative genre or manner of speech invoked in it.

These differences in approach to the study of genre represent more of a shift in emphasis than a new understanding of genre. Multiple emphases exist in genre study, some addressing the speakers within texts and some addressing the readers of texts. Genre may provide a speaker with a way of communicating and framing his or her perception of a situation or a reality. Genre may also provide a reader with a way to classify and frame his or her perception of a text. Even though biblical scholars have traditionally emphasized a text's formal properties when studying genre throughout the last century, they have often tried to reconstruct how genres operated within a particular situation in life in the ancient Near East (setting-in-life or *Sitz im leben*). In this sense, such studies do not ignore the rhetorical functions of a genre even when trying to isolate its pure or ideal form. Thus, we should not press the distinction between form and function to contrast traditional and more recent approaches to genre within biblical scholarship. For purposes of this book, we follow recent developments that emphasize genre as a means of rhetorically orienting a biblical speaker's message(s) within the present text. Our approach to genre may not represent an entirely new use of the term as much as a renewed emphasis on its function.

Due to this emphasis on genre as providing a rhetorical orientation for a text or speech rather than as the categorization of a text or speech, the following chapters will not attempt to reconstruct a pure or ideal form of the genres under consideration. It is more important to show how the particular narratives invoke and recall particular genres in order to supply additional force to the speaker's point(s). Thus, the following chapters spend more space discussing the rhetorical use of particular genres or modes of speech in the ancient Near East than they do showing how the discussed narratives conform to an idealized structure of a genre. For example, when discussing the parables in 2 Samuel 14 and 1 Kings 20, we consider the situations in which people in the ancient Near East invoked the petitionary narrative genre instead of the precise form of the petitionary narrative. To be sure, we do not discuss genres in an ahistorical manner. Rather, we understand genres as products of particular sociohistorical settings that biblical authors would have recognized or at least imagined and tried to re-create, whether accurately or not.

Our approach to genre helps clarify the function(s) of parables in the Hebrew Bible. In the prose sections of the Hebrew Bible, none of the genres of the narratives that become parables represents modes of speech whose primary rhetorical orientation is didactic (unlike the *meshalim* in Psalm 49, 78; Job 27; 29–31).[22] Judges 9 creates a parable out of a curse, 2 Samuel 14 and 1 Kings 20 out of a petitionary narrative, and 2 Kings 14 and 2 Chronicles 25 out of a disputation text. These genres have a variety of rhetorical orientations. Since a parable is a function rather than a genre (such as a wisdom saying), we cannot argue that the rhetorical orientation of parables remains primarily didactic or aims to resolve conflicts through commonly acknowledged wisdom simply because they are parables. Nor do the parables clarify a particular lesson by way of comparison. Instead, we must examine the rhetorical orientation of the specific genre that the parable invokes to understand how it relates to the corresponding situation or addresses a conflict in the surrounding narrative.

The following chapters contain case studies that focus on close readings of selected parables. These studies focus on the particular genres invoked in the short stories that a speaker turns into parables (e.g., curses, petitions, taunts, and so forth). The study of these genres becomes central to understanding the way a parable helps communicate its speaker's message. To understand the relationship between a parable and the conflict it addresses, we must examine why and how a speaker invokes a particular genre as the basis for his or her parable and how a particular genre meets the needs of the communicative situation of a particular parable, to use Sweeney and Ben Zvi's words. Biblical scholars have paid little attention to the contribution made by the genre invoked by the short story that becomes a parable. Often, however, its speaker employs a particular genre to facilitate or intensify his or her rhetorical point(s).

DID THE PARABLES EVER EXIST AS INDEPENDENT NARRATIVES?

In the early part of the 20th century, scholars who studied parables as a genre assumed that to uncover their sociohistorical settings, we must recover their setting in life prior to their present literary location.[23] Yet this method resulted in an unfortunate focus on the question of whether these parables existed independent of the narratives that currently surround them. Such a question is immaterial for the present study because a narrative does not become a parable until one uses it as a comparison, and the formation of a comparison requires some external literary context. Nonetheless, although no manuscript evidence exists to support the original independence of the biblical parables, some scholars argue for this conclusion because both biblical and comparative ancient Near Eastern literature cite several popular proverbial *meshalim* to support their larger points (cf. Jer 31:39; Ezek 12:22; 18:2; Esarhaddon's letter to the "non-Babylonian" inhabitants of Babylon; the Mari letters).[24] Nevertheless, though these proverbial *meshalim* originally existed independent of their present literary contexts, they are not short stories that create explicit comparisons. Therefore, they do not qualify as parables.

Scholars also argue for the original independence of the parabolic materials based on the parables' general lack of correspondence with their surrounding conflicts. Nonetheless, the parables do not mirror the surrounding conflicts in terms of parallel content because the speakers rarely present them as pure allegories with a one-to-one correspondence to these conflicts. This concern over a lack of strict correspondence mistakes parables for allegories (see below).

Furthermore, Egyptian literature provides at least one parable embedded in a larger narrative that does not correspond well with the surrounding conflict it addresses. In the story of "Horus and Seth," both these gods lay claim to the deceased Osiris' throne since Horus is Osiris' son and Seth is his brother. To show Seth the illegitimacy of his claim, Horus' mother, Isis, presents Seth with a story. She encounters him incognito and claims that her husband is dead and that a stranger threatens to take her husband's livestock from her son by force. Against the stranger, Seth sides with the son in her story. Then, Isis declares that he has judged against his own actions. In other words, she turns her story into a parable that addresses the conflict in the surrounding narrative. Yet, as with several examples of Hebrew Bible parables, the details of Isis' story differ considerably from the conflict between Horus and Seth. This example from Egyptian literature suggests that parables could originate within a larger composition without a high degree of correspondence to the conflict in the surrounding narrative. We will return to this Egyptian parable in chapter 4 of this book.

In summary, other comparative ancient Near Eastern material reveals little about whether the narratives that become parables in the Hebrew Bible originated independent of larger written compositions.

THE TERM "PARABLES" AND RELATED TERMS

Parables and Taunts

When used as comparisons, taunts in the Hebrew Bible help clarify how parables relate to matters both of genre and of conflict. Throughout the Hebrew Bible, characters use taunts to mock their enemies. As with *meshalim*, taunts come in a variety of forms, such as proverbs, songs, and humiliating actions. Several examples of taunts appear in extant Sumerian literature. Sumerian "Disputation Texts" record long series of taunts and insults between various animals, plants, tools, and elements of nature (*COS* 1.180–83:575–84). In addition, a number of taunts surface in Sumerian "School Dialogues" (*COS* 1.184–85:588–92). In the Hebrew Bible, different words appear as labels for a taunt, including *sheninah* (1 Kgs 9:7; Jer 24:9), *gedupah* (Ezek 5:15), *hereppah* (Neh 6:13), and *melisah* (Hab 2:6). In addition to these labels, several passages label a taunt as a *mashal*. In other words, biblical characters may use a comparison to create a taunt. In fact, outside of wisdom literature, comparisons function primarily as taunts when the Hebrew Bible labels comparisons specifically as *meshalim* (see chapter 6). These *meshalim* function as a means of mockery and reproach.[25]

These taunt *meshalim* come in several forms. Among them, scholars have labeled several as "satirical taunt songs" (e.g., Isa 14:4; Mic 2:4; Hab 2:6; cf. Num 21:27–30).[26] These songs describe a divine judgment by inviting addressees to draw a comparison between themselves and certain images from the songs that serve as exemplars of humbled arrogance. Elsewhere, a person or a nation may become a taunt *mashal*. These persons or nations serve as objects of judgment to which others may compare themselves (cf. Deut 28:37; 1 Kgs 9:7; Jer 24:9; Ezek 14:8; Ps 44:15; 69:12; Job 17:6).[27] Throughout the Hebrew Bible, speakers use such *meshalim* as a rhetorical technique to intensify condemnations or to justify hostile actions taken against their addressees rather than as a means of conflict resolution. Many parables in the Hebrew Bible also appear to serve this function.

To better understand the connection between parables, taunts, and conflicts, we should examine the use of nonparabolic taunt *meshalim* appearing within conflicts in the Hebrew Bible's prose sections. Some scholars suggest that certain short nonnarrative comparisons such as proverbs or sayings function as diplomatic language that helps diffuse tense situations (cf. Judg 8:2, 21; 1 Sam 16:7; 24:14; 1 Kgs 20:11).[28] Fontaine comments, "The traditional saying is apt to be found operating in areas of perceived conflict . . . it is tempting to infer that there may have existed a common body of 'traditional wisdom' upon which one may draw to settle disputes, and which was known and acknowledged by all."[29] For example, in 1 Samuel 18–24, Saul tries to kill David repeatedly, despite the fact that David is his son-in-law. In 24:13–14, David confronts Saul and says to him, "May YHWH judge between me and you! May YHWH avenge me regarding you; yet my hand will not be against you. As the ancient proverb (*mashal*) says, 'From evil doers issues evil deeds'; yet my hand will not be against you." Some argue that David directs this proverb at Saul with the goal of convicting the king of his evil ways, thus resulting in a change in Saul's behavior.[30] David uses it to sum up a pattern of negative behavior, namely Saul's repeated attempts to kill David. Rather than resorting to violence, he hopes Saul will compare himself to the evil doer of the proverb and thus become convinced of his wrongdoing.

Yet proverbial or parabolic comparisons do not always settle conflicts or convince one party of the other's point(s). For example, Ahab quotes the following proverb to Ben-Hadad in 1 Kgs 20:11: "The one who puts on [armor] should not boast like one who takes off [one's armor]." Ahab may intend for Ben-Hadad to draw a comparison between himself and a foolish warrior who overestimates his capabilities. This proverb does not diffuse tensions between the two kings but rather escalates them. When a drunken Ben-Hadad hears the proverb he orders his troops to attack Ahab's city (20:12). (We examine 1 Kings 20 in detail in chapter 5 of this book.) Likewise, Saul's conviction regarding his behavior toward David appears short-lived, although he seems convicted immediately following David's speech (1 Sam 24:17–21). In 1 Sam 26:1–2, he resumes his hunt for David and appears just as intent on killing David as ever.

Thus, in the context of the surrounding narrative, David's proverbial *mashal* does not seem to diffuse tensions in the long run. One may come to the same conclusion for parabolic *meshalim* throughout the Hebrew Bible. Rhetorically, they do not function to diffuse tensions. Instead, like taunts, they promote tensions and escalate conflicts.

Parables and Fables

Instead of using the label parables, some scholars prefer to use the label fable for short stories that employ animals and plants as central characters (e.g., Gen 37:6–8; Judg 9:7–21; 2 Kgs 14:8–14 [cf. 2 Chr 25:1–28]; Ezek 17:2–10; "The Heron and the Turtle" [*COS* 1.178:571–73]; some stories in "The Teachings of Ahiqar" [*ANET* 427–30]). They reserve the label parable for the stories involving humans primarily.[31] For purposes of the present book, however, fables and parables do not describe two different types, or genres, of short stories. Rather, the term fable describes a certain type of narrative involving animals or plants (Gen 37:6–8; Judg 9:7–21) and at times their interactions with humans (2 Sam 12:1–4; Isa 5:1–7), whereas the term parable describes a function of any type of narrative, including fables (fable *meshalim*).[32] Since all of the biblical short stories treated in this book evoke a comparison by some character within the surrounding text, we label them all as parables, including those that use fables to evoke a comparison (2 Sam 12:1–4; Isa 5:1–7; Ezek 17:2–10; and so on). Most fables in ancient Near Eastern literature outside of the Hebrew Bible do not contain an explicit comparison to a situation within a larger narrative context. Therefore, they do not qualify as parables. These types of fables exist both on their own and within larger pieces of extant comparative literature. A Sumerian story entitled "The Heron and the Turtle" appears independent of a larger literary context, whereas fables involving brambles, animals, and humans appear within a largely non-prose Aramaic composition entitled, "The Teachings of Ahiqar."

Parables and Allegories

Some scholars argue for a more rigorous distinction between parables and allegories than necessary. Pure allegories are stories in which each element in the narrative represents a corresponding reality. Some claim that parables, unlike allegories, intend to illustrate just one central point.[33] Although this position was popular throughout the 20th century, recent scholarship has moved away from this distinction. Some note that we could understand the parables in several Hebrew Bible texts as allegories since we could derive a number of different lessons from them.[34] Others observe that the term *mashal* applies to both parables and allegories and that the biblical writers did not differentiate between the terms sharply.[35]

We argue that every parable requires some allegorical interpretation to accomplish its role as a comparison. The character(s) making the comparison must employ some allegorization to connect the parable and the related situation. Even if the speaker of the parable intends to communicate one point through a parable (although not necessarily so), the addressee can access that point only by creating some type of allegory. Nevertheless, since not every element in the parable may correspond to a related situation, the parable invites only limited allegorical interpretation. They do not represent pure allegories.[36] This phenomenon creates interpretative challenges since the short stories that become parables may include multiple images. A limited allegory may not draw a comparison with each image in the story. Thus, it remains possible for the speaker and the addressee to understand the story as communicating different points if they each allegorize different images in the story or if they allegorize the same image differently.[37]

In this way, a parable may function to epitomize a speaker's point, but inevitably the form of its delivery (a short story) obscures its point. For example, in Ezek 17:2–10, the prophet tells a short story that invites the house of Israel to draw a limited allegory with its own situation (vv. 9–10). The story involves two great eagles and the planting of a vine. In vv. 11–21, Ezekiel provides a commentary on his story that offers an allegorizing explanation of factors that contributed to the house of Israel's present circumstances. In this sense, Ezekiel tells the story to communicate and to epitomize certain truths about Israel's situation. Nonetheless, it remains possible for the addressees to draw different point(s) than the ones Ezekiel explains in vv. 11–21. When making their own comparison, they may allegorize different elements of the story than Ezekiel does or the same elements differently. For example, as Timothy Polk has shown, we could read the images of the "great eagles" and the "king of Babylon" (vv. 3, 12) as either Nebuchadnezzar or YHWH.[38]

Since parables function as limited allegories, we run the risk of over-allegorizing or under-allegorizing the parable and missing the speaker's intended point(s). In this sense, like other types of *meshalim*, a speaker may use a parable to help communicate a particular point regarding the addressee's circumstances, but what the parable communicates for its speaker may not seem readily apparent to its addressee.[39]

Parables and Riddles

Given the ambiguity of parables, recent scholarship has stressed their mysterious and elusive qualities.[40] We should note that Ezek 17:2 labels the short story in the following verses not only as a comparison (*mashal*) but also as a riddle (*hidah*). This is not a unique situation since the Hebrew Bible labels several other proverbs, prophecies, or songs both as comparisons (*meshalim*) and riddles (*hidot* [the plural form of *hidah*]) (e.g., Hab 2:6; Ps 49:5; 78:2; Prov 1:6; cf. Wis 8:8; Sir 39:3; 47:17). As with *meshalim*, *hidot* come in a variety of forms. Although the words *mashal* and *hidah* have two distinct meanings that we should not confuse,[41] they can both describe the multiple functions of a single proverb, song, or parable. As this book demonstrates, every parable appearing within Hebrew Bible prose sections functions as both a *hidah* and a *mashal*. In other words, the parables we examine in the following chapters function as riddling comparisons.

According to Eccl 12:9, one of the roles the sages played in the Hebrew Bible was to interpret *meshalim*. In fact, Prov 26:7 implies that a *mashal* is useless when spoken or interpreted by a fool: "The legs of the lame languish, so does a proverb in the mouth of a fool" (cf. Prov 26:9; Sir 20:20).[42] In contrast, one could demonstrate his or her wisdom by understanding *meshalim* or *hidot* properly (Prov 1:6; cf. 1 Kgs 10:1; Dan 8:23; 2 Chr 9:1; Wis 8:8; Sir 39:3; 47:17). In this sense, a speaker may tell a *mashal/hidah* to challenge the addressee to draw out the speaker's intended comparison. Often, the parables within the Hebrew Bible's prose sections serve this function. They challenge the addressee to make the proper comparison and thereby they test the addressee's discernment. In most cases, the addressee's discernment comes up short and a hostile judgment ensues.

Aside from Ezek 17:2–10 and 24:3–5, no parable in the Hebrew Bible carries an explicit label (i.e., *mashal, hidah,* or both). Thus, we should consider the possibility that the unlabeled parables studied in this book function as both *meshalim* and *hidot,* just as Ezek 17:2–10 does. This suggestion finds support when we compare the narratives that surround several parables to the one occasion in which a speaker tells an explicitly labeled riddle (*hidah*) within the Hebrew Bible's prose sections. In Judg 14:12–14, Samson challenges his Philistine wedding guests to solve the riddle he tells them. Although Samson's riddle does not qualify as a parable since it lacks a short story, the surrounding narrative contains several elements characteristic of the conflicts surrounding the parables in the Hebrew Bible's prose sections. For example, as with several of the parables, the surrounding prose context in Judges 13–16 suggests multiple interpretations that may obscure Samson's intended solution.[43] In addition, Samson's addressees are unable to interpret his riddle (cf. 2 Sam 12:1–7; 2 Kgs 14:8–11). Furthermore, rather than defuse the tensions between the Israelites and Philistines (14:3–4), Samson's riddle operates more as a taunt of the Philistines that becomes a catalyst for the intensification of their conflict (14:18b–19; cf. 15:9–11).

The contextual similarities between the larger narrative setting of Samson's riddle and those of the parables suggest that the parables possess a similar riddling quality in relation to their respective narrative settings. As seen in the following chapters, in certain cases a parable's addressees betray their mishandling of complex and ambiguous conflicts within the larger narrative through their mishandling of complex and ambiguous parables. The mishandling of the parable provides an opportunity for the speakers to pass judgment or to take a hostile action against their addressees. We see this use of a parable especially in 1 Kings 20.

In sum, we have made four related arguments regarding the relationship between parables and other terms we have covered over the last several sections. First, as with some other nonparabolic taunt *meshalim,* parables may function to promote conflict rather than resolve it. Second, parables refer to the comparative use of short stories, whereas fables refer to short stories whose central characters are animals or plants. Third, we should not distinguish too strictly between parables and allegories since all parables require limited allegorical interpretation. Fourth, although the terms comparison (which includes parables) and riddle should remain distinct, we find that often parables possess a riddling quality. We best understand the parables as riddling comparisons. Discussing parables in relation to these other terms sharpens and adds precision to this book's discussion of parables in the Hebrew Bible. Yet, before turning to an overview of the following chapters, a brief discussion of how comparisons (including parables) meet the needs of the communicative situations within Hebrew biblical contexts is in order.

THE INTENSIFYING FUNCTION OF PARABLES AND OTHER *MESHALIM*

Within the prose sections of the Hebrew Bible, parables do not function rhetorically as appeals to change one's behavior or primarily as a means of teaching a lesson or diffusing tensions. Rather, the parables intensify and even justify judgments or hostile actions against their addressees. In his book, *The Parables of Jesus in the Light of the Old Testament*, Claus Westermann comments on the function of comparisons (*meshalim*) in general in the Hebrew Bible. He writes, "The comparisons are meant to ensure that the Psalm or prophetic oracle is listened to.... Comparisons in the indictment of God intensify it, as do those in the I-lament, while comparisons in the Confession of Trust confirm what the worshipper puts his trust in, and the Praise of God are meant to exalt God."[44] Following Westermann, the comparison intensifies its speaker's larger message, be it an indictment, a lament, a confession, or so forth. For example, if the comparison appears within a didactic discourse, it helps convey a lesson, but if it appears within a larger condemnation or judgment, it helps intensify the condemnation or judgment. Westermann's observation holds true for the function of parables, since they appear in contexts of severe conflict. Often, they help justify hostile actions or judgments toward their addressees.

We are not suggesting that parables within the prose sections serve a unique or idiosyncratic function seen nowhere else in the Bible or comparative ancient literature. In addition to parables, we see this function of intensifying of hostile actions or judgments in various types of *meshalim* mentioned throughout this chapter, including satirical taunt songs, certain proverbial *meshalim* within larger narratives, and passages in which the speaker refers to humiliated peoples or cities as *meshalim*. In comparative ancient Near Eastern material, comparisons also intensify judgments and admonishments. We see this tendency in an extant parable from the Qumran writings (4Q302)[45] as well as in proverbs in an extant letter from the archives of Nineveh.[46] In other words, although the parables do not primarily aim to convince or convict the addressee of a correct position or course of behavior as some other examples of *meshalim* do (Psalm 49, 78; Job 27, 29–31), the parables share common functions with certain *meshalim* found elsewhere in the Hebrew Bible and ancient Near Eastern comparative material.

OVERVIEW OF THE ESSAYS IN UPCOMING CHAPTERS

In this chapter, we presented a definition of parables in the Hebrew Bible and considered their rhetorical function in relation to conflicts. The essays in the following chapters help flesh out this chapter's discussion. They work out the abstract conclusions presented thus far through close studies of specific parables and related conflicts. The specific conflict and communicative situation in which any given parable appears differs from the conflicts and contexts that surround other parables. In addition, the manner in which the parable intensifies a particular condemnation or justifies a hostile action depends largely on the specific conflict and the genre invoked by the parable. Thus, we must examine each parable and its context on a case-by-case basis to understand the specific dynamics involved in the surrounding conflict and how a given parable relates to that conflict.

The second chapter examines Jotham's parable and the story of Abimelech in Judges 9. This episode contains several features that will reoccur in most of the contexts of other parables within the Hebrew Bible's prose sections. Jotham's parable does not try to convict or bring about a change of behavior among its addressees. As with a number of the other parables, the conflict this parable addresses continues to intensify even after the parable. The parable does nothing to dissipate this intensification. Additionally, Jotham's story contains many multivalent images that lend themselves to various interpretations.

In Jotham's story, a group of trees offers the crown to several different types of trees. After repeated refusals, they offer it to a bramble. The bramble threatens the other trees with a curse if they make their offer in bad faith. Although an interpreter may compare any number of the images in this story to a variety of situations in the surrounding narrative, Jotham creates his comparison out of the curse with which the bramble threatens the other trees. Through this comparison, he suggests that his addressees risk receiving a curse just as the trees in his story risk receiving a curse. In other words, the parable helps Jotham intensify the declaration of his curse. His parable allows him to introduce a curse into the story, and the rest of Judges 9 works out the fulfillment of this curse. A genre that Jotham's parable invokes (a curse) becomes essential for understanding the parable's relationship with the larger conflict.

Chapter 3 explores Nathan's parable spoken to David in the context of 2 Samuel 11–12. We address matters of the parable's genre by putting it into conversation with parabolic fables and dreams in Genesis, Ezekiel, Isaiah, and Daniel. Most scholars assume that David treats the story as an actual legal case rather than as a fable. Against this general consensus, we argue that Nathan presents his short story to David not as a legal case but as a standard prophetic fable and that David recognizes it as such. The fable allows Nathan to reframe David's actions in 2 Samuel 11 as destroying familial networks. Through limited allegorical interpretation (cf. Ezekiel 17; Isaiah 5), Nathan applies a fable that focuses on the unity and subsequent destruction of a familial network to David's situation. This allows Nathan to announce both a hostile divine action against David's house and the intensification of conflict within David's familial network (12:9–15).

Chapter 4 explores the parable that the wise woman of Tekoa tells David in 2 Samuel 14. Although it seems that the parable aims to resolve David's conflict with his son Absalom, the actions in this chapter actually lead to much greater conflict in the following chapters. In this study, we find that the wise woman does not actually advise David to take a particular course of action to resolve his conflict with Absalom. Rather, following a brief review of the "petitionary narrative" genre's features, we see how the wise woman uses a fictitious petitionary narrative to repeatedly expose David's mishandling of his son Absalom's situation. The wise woman of Tekoa's use of the petitionary narrative genre allows her to frame the situation in a variety of ways, but each time David's response proves inadequate. In the end, she exposes David's inability to handle complex conflicts properly. He simply defers to Joab's plan for handling the situation.

Chapter 5 examines a parable in the midst of an international conflict involving the Israelite king Ahab and the Syrian king Ben-Hadad in 1 Kings 20. In this chapter, we examine how Ahab has interpreted situations in the previous conflict leading up to his encounter with an unnamed prophet. The prophet's parable functions to expose Ahab's inability to discern the proper course of action in a complex situation. Often, scholars identify the parable as a juridical parable because a prophet presents a petition to Ahab while disguised as a wounded solider. Yet they do not ask why the prophet creates his parable out of a petitionary narrative rather than some other genre of speech. The use of the petitionary narrative genre helps to foreground Ahab's inability to read the situation that he faces in 1 Kings 20 properly. Ahab shows mercy to his enemy Ben-Hadad, but not to his own wounded solider, who presents a petition to him. The parable helps illustrate that Ahab does not know when it is appropriate to extend mercy.

In 2 Kings 14 and 2 Chronicles 25, a parable appears once again in the context of international conflict. Here, the conflict involves Israel, Judah, and Edom. Often, scholars suggest that the Israelite king uses his parable to warn the Judean king against excessive pride and a foolish military campaign. Yet, the parable has little correspondence with the conflict in the surrounding narrative. Given that we may interpret it in a variety of ways, it seems to muddle the warning rather than clarify it. With these interpretative issues in mind, we reconsider how the parable functions rhetorically. Elsewhere in the Hebrew Bible, kings use various types of comparisons to taunt others during diplomacy efforts that often precede wars (e.g., Ahab and Ben-Hadad in 1 Kings 20). After examining taunt comparisons in biblical and other ancient Near Eastern literature in greater detail, we find that the Israelite king does not use his parable to intensify his warning. Rather, he uses it to intensify his taunt of the Judean king. Rather than defusing tensions, the parable escalates them and thereby allows its speaker to take hostile actions against its addressee in the following verses.

The final chapter expands on the conclusions of the previous chapters and examines their implications for the study of parables found elsewhere in the Hebrew Bible, especially in the Latter Prophets. Moving beyond the prose portions of the Hebrew Bible, this chapter will test this book's thesis further through a brief examination of selected parables from Ezekiel and First Isaiah. We use Isa 5:1–7 and Ezek 17:1–21 as test cases to show that this book's close studies of parables within the Hebrew Bible's prose portions shed light on the communicative situations that provoke parables in the Latter Prophets. As with their counterparts within biblical prose, these prophetic parables appear in situations of conflict and they function to intensify announcements of judgment. Furthermore, the genres invoked within these parables provide particular rhetorical orientations that add force to their prophetic announcements. This final chapter shows that the studies throughout this book have great implications for the study of parables used throughout the Hebrew Bible.

2

Devouring Parables: Jotham's Parabolic Curse in Judges 9

"The fable is used to pour scorn on Abimelech... to prepare the way for the pronouncement of Jotham's curse in v. 20."

–Barry G. Webb, *The Book of Judges: An Integrated Reading*

"It will become clear that the primary focus of the chapter is not upon kingship as such, but upon the mutual conflict between Abimelech and the men of Shechem."

–Graham S. Ogden, "Jotham's Fable: Its Structure and Function in Judges 9"

Jotham's parable in Judges 9 provides an excellent point of entry into this book's study of Hebrew Bible parables. Jotham is the lone survivor of his brother Abimelech's massacre of 70 of his siblings (v. 5). As with the parables in 2 Samuel 12 and 14, Jotham's parable addresses a conflict, specifically a murder that nearly destroys a kinship network. Yet, clearly, Jotham does not intend his parable to prompt any change of behavior among his addressees, namely the lords of Shechem. Nor does he show any concern for conflict resolution through his parable. He shows no interest in hearing how the Shechemites understand his parable. In fact, after he speaks his parable, he leaves immediately, without even giving them an opportunity to respond (v. 21).

Instead, the parable helps strengthen the judgment that Jotham calls down upon Abimelech, the house of Millo, and the lords of Shechem. By comparing their situation to the curse portion of his story, Jotham reinforces the negative judgment that his addressees face. In this chapter, we show that his parable does not resolve or dissipate the growing conflict.

Instead, his parable intensifies that conflict in the surrounding narrative. To understand this intensifying function, we must pay close attention to more than the genre of his story as a whole (a fable in vv. 7–15). More importantly, we need to examine the genre invoked by the specific part of the story from which he creates his comparison, namely the curse in v. 15. For our reading of the relationship between the parable and the larger conflict in Judges 9, we must remember that Jotham builds his parable (his comparison) specifically around the curse rather than around the other genres invoked in his story.

First, we discuss the literary context and genre of Jotham's speech and note how scholars have used issues of context and genre to comment on the parable's function within Judges 9. Second, we consider the content of Jotham's parabolic curse and the object against which he actually directs this curse. Third, we examine how Jotham's choice to turn a curse into a parable helps intensify the conflict in the surrounding narrative and bring a negative judgment upon his addressees. As the narrative in Judges 9 works out the implications of this judgment and the realization of the curse that the parable helps to declare, we see an increase in hostility and destruction among its addressees instead of an increase in insight or perspective. Fourth, building on this reading of Judges 9, we conclude this chapter with observations about ways that this chapter sets the tone for the book's interpretations of the parables treated in the following chapters.

MATTERS OF BACKGROUND AND GENRE FOR JOTHAM'S PARABLE

The opening verses of Judges 9 narrate Abimelech's rise to power. Abimelech is one of over 70 of Gideon's sons and is related to the Shechemites through his mother. Reminding the Shechemites of this family connection, he asks them whether it is better for one person to rule over them or 70 people (i.e., his brothers). The Shechemites agree to follow Abimelech and note that "he is our brother" (v. 3b). Then, Abimelech hires a gang of thugs with funds provided to him by the Shechemites and slaughters 70 of Gideon's other sons, who are also Abimelech's brothers, on a single stone (*'eben*; v. 5). Dennis T. Olson observes the irony of this slaughter. He writes, "The Shechemites, who felt secure in their support of Abimelech because, 'he is our brother,' should have learned from this massacre how Abimelech treats his 'brothers.' Indeed, Abimelech will eventually attack and kill all his Shechemite 'brothers' just as he had killed his brothers who were the sons of Gideon (vv. 3, 34–49, 57)."[1]

Abimelech's youngest brother, Jotham, escapes the massacre and goes into hiding. When Jotham hears that the Shechemites and the house of Millo made his murderous brother their king at the oak (*'elon*) of the pillar at Shechem, he ascends Mount Gerizim and tells a fable (a narrative that involves animals or plants, see chapter 1) that he compares (applies parabolically) to Abimelech's rise to power.

From atop Mount Gerizim, Jotham tells the following fable:

7b. Listen to me, Lords of Shechem, so that God may listen to you! 8. The trees went forth to anoint a king over themselves. They said to the olive tree, "Reign over us." 9. But the olive tree said to them, "Should I bring to a halt my fatness in which gods and mortals find honor and go wave over the trees?" 10. The trees said to the fig tree, "Go, you reign over us." 11. But the fig tree said to them, "Should I bring to a halt my sweetness and good fruit and go wave over the trees?" 12. The trees said to the vine, "Go, you reign over us." 13. But the vine said to them, "Should I bring to a halt my new wine that makes gods and mortals happy and go wave over the trees?" 14. All of the trees said to the bramble, "Go, you reign over us." 15. The bramble said to the trees, "If in truth you are anointing me as king over you, come, seek refuge in my shade. But if not, may fire come out from the bramble and devour the cedars of Lebanon."

In the verses that follow, Jotham creates a parable out of this fable by comparing it to the relationship between his brother Abimelech and the Shechemites and the house of Millo.

16. Now therefore, if you acted in truth and integrity when you made Abimelech king and if you acted well with Jerubbaal [Gideon] and his house and if according to the dealing of his hand you did to him. 17. (After all, my father fought for you and risked his life and rescued you from the hand of Midian, 18. but you rose up against the house of my father today and killed his sons, seventy men upon one stone. You made Abimelech son of his maidservant king over the lords of Shechem because he is your brother.) 19. If you acted in truth and integrity with Jerubbaal and his house this day, be happy with Abimelech and may he be happy with you. 20. But if not, may fire come out from Abimelech and devour the lords of Shechem and the house of

Millo and may fire come out from the lords of Shechem and the house of Millo and devour Abimelech.

After Jotham finishes his speech, he flees in fear of Abimelech. Unlike the parables in Samuel and Kings (see the following studies in this book), the reader does not have access to the reactions of the lords of Shechem to Jotham's parable. His refusal to wait for their response suggests that Jotham does not intend his parable to lead to any change of behavior on his addressees' part or to promote conflict resolution. This leaves the question of the parable's function unanswered. Thus, many scholars have attempted to discern its function by (1) exploring its attitude toward kingship or (2) examining its literary genre.

When read within the larger context of the book of Judges, scholars have debated whether Jotham's parable functions as a condemnation of the institution of kingship. Martin Buber referred to the parable as "the strongest anti-monarchical poem of world literature."[2] On the other hand, Eugene H. Maly reads it as "clearly not directed against kingship itself, but against those who refused, for insufficient reasons, the burden of lordship [represented by the olive tree, fig tree, and vine]."[3] In considering this debate, Larry L. Lyke notes correctly that the parable "contains such a mixed message that either of these positions represents a reasonable and internally consistent reading."[4]

Expanding on Lyke's observation, we argue that we find mixed messages because Jotham does not intend to present a clear message about the merits of monarchy or any other institution through his parable. It does not function as a lesson regarding the proper form of leadership for his addressees. Instead, it functions as a condemnation of the choices that his addressees have already made. To be sure, the parable may participate in the book of Judges' larger discourse on the merits of various institutions of leadership. Yet only the readers of the book have access to this discourse. The addressees of Jotham's parable, who are characters within the book, do not have the same access. Scholarly discussions of Jotham's position on the merits of a monarchical system may help the reader understand larger themes in the book of Judges as a whole, but they are not helpful for understanding how his parable addresses the immediate conflict in Judges 9.

Other scholars have spent much time discussing the genre(s) of Jotham's speech as another way of getting at its function within the conflict of Judges 9. Although some label Jotham's story in vv. 8–15 as a parable, allegory, or apologue, the majority of scholars prefer to see it as a fable since it focuses on personified plants rather than humans.[5] Many argue that this fable originally existed independent of its present literary context. Although no textual evidence exists to support this argument, several stories involving talking plants and trees, including brambles, exist in comparative ancient Near Eastern literature.[6] Unlike Jotham's fable, most of these parallels do not appear as part of a larger narrative. Rather, they often appear as freestanding compositions or appear among collections of wisdom sayings. It is possible that the author of Judges 9 could have incorporated a popular fable into his or her telling of Abimelech's rise to power. Consider the following example from the Assyrian "Sayings of Ahiqar" (7th century BCE): "A thorn bush [or bramble] asked a pomegranate tree, 'Why so many thorns to protect so little fruit?' The pomegranate tree said, 'Why so many thorns to protect no fruit at all'?"[7]

Furthermore, the claim for the original independence of Jotham's fable rests partly on the fact that Jotham does not create a pure allegory with his parable.[8] Rather, major differences exist between Jotham's fable and the conflict in the surrounding narrative. For example, since at least the time of Redaq, some interpreters have suggested that the first three trees that refuse the offer of kingship (9:8–13) may represent Gideon, his son, and his grandson, whereas the bramble represents Abimelech.[9] In 8:22, the Israelites request that Gideon, his son, and grandson rule over them with vocabulary similar to that of the trees in the fable. Like the first three trees in the fable, Gideon refuses their request (8:23). In the fable, however, the trees approach the bramble and offer it the kingship (9:14), but in the surrounding narrative, Abimelech approaches the Shechemites and convinces them to make him king (9:2).[10] This suggests to some scholars that Jotham's fable does not match the conflict it addresses well enough to support the idea that it was originally part of Judges 9.[11]

Convinced of the original independence of the fable in vv. 8–15, some scholars have concentrated on its genre(s) to better understand Jotham's rhetorical intention in incorporating this fable into his speech. For example, Barnabas Lindars has argued for both the original independence of Jotham's story and the independence of v. 15b from the rest of the story. Although we will not review most of the scholarly discussion of the fable's genre because such discussion remains largely immaterial to our present study, Lindars' argument merits special attention for our reading of Judges 9 because he focuses on the verse from which Jotham creates his parable (his comparison). Lindars sees vv. 8–14 as an originally independent fable and v. 15 as an addition by the narrator to serve his or her narrative goals of connecting the fable to the curse that is developed further in vv. 21–57.

For Lindars, v. 15b ("may fire come out from the bramble and devour the cedars of Lebanon") represents a "separate proverb" that means, "A small spark can kindle a huge blaze."[12] He suggests that the proverb allows the narrator to continue the fable's arboreal imagery. In addition, it allows him or her to introduce a curse into the larger narrative by transforming the proverb into the conditional statements of v. 15. He writes, "It is this proverb which is the most important thing from the narrator's point of view, because it can be used as a curse, and the whole narration turns on the fulfillment of the curse."[13] Although Lindars does not do so, we should note that the root *qll* is often translated as "curse" (Judg 9:27, 57; cf. Deuteronomy 27–29) and that this root can appear as a parallel for the root *mshl*, which is often translated as proverb (cf. Jer 24:9). In other words, proverbs may serve as curses elsewhere in the Hebrew Bible.

Nevertheless, much of Lindars' reconstruction of the prehistory of vv. 8–15 remains overly speculative. As seen throughout this book, parables in the Hebrew Bible help intensify their speakers' point(s) by comparing the addressees' present situation to a narrative involving some equally complex, although not exactly parallel, conflict. In the case of Judges 9, Jotham's comparison of the Shechemites to the trees reinforces the notion that both parties have mishandled a complex situation. The parable does not have to represent a pure allegory to perform this function. Therefore, the tensions that Lindars and other scholars perceive between these verses and their present literary context do not necessarily provide evidence of the original independence of these verses. Instead, such tensions represent a standard feature of all Hebrew Bible parables and of some ancient Near Eastern comparative literature that contain parables embedded in larger stories of conflict (cf. the Egyptian story "Horus and Seth" discussed in chapters 1 and 4 of this book). Furthermore, as with these other parables, Jotham's parable appears very integrated in the surrounding narrative through common vocabulary, motifs, and themes (we will return to a number of these commonalities later).[14] Thus, we may explain perceived tensions between the parable and the surrounding narrative without appeals to redactional speculations.

Having stated this qualification about his redactional conclusions, Lindars' work helps focus our attention onto the central status of the curse in the parable. Curses represented a well-known and recognizable speech genre in ancient Near Eastern cultures. Many examples of curses remain extant.[15] The curse is the one element of the story from which Jotham creates a direct comparison with the Shechemites' current situation. He compares the bramble's curse of the trees in v. 15b ("But if not, may fire come out from the bramble and devour the cedars of Lebanon") to his curse of the lords of Shechem, the house of Millo, and Abimelech in v. 20 ("But if not, may fire come out from Abimelech and devour the lords of Shechem and the house of Millo and may fire come out from the lords of Shechem and the house of Millo and devour Abimelech"). In other words, the curse is the element within the fable that he turns into a parable. As a parable, Jotham's fable helps introduce and intensify the curse against the Shechemites, the house of Millo, and Abimelech's relationship.

The narrative framework of Jotham's speech draws explicit attention to the curse in his speech. He delivers his speech from on top of Mount Gerizim. The Hebrew Bible associates Mount Gerizim and Mount Ebal with places where Moses and Joshua proclaim blessings and curses (*qll*) on the Israelites (Deut 11:19; 27:12; Josh 8:33). By setting his speech on Mount Gerizim, the narrative connects his speech to these traditions of cursing and blessing people.[16] Jotham offers his addressees both a blessing (v. 19) and a curse (v. 20).

Although Jotham sets up both vv. 16 and 20 as conditional statements, he does not present the curse as a warning against acting in bad faith or as a motivation to do otherwise in the future. Clearly, he sees the damage as already done. He rehearses the Shechemites' behavior toward the house of his father Gideon in v. 18. He makes a point of noting that they killed 70 of Gideon's sons upon one stone, even though Gideon risked his life to save them. Their behavior would not qualify as acting in good faith. Jotham's speech does not warn or motivate. Instead, it aims to condemn their previous actions. The conditional statements simply add rhetorical force to his negative judgment. As with his drawn out story of the trees searching for a king, taking the time to review the Shechemites' actions in detail in v. 18 allows Jotham to intensify his condemnation. The conditional presentation of his curse does not present hope for the parties facing the curse.[17] Rather, as with its comparison to the bramble's curse, it highlights the curse itself.

Furthermore, after both the Shechemites and Abimelech die, vv. 56–57 state, "God returned the evil that Abimelech did to his father in regards to killing his seventy brothers. 57. God returned the evil of the people of Shechem on their heads. The curse (*qll*) of Jotham son of Jerubbaal [Gideon] came on them." Rather than labeling his speech as a warning, allegory, or apologue, the biblical narrative labels it a "curse." As Jan P. Fokkelman writes, "The narrator assigns a genre name to Jotham's speech afterward, in the line that points out the downfall of Shechem and Abimelech as the fulfillment of 'Jotham's curse' (v. 57b)."[18] In other words, the biblical text views the genre of the speech from which Jotham creates his parable (his comparison) as a curse. The narrative not only sets his speech in a geographic location associated with blessings and curses, it also explicitly identifies it as a curse. These narrative techniques help the curse portion become the emphasis of Jotham's speech regarding the surrounding conflict.

To summarize, regardless of whether Jotham uses a preexisting fable, we should take seriously the fact that the biblical text presents Jotham's speech as a curse. The curse becomes a central aspect of Judges 9. The slow, drawn out pace of the story of the trees culminating in the bramble's curse and then its comparison to the curse against Jotham's addressees adds rhetorical intensity to Jotham's curse in v. 20. We see this technique of highlighting the importance of a moment or event through a slowed down, highly repetitive, narrative pace elsewhere in Biblical Hebrew prose (e.g., Genesis 22; 2 Kings 3).

THE CONTENT AND OBJECTS OF JOTHAM'S CURSE

Once we identify the parable's genre as a curse, we should ask why Jotham uses a curse as the basis for his parable. To appreciate how the curse functions within the larger conflict in Judges 9, we should have a firm grasp on the content and objects of the curse. Although Jotham speaks to the lords of Shechem according to v. 7b, his curse does not concern them alone. Rather, it involves the *relationship* between the lords of Shechem, the house of Millo, and Abimelech. In v. 19, Jotham calls for each party to "be happy" with one another if they have acted with integrity. At best, they should accept the relationship they have entered. They should live with the consequences of their actions. Yet, in the following verse, he curses this new relationship. According to v. 20, the curse calls for fire from each party to come out and devour the other party. Ogden observes that "both parties act upon one another. The men of Shechem and Abimelech are to 'rejoice in' one another, meaning they each will destroy the other.... The mutual destruction of Abimelech and the people of Shechem is the 'curse' (v. 57) which Jotham calls down. Vv. 26–55 demonstrates the curse's outworking."[19]

Expanding on this interpretation, we should note that Jotham does not aim his curse at any one of these parties alone. Rather, he curses the relationship between these parties. According to vv. 23–24, God attacks this relationship. As the narrative explains, "God sent an evil spirit between Abimelech and the lords of Shechem. The lords of Shechem dealt faithlessly with Abimelech so that the violence against the 70 sons of Jerubbaal [Gideon] and their blood would be set upon Abimelech, their brother who killed them and upon the lords of Shechem who made strong his hand in order to kill his brothers." Whereas elsewhere in the book of Judges a divine spirit tends to come upon an individual (cf. 3:10; 6:34; 11:29; 14:6, 19; 15:14, 19; 16:9), in this case, a divine spirit influences the relationship "between" peoples.[20] The remainder of Judges 9 narrates the way in which this divinely corrupted relationship results in the mutual destruction of Abimelech, the house of Millo, and the Shechemites.

We may read the divine action in vv. 23–24 as connected to Jotham's parable. In the speech's opening, Jotham informs the lords of Shechem that he speaks to them so that "God may listen to you!" (v. 7b). In other words, God will hear Jotham's case against the lords of Shechem. Thus, v. 7b sets this divine attack in the context of Jotham's parable against the relationship between Abimelech, the house of Millo, and the Shechemites. Jotham's parable helps justify God's attack. It declares, and possibly even evokes, hostile divine actions against an ill-conceived relationship.[21] The divine actions following Jotham's parable provide additional evidence that the parable does not intend to introduce a change of mindset among the Shechemites but a hostile action from God. Nor does it help resolve conflicts over leadership and within kinship relations that run throughout Judges 9. Instead, the parable helps provoke further and more severe conflict through God's hostile actions in the last half of Judges 9.

THE GROWING CONFLICT AS THE REALIZATION OF A CURSE (JUDGES 9:23–57)

By employing several of the parable's images in its narration of the fatal conflict between Abimelech and the house of Millo and the Shechemites, the last half of Judges 9 underscores the way the parable reinforces the curse. To support this point, this section examines details of the conflict between Abimelech and his opponents in the wake of Jotham's parable. We see the effects of the evil spirit beginning in v. 25, when Abimelech learns that the lords of Shechem have set ambushes for him in the mountaintops. Although this suggests trouble on the horizon, the narrative does not record Abimelech's reaction. Instead, it moves to the arrival in Shechem of a man named Gaal and his household (v. 26). The Shechemites put their trust in him even though the text does not clarify Gaal's relationship to them. Nevertheless, as with Abimelech before him, Gaal stresses his relationship to Shechem. He includes himself within their ranks through his repeated use of the pronoun we when speaking to the lords of Shechem (v. 28).[22] Here, the people, presumably Gaal's household and the Shechemites, curse (*qll*) Abimelech. The text records the content of Gaal's curse of Abimelech in vv. 28–29:

Gaal the son of Ebed said, "Who is Abimelech and who is Shechem that we should serve him? Did not the son of Jerubbaal [Abimelech] and Zebul his deputy serve the people of Hamor, the father of Shechem? So why should we serve him? 29. If only this people were given into my hand, I would remove Abimelech. He said to Abimelech, "Increase your army and come out!"

Like Abimelech, Gaal appeals to them to make him their leader. He claims that he would remove Abimelech from power. Once again, a bid for power over Shechem involves the violent removal of anyone with opposing claims to leadership (cf. v. 5).[23] Clearly, his curse intends to provoke further conflict by drawing Abimelech into a military confrontation. This strategy works well. When Zebul hears word of Gaal's curse, he becomes enraged and informs Abimelech that Gaal and his household are turning the Shechemites against him. He advises Abimelech to set an ambush against the city at night and make a raid on it in the morning (vv. 30–33). In v. 34, Abimelech enacts Zebul's plan.

We should note that, as with Jotham's parabolic curse, Gaal's curse fuels the growing conflict. Both curses contribute to the increase in verbal sparring that becomes a catalyst for an extremely bloody war in the last half of Judges 9. This point surfaces most clearly during Gaal's and Zebul's exchange in vv. 35–39, not only in what they say but in the imagery they use.

Standing at the city gate, Gaal spots Abimelech's army coming out of its ambush. He says to Zebul, "Look! People are descending from the tops of the mountains" (v. 36a). Zebul responds with a lie when he claims that "you are seeing the shadows (*tsel*) of the mountains that are like people" (v. 36b). Zebul's use of "shadow" (*tsel*) to cover up the advance of Abimelech's troops picks up on the bramble's (Abimelech's) use of the same word to describe the "refuge" that his "shade" (*tsel*) would provide to the other trees (the Shechemites) in v. 15. It is ironic that, in the end, shade/shadows do not describe any refuge Abimelech provides for the Shechemites. After all, the bramble seems too small to provide real shade for all the tall cedars of Lebanon. Rather, shade/shadows describe Abimelech's forces sent to destroy the Shechemites instead of protecting them.

Gaal does not believe Zebul's attempt to dismiss the advancing army as mere shadows. In v. 37, he insists that the shadows are people coming down in two companies – one from Tabbur-erez, and one from Elon-meonenim ("the oak [*'elon*] of Meonenim"). Gaal's use of *'elon* continues the arboreal imagery that runs throughout Judges 9, especially in Jotham's parable. In v. 6, the "oak" (*'elon*) of the pillar of Shechem is the location where the Shechemites and the house of Millo make Abimelech their king. Yet, in v. 37, the "oak" (*'elon*) of Meonenim is the location from which some of Abimelech's troops advance against the Shechemites. As with the shade/shadow imagery, the repetition of this "oak" image helps signal the change in the relationship between these parties. As the conflict builds in the wake of Jotham's parable, we see that the narrative continues to employ arboreal imagery to articulate the deadly breakdown of the relationship between Abimelech, the Shechemites, and the house of Millo.

After Gaal insists that people are advancing toward them, Zebul turns on him and taunts him. In v. 38, he says to Gaal, "Where is your mouth now, that you said, 'Who is Abimelech that we should serve him?' Isn't this the people that you despised? Go out please and fight against him." Zebul calls Gaal to back up his previously stated curse against Abimelech. He goes as far as quoting Gaal's curse back to him, although his reference is inexact. Zebul continues the verbal sparring that began with Jotham's parable earlier in the chapter. This sparring promotes tensions until they reach a boiling point. (Similar phenomena occur in 1 Kings 20 and 2 Kings 14, as seen in chapters 5 and 6 of this book.) Following Zebul's mockery of him, Gaal leads his troops into battle against Abimelech, but Abimelech defeats him soundly and Zebul expels them from Shechem (vv. 39–41).

Abimelech's defeat of Gaal, however, does not satisfy him. The next day, he sets an ambush for the people of Shechem who had come out of the city into the fields. He kills all of these people in the fields (vv. 43–44). Then he turns his attention to the city itself and destroys it. He launches a day-long campaign in which he kills everyone in the city, razes the city, and salts the ground so that nothing can grow there again (cf. Deut 29:22).

When the lords of Shechem hear what Abimelech has done, they flee to the stronghold of the house of El-berith. When Abimelech learns of their location, he leads his troops to nearby Mount Zalmon. In v. 48, the narrative slows its pace when it recounts how Abimelech cuts off portions of trees. "Abimelech went up Mount Zalmon, he and all the people that were with him. He took an axe in his hand and cut off a branch of trees, lifted it, and set it upon his shoulder (*shekem*). He said to the people that were with him, 'What you saw that I have done, quickly do likewise'." As the narrative reaches its climactic moment, it returns to its arboreal imagery. This imagery focuses the reader's attention on Abimelech's use of his axe against a group of trees, an image that functioned as a cipher for the lords of Shechem in Jotham's parable. This verse hints at the association of the trees and the Shechemites in Jotham's parable through a play on words. The name "Shechem" (*shekem*) sounds very similar to the word "shoulder" (*shekem*), the place where Abimelech sets the now-dead tree branches.

Abimelech's cutting of the trees near Shechem is more than a symbolic fulfillment of Jotham's parable. He not only attacks the metaphorical representations of the lords of Shechem. In v. 49, he uses the tree branches to start a fire that burns the stronghold where the actual lords of Shechem had fled. The narrative reports that all the people in the stronghold died in the fire, "about one thousand men and women." Lyke captures the irony of this situation when he writes, "Verses 48–49 describe Abimelech cutting the branches from the trees [*shobat 'etsim*] for fuel to burn the Shechemites. This imagery is fascinating because the 'trees', as ciphers for the Shechemites, supply the fuel for their own demise."[24] The use of arboreal imagery in Jotham's parable contributes rhetorical force to the fulfillment of his curse in a way that would be lacking if he had simply delivered his curse without comparing it to the curse in the accompanying fable.

The fire that destroys the lords of Shechem, however, creates a far less subtle connection with Jotham's parable. Jotham created his parable through a comparison between the bramble's call for fire to come forth from the bramble to destroy the cedars of Lebanon and Jotham's own call for fire to come forth from Abimelech to destroy the Shechemites and the house of Millo (vv. 15, 20). Although the house of Millo does not appear in this episode,[25] Abimelech's burning of the Shechemites provides a close fulfillment of Jotham's curse on the relationship between these parties.

Following his brutal attack on the Shechemites, Abimelech launches a campaign against the city of Thebez. To this point, Thebez has not appeared in the story and has had no direct involvement in the prior conflict. Abimelech seems to be out of control. As Olson observes, "One senses that Abimelech is randomly slaughtering people for no apparent reason."[26] The only discernable connection between Shechem and Thebez lies in the fact that both cities have a tower. After Abimelech conquers Thebez, all of the men, women, and lords of the city flee to the tower, shut themselves in it, and go up to the tower's roof (v. 51). Abimelech advances toward the tower to burn it just as he had burned the stronghold at Shechem (v. 52). Yet this time his attempt to burn down a tower is thwarted. According to v. 53, "one woman threw an upper millstone upon Abimelech's head and crushed his skull."

The report of this near fatal blow contains a number of images and motifs that recall Jotham's parable. Although the word for "millstone" (*pelah*) in v. 53 is different from the word for "stone" (*'eben*) in vv. 4 and 18, all three verses note the involvement of some type of rock in the deaths of Abimelech and his brothers. Abimelech had 70 of his brothers killed on one stone (vv. 4, 18), and now one woman drops a stone on his head (v. 53).[27] We should note that "one" woman drops the stone since this number appears in reference to (1) Abimelech's suggestion to the Shechemites that "one" person (i.e., him) rather than 70 persons should rule over them; (2) the "one" stone upon which Abimelech kills his brothers; and (3) the "one" company of troops that he sends from Elon-meonenim to attack Gaal in v. 37.[28] Whereas previously the number "one" appears in Abimelech's campaigns to eliminate others, here it appears in the woman's attempt to eliminate him.

Furthermore, that the narrative specifies that the stone lands on Abimelech's "head" (*ro'sh*) connects this verse to the gradual breakdown of the relationship that Jotham curses earlier in the chapter. Previously, the narrative used the word *ro'sh* to refer both to mountaintops and Abimelech's military companies.[29] From the "top" (*ro'sh*) of Mount Gerizim, Jotham delivers his parabolic curse. In the wake of this curse, mountaintops are where the Shechemites set ambushes for Abimelech (v. 25) and the place from which Abimelech's troops descend upon Shechem (v. 36). Throughout Judges 9, military companies refer to Abimelech's troops who ambush and massacre the Shechemites (vv. 34, 37, 43, 44).

The final use of *ro'sh* within Judges 9 refers to the Shechemites' heads. Verses 56–57 read, "God returned the evil that Abimelech did to his father in regards to killing his seventy brothers. 57. God returned the evil of the people of Shechem on their heads (*ro'sh*). The curse (*qll*) of Jotham son of Jerubbaal [Gideon] came on them." In vv. 53 and 57, the narrative uses the word *ro'sh* in connection with the unpleasant fates of both Abimelech and the Shechemites' heads – both sides of the cursed relationship. The use of *ro'sh* links a handful of verses that help articulate the destruction of the relationship, which was what Jotham had declared from "atop" (*ro'sh*) Mount Gerizim. The vocabulary and imagery of vv. 53 and 56–57 strengthen the link between Jotham's curse and the fate of the cursed relationship.

Between vv. 53 and 56, Abimelech attempts to cover up the circumstances of his demise. Before he dies, he instructs his armor bearer, "Draw your sword and kill me, lest they say about me, 'A woman killed him'" (v. 54a). His armor bearer follows his command and strikes him dead. Had Abimelech's plan worked, the story of his death would not be remembered. This would sever the ironic connection between the fatal blow to his head via one woman with a stone and Jotham's condemnation of his slaughter of his 70 brothers on one stone from atop Mount Gerizim. Nevertheless, despite Abimelech's final command, the narrative of Judges 9 assures that this connection will be remembered. In fact, the only other biblical reference to this Abimelech outside of Judg 8:23–10:1 occurs when King David recalls that he was killed by a woman who dropped a millstone upon him (2 Sam 11:22; cf. chapter 3 of this book). David never mentions that Abimelech's armor bearer struck him down. Abimelech proves unable to revise his fate or to present it as anything less than the outcome of Jotham's curse (v. 56). Judges 9:23–57 work out the implications of Jotham's parabolic curse through a series of ironic connections leading to Abimelech and the Shechemites' mutual destruction.

CONCLUSIONS AND IMPLICATIONS

We began this chapter by observing that Jotham's parable provides an excellent point of entry into the study of parables in the Hebrew Bible. We found that Jotham shows little concern that his addressees gain perspective and change their ways after hearing it. Rather, he uses his parable to strengthen a curse against the relationship that led to the massacre of his 70 brothers. Not every element of the fable of the bramble's curse of the trees has a direct parallel to Abimelech's conflict in the surrounding narrative. Yet, the fable adds force to Jotham's curse since it introduces a curse into the arboreal imagery that runs throughout the chapter's narration of Abimelech's rise and fall. The fable that becomes a parable allows Jotham's curse to connect with the surrounding conflict through both its content and its imagery.

Our focus on the centrality of the curse as key to understanding how the parable addresses the larger conflict in Judges 9 does not represent a significant break with previous conclusions of certain scholars. As seen throughout this chapter, a number of them argue that Jotham's parable aims to condemn his addressees instead of instructing them (cf. the epigraphs for this chapter). Nevertheless, we should reinforce this point because it holds true for the rest of the parables we will examine in upcoming chapters.

Another reason exists for focusing on how Jotham uses the bramble's curse to create his parable. This focus highlights the importance of the particular invoked genre (in this case, a curse) that serves as the basis for understanding how the comparison addresses the surrounding conflict. In the case of Judges 9, it seems obvious that Jotham's parable would not have the same effect if he created his parable from a narrative that did not involve a curse. In other cases, however, the impact of a genre invoked in a parabolized narrative may seem less than obvious (e.g., 2 Samuel 14 or 1 Kings 20). Yet, as with the curse in Judges 9, recognizing the impact of the invoked genre in subsequent parables remains essential for understanding the relationship between a given parable and its surrounding conflict in the chapters to come. Thus, we have emphasized the more obvious use of a genre in Jotham's parable to focus our attention on the importance of the genres used to create the parables studied throughout this book.

We have also emphasized the fact that Jotham's parable addresses a severe conflict within its surrounding narrative. This feature sets the tone for the use of parables throughout the Hebrew Bible. Furthermore, the murderous conflict in Judges 9 threatens to destroy a kinship network.[30] Although this may be a coincidence, parables in 2 Samuel also address murderous conflicts that threaten kinship networks. As in Judges 9, the conflicts that provoke parables throughout the Hebrew Bible are much more severe than mere squabbles. At minimum, someone always meets an untimely demise. In fact, in a number of cases, they involve multiple killings.

Although Judges 9 shares several notable features with the literary contexts of other parables in Hebrew Bible prose, important differences remain. One key difference between Jotham's parable and the parables studied in the following chapters is that we do not have access to the Shechemites' reaction to Jotham's parable, whereas we do have access to the addressees' reactions in a number of other parables. On the surface, this seems to provide us with a window into the mindset of the parable's addressee.

Nonetheless, such recorded reactions give us access only to the addressees' words and external behavior. The characters' motivations or mindset behind their reactions are still a matter of speculation. For example, even though the text records King David's reactions to parables in 2 Samuel 12 and 14, we cannot discern his mindset in these cases with any more certainty than we can discern the Shechemites' mindset in Judges 9. For that matter, we could make the same claim about the speakers of parables' mindsets. What would inspire a character to speak in parables or create parables out of particular genres of speech? We face the dilemma that any conclusions about a character's motivations remain speculative. Nevertheless, some speculation is necessary if we want to arrive at any interpretation of the text at all.

Unlike in Judges 9, the speakers and addressees of parables in the following studies interact more directly with the parable itself. For this reason, our readings of the parables in the following chapters require a greater amount of acknowledged speculation as we attempt to uncover subtexts beneath the terse exchanges between parable speakers and their addressees. At best, we should interpret a character's motives in a way that provides continuity with that character's words and actions elsewhere in the text. While recognizing that our interpretations do not represent the only way to read a given character's motivations, we aim to provide interpretations that are both compelling and consistent with characters' speech and behavior in the surrounding narrative.

Although we cannot make definitive statements about the characters' mindsets, we do have a good picture of how well the addressees discern the parables and the larger conflicts that confront them. In a word, the addressees fail repeatedly to understand either one very well. The parables further illustrate and reinforce the incompetence of the addressees in this regard. Once again, Judges 9 sets the tone for the following studies. From the beginning of Judges 9 on, the Shechemites make a series of poor choices that call into question their ability to manage or resolve the complex conflict that involves them. Even though we do not know how they understand Jotham's parable, like the trees that serve as a cipher for them the Shechemites demonstrate poor judgment in choosing their leaders.

This lack of judgment sets a precedent for the addressees of subsequent parables. Other Hebrew Bible parables continue to expose failure rather than provide insight, although each one does so in a different way. For example, while the Shechemites offer no interpretation of Jotham's parable in Judges 9, David offers an overinterpretation of Nathan's parable in 2 Samuel 12. Both reactions contribute to a series of disastrous consequences for each party. To return to the epigraph of chapter 1, as characters engage parables more directly, we have greater opportunities to structure the characters' defeat, and to chart the contours of their ignorance. The following chapter shows how a close study of David's engagement with Nathan's parable in 2 Samuel 11–12 provides us with such an opportunity.

3

Overallegorizing and Other Davidic Misinterpretations in 2 Samuel 11–12

"How good and delightful it is when kin dwell together in unity!"
—Psalm 133:1b

"[T]he fable, according to its proper character, does not pursue moral goals but tries simply to present a truth, a reality, something as typical and which is as it is. Frequently, the discourse of the truth drives it into the realm of cruelty."
—Gerhard von Rad, *Wisdom in Israel*

The parable that Nathan tells David in 2 Sam 12:1b–4 is arguably the best known parable in the Hebrew Bible. It reads:

Two men were in one city; one rich and one poor. The rich one had very many flocks and cattle, but the poor one had nothing except one small ewe-lamb that he purchased. He raised her. She grew up with him and his sons together. From his morsel she ate, from his cup she drank, and in his bosom she slept. She was like a daughter to him. Now a traveler came to the rich man, but it seemed a pity to him to take from his own flocks and cattle to prepare for the wayfarer who came to him. Instead, he took the poor man's ewe-lamb and prepared her for the man who came to him.[1]

Many readers can connect the parable to the events of the previous chapter (2 Samuel 11) concerning David and Bathsheba even before Nathan makes these connections in vv. 7–12. Israel's war with Ammon provides the setting for the events in 2 Samuel 11. Against the backdrop of this larger conflict, the chapter focuses on how David destroys a family unit. He orchestrates an affair with Bathsheba, and after he learns that he has impregnated her, he arranges for the murder of her husband Uriah. At the conclusion of 2 Samuel 11, the narrator notes, "The thing that David did was evil in the eyes of YHWH" (11:27b). The next verse opens chapter 12 with YHWH sending Nathan to David. Thus, we may expect the prophet to condemn David's actions in the following verses. Yet the condemnation of David's handling of this "familial" conflict begins with a parable.

We begin this chapter by examining the genre of Nathan's speech that he turns into a parable, arguing that we best understand it as a fable. A general consensus among scholars holds that David misunderstands Nathan's fable. Most scholars assume that this misunderstanding results from David's treatment of it as an actual legal case or petition.[2] We argue that David recognizes Nathan's story as a fable but that he does not interpret it as Nathan intends. Rather, David overallegorizes the fable and then tries to condemn Joab for the murder of Uriah in vv. 5–6. This misinterpretation exposes his inability to handle complex conflicts with discernment. Finally, we examine Nathan's application of his parable to David's situation in vv. 7–15. He uses his fable about a disrupted family unit to introduce his judgment against David's family unit.

THE GENRE OF NATHAN'S SPEECH IN 2 SAMUEL 12:1–4

The notion that David interprets Nathan's story as a legal case has been popular since Uriel Simon suggested that Nathan's story belongs to the genre of juridical parables.[3] According to Simon, a juridical parable contains a realistic story about a legal violation told to someone who has committed a similar offense in the hope that the person will unsuspectingly pass judgment on himself or herself. The offender will be caught in the trap only if he or she does not detect prematurely that the parable condemns him or her. Thus, the speaker disguises the parable as a legal case and creates some discrepancy between the parable and the offender's situation to trap the offender.[4]

Although some scholars question whether Simon has identified an actual genre of parables,[5] his notion that the juridical setting of Nathan's story conceals its parabolic quality remains influential.[6] Yet, as Hugh Pyper observes, only the surrounding narrative provides the juridical setting for the parable. If we bracket David's reaction to the parable in vv. 5–6, nothing in the parable itself (vv. 1b–4) suggests that it is a legal case.[7]

The parable does not have any of the typical features of a legal proceeding, such as specific details, witnesses, or testimony (cf. 1 Kgs 3:16–30).[8]

In addition, important differences exist between Nathan's story and the two most convincing parallels that Simon cites. In the case of the wise woman of Tekoa (2 Sam 14:1–24) and the unnamed prophet disguised as a wounded soldier (1 Kgs 20:35–43), the one who relates the veiled parable comes to the king disguised as an injured party seeking mercy from the king.[9] The wise woman of Tekoa, disguised as a bereaved mother, presents her case as a dispute among her family members.[10] Disguised as a wounded soldier, the prophet presents his case as an incident that happened to him in war (we provide detailed studies on these two texts in the following chapters). Yet, in 2 Sam 12:1b–4, Nathan, who is not disguised, tells a story about two men who have no apparent relation to him. Since no other biblical prophet presents another person's legal case to a king, we have little reason to believe that Nathan provides an exception. In other words, compared to other examples of a parable disguised as a legal case, Nathan does a poor job of disguising his parable.

Of course, Nathan may not intend to present a disguised parable but rather a fable-*mashal* (fable comparison) with the aim of convicting David directly. The poetic style and vocabulary in vv. 1b–4 link the story more closely with proverbs and fables than with legal petitions. For instance, outside of Nathan's story, the book of Proverbs (*meshalim*) contains the only other occurrences of the words "rich" (*'ashir*) and "poor" (*ro'sh*) in the same biblical verse (cf. Prov 10:4; 13:7, 8; 14:20; 18:23; 22:2; 28:6). As many scholars note, the literary character of Nathan's story breaks from the surrounding narrative. Although Jan P. Fokkelman argues that David takes the story as a historical event and not a parable, he still draws the reader's attention to its "unified rhythm" and its cluster of phonetic devices such as rhyme and consonantal alliteration.[11] The poetic quality, the third-person narration, and the personification of animals in Nathan's story resemble other fables that prophets turn into parables (fable-*mashal*), such as Isa 5:1–6 or Ezek 17:2–10.

In these other cases of fable-*meshalim*, the prophet does not use a fable to disguise his message. Rather, as with Jotham in Judges 9, the fable adds rhetorical force to the judgment that the prophet announces and heightens its ability to condemn the audience. The success of such a rhetorical function rests on the addressees' ability to recognize that the prophet's fable somehow applies to their current situation. The prophet's parable depends on limited allegorical interpretation to explain certain elements in the fable (Isa 5:7; Ezek 17:11–21).[12] We are not suggesting that Isa 5:1–6 or Ezek 17:2–10 contain pure allegories in the sense that each element represents a corresponding reality. Instead, we argue that certain elements or images such as the vineyard (Isa 5:7) or the eagle (Ezek 17:7) invite allegorical-interpretation from their addressees. Although such parabolic fables used to relate judgments in prophetic literature tend not to include the addressees' reactions, we may safely assume that the addressees would have been sophisticated enough to recognize that the fable invites some allegorical interpretation that applies to their situation. Ezekiel routinely applies fables to his addressees' situations to add rhetorical force to his judgments on them (Ezek 15:1–28; 16:1–58; 17:1–10; 19:2–14; 23:1–29; 21:1–4; 24:3–14). More importantly, his addressees recognize this technique so well that, in Ezek 21:5, Ezekiel complains that they dismiss him as simply "one who makes comparisons (*memashel meshalim*)." Likewise, after witnessing Ezekiel perform a sign-act, the people ask him, "Why don't you tell us what these things that you are doing mean for us?" (24:19). Thus, we have reason to doubt that the addressees would have been surprised when a prophet applies a fable to their situation, especially if the use of such fables functioned as a standard prophetic rhetorical technique. Against Simon, it seems odd to suggest that the juridical parable represented a recognized genre familiar to addressees in the Hebrew Bible since the genre's use supposedly surprises the same addressees every time a speaker employs it.

Given Nathan's use of proverbial language and lack of legal disguise, we have little reason to suppose that David does not see his story as this type of prophetic fable that requires limited allegorical interpretation. After observing that the story employs several terms relatively rare in prose narrative, Robert Alter muses, "It is a little puzzling that David should so precipitously take the tale as a report of fact requiring judicial action."[13] Yet it is far less puzzling if we argue that David recognizes this story as a fable rather than as a legal case.

By contrast, Simon B. Parker objects to classifying Nathan's speech as a fable or parable. He argues that it does not qualify as a fable or parable because of its "incompleteness." He notes that it does not include any consequences or lack thereof for the rich man's actions that may illustrate a lesson of some sort.¹⁴ Parker suggests that whereas 2 Samuel 14 and 1 Kings 20 contain "petitionary narratives" in which an injured party petitions the king for mercy due to an unusual legal circumstance, 2 Samuel 12 contains "a variation on the standard petitionary narrative that I shall call the hypothetical petitionary narrative."¹⁵ According to this theory, David would have recognized the petition as hypothetical and as a standard test of his discernment and commitment toward justice for the oppressed (cf. Ps 72:2).

Although Parker is correct that David takes Nathan's speech as fictitious, there are at least two difficulties with labeling it a hypothetical petitionary narrative instead of a fable or parable. First, this argument assumes that fables or parables in the Hebrew Bible always convey a lesson. On the contrary, as seen below, Nathan's story intensifies a condemnation and thus does not need to include a consequence or lesson to qualify as a parable. Second, according to 12:5a, David becomes angry after hearing Nathan's speech. It seems odd that David would get upset over a speech that he recognizes as a hypothetical test case. The style and vocabulary of Nathan's speech suggest that David may easily recognize the story as a fable aimed against him. This would explain why he gets so upset after hearing the fable. As seen in the following chapters, Parker's petitionary narrative better explains the genres of the parables in 2 Samuel 14 and 1 Kings 20 than Simon's juridical parable does. Yet, the label hypothetical petitionary narrative does not work as well as fable does for 2 Sam 12:1–4.

Furthermore, David interprets Nathan's speech more like a prophetic fable in need of allegorization than a legal case or hypothetical petition requiring witnesses or testimony. Instead of calling for additional witnesses as he does with the petition in 2 Sam 14:10, he interprets Nathan's story based on a pun. In v. 6, he convicts the rich man because "he showed no pity" (*l'o-hamal*).¹⁶ This conviction plays on Nathan's description of the rich man in v. 4: "Now a traveler came to the rich man, but it seemed a pity (*wayyahmol*) to take from his own flocks and cattle to prepare for the wayfarer who came to him." Likewise, prophets employ word plays to interpret fables and turn them into parables elsewhere in the Hebrew Bible. When allegorizing his own fable, Isaiah builds his interpretation around a word play in 5:1–7. Just as the gardener "waits" (*qawah*) for his vineyard to produce grapes (5:2, 4), YHWH "waits" (*qawah*) for the people to do justice (5:7).

Word play is a deductive method of allegorical interpretation for various enigmatic narratives including visions, dreams, riddles (Num 12:6–8), and fables.[17] Regarding dreams, Scott B. Noegel has reconsidered the widely held scholarly opinion that dream interpretation represented an inspired form of divination as opposed to a deductive form. He writes, "[Dream interpretation] is a deductive process, one based not on the observation of physical phenomena, but on the study of words, which the ancients perceived as equally 'empirical'."[18] Noegel supports this claim by noting the frequent use of puns based on polyvalent readings of written cuneiform signs as well as the bilingual nature of many dream omens. He also sees this dynamic at work in biblical dreams that become comparisons (cf. Judg 7:13–15; Genesis 37–41; Daniel 2, 6). In this sense, as with fables, interpreters may create a comparison (*mashal*) out of dream narratives through word play.

The similarities in interpretative approaches to dream-*mashal* and fable-*mashal* help explain why David fails to interpret Nathan's fable correctly. As with other types of *meshalim* in the Hebrew Bible (cf. Eccl 12:9), a number of the dreams, especially those presented to Joseph and Daniel, challenge the interpreter to create a proper allegory through learned deduction instead of private inspiration alone. In the prose portions of the Hebrew Bible, a ruler's (in)ability to handle the complex nature of a dream reflects a ruler's (in)ability to handle the complexities of situations facing the character in the surrounding narrative. This holds true for the rulers who recount their respective dreams to Joseph and Daniel (Genesis 41; Daniel 2, 6). In this sense, their lack of interpretative skill highlights the limits of their discernment. Other narrative genres that become parables, including fables, also test the addressee's ability to deduce the proper play on words and expose the limits of their wisdom if they fail.[19] Instead of a legal case or petitionary narrative, David approaches Nathan's speech like a dream, riddle, vision, fable, or other type of limited allegory typically employed by prophets and deduced from word plays. Yet, in the following sections, we see how David misinterprets the fable by overallegorizing it.

HOW DAVID OVERALLEGORIZES THE PARABLE

If David recognizes Nathan's speech as a fable, how might he have allegorized it? Any attempt to answer this question involves great speculation.

We will never ultimately know how David interprets Nathan's fable, especially since we have little access to the motivations behind David's speech and emotional display.[20] Nonetheless, we must engage in some speculation if we are to offer any interpretation of David's response at all. At best we can answer this question in a manner that remains consistent with David's speech and actions elsewhere in the David story.

As scholars often note, we may connect the way the rich man "takes" (*laqak*) the lamb from the poor man in 12:4 with the way David "takes" (*laqak*) Bathsheba from Uriah in 11:4.[21] Based on Nathan's reply to David in vv. 7–12, the prophet seems to intend the rich man to represent David, the poor man to represent Uriah, and the ewe-lamb to represent Bathsheba.

Yet Nathan's reply does not clarify every major element of the fable. For example, it does not account for the traveler who visits the rich man. Interpreters have puzzled over this issue since antiquity. In one Talmudic discussion, the rabbis identify the traveler as the Evil Inclination who visits or influences David (*b. Sukkah* 52b). Both Rashi and Redaq follow the sages in this identification.[22] More recently, Larry L. Lyke has suggested the traveler may refer to Uriah himself based on the similarity between the participle for "traveler" (*'oreh*) and the proper name Uriah (*'uriyah*), and the fact that Uriah is the one who comes (*bo'*) to David in 11:7 just as the traveler comes (*bo'*) to the rich man in 12:4.[23] Both Lyke and Robert Polzin note that in Nathan's reply, David resembles the traveler for whom the lamb is taken when Nathan tells him that YHWH gave Saul's wives to David (v. 8).[24] Yet, even before Nathan's reply, David could have understood himself as the traveler in the parable, the one for whom the lamb was killed. We will return to this possibility below.

Hermann Gunkel observes another issue complicating Nathan's application of the parable to the situation in chapter 11. According to Gunkel, 2 Samuel 11 focuses on the murder of Uriah, but the parable does not contain a murder. Thus, he concludes that the parable originally existed independent of chapter 11.[25] By contrast, other scholars suggest that the ewe-lamb must represent Uriah since it is the only one that presumably dies in the parable.[26] Indeed, David may connect the ewe-lamb with Uriah, given the similar vocabulary in chapters 11 and 12. The three verbs Nathan uses in 12:3 to describe the ewe-lamb's actions toward the poor man ("eat" [*'okal*], "drink" [*shatah*], "lay down" [*shakab*]) are the same verbs Uriah uses to describe his potential actions toward Bathsheba while speaking to David.[27] In 11:11, Uriah says to David, "The ark, Israel, and Judah are dwelling in booths. My lord Joab and the servants of my lord are camping upon the face of the open field. Should I myself come to my house to eat (*'okal*) and to drink (*shatah*) and to lay down (*shakab*) with my wife?!! As you live and your entire being lives, I will not do this thing."

Unlike the reader, David has no access to the narrator's connection between his "taking" of Bathsheba (11:4) and the rich man "taking" the ewe-lamb (12:4). Nor does Nathan make this connection for him until 12:9. Nevertheless, David may connect Nathan's description of the ewe-lamb to Uriah's description of himself, since he hears both Uriah and Nathan use the same series of verbs. If David understands the slaughtered lamb as the murdered Uriah, then he may identify the poor man as Bathsheba. As the poor man is the ewe-lamb's object of affection, Bathsheba is Uriah's object of affection.

Whom would David identify as the traveler and the rich man? If he understands the fable as a parable about Uriah's murder, then the rich man who arranges the murder of the ewe-lamb (Uriah) to please the traveler would be the only other named character in 2 Samuel 11: Joab. Joab arranges the murder of Uriah for David just as the rich man arranges the slaughter of the lamb for the traveler. Unlike Nathan's explanation in vv. 7–12, this interpretation accounts for every named character in 2 Samuel 11.[28] The rich man (Joab) takes the ewe-lamb (Uriah) from the poor man (Bathsheba) and slaughters it to please the traveler (David). Certainly, given Nathan's reply, the prophet does not intend this understanding of the fable. Since the speaker may intend to draw a single point of comparison, the hearer should not search for parallels for each element of the narrative.[29] Nonetheless, this understanding of the fable is probably what David hears if he understands the story as a typical prophetic fable requiring allegorical interpretation.

If David assumes that Nathan identifies him as the traveler, David may believe that Nathan is implying that Joab (the rich man) carried out the murder for the king's (traveler's) benefit. In other words, David may think that Nathan suspects that he has orchestrated Joab's actions. After all, David may have devised other politically advantageous murders to be carried out by Joab. Since at least the time of Talmud (*b. Sanh.* 20a), interpreters have suspected Davidic support of Joab's murder of Abner, Saul's general (2 Sam 3:27).³⁰ Yet, David insists that Joab acted alone and distances himself from Joab by publicly condemning him for this murder and cursing his entire house (3:28–29). This technique seems to work effectively since the narrator reports that everyone believed David had nothing to do with Abner's murder (3:38). Later, Joab murders Amasa, Absalom's general (2 Sam 20:10). As with Abner's death, this murder strengthens David's political position. Again, David distances himself from Joab by condemning him strongly for this murder. David tells Solomon that Joab should be put to death for both of these murders (1 Kgs 2:5–6).

Since David portrays Joab publicly as a cold-blooded killer acting on his own in these other cases, we would expect him to condemn Joab publicly for Uriah's death in chapter 11. Yet, when David hears of Uriah's death, he does not condemn Joab.³¹ Rather, he tells Joab, "Do not worry about this thing, because the sword devours one just like the other" (11:25a). To be sure, though David's words aim to comfort Joab, to an uninformed third party they seem to place implicit blame for Uriah's death on Joab, even if the death appears accidental. Nonetheless, David leaves room for Nathan to suspect him of being involved in Uriah's death since he offers no strong public condemnation of Joab and even marries and has a child with Uriah's widow soon after the event (11:27).

Upon hearing the parable, David may desire to correct this dangerous oversight. If he thinks Nathan sees him as the traveler, he may want to emphasize that, like the traveler, he did not call for the slaughtering. He could create such emphasis through a strong condemnation of the rich man, whom he identifies as Joab. Thus, David falls back on a proven technique that worked well for him in Saul's death (1:14–26), Abner's death (3:28–35), and Ishbosheth's death (4:9–11).³² In vv. 5–6, he delivers an emotionally charged condemnation of the murderer, something he neglected to offer in 11:25.

DAVID'S REACTION BASED ON HIS OVERALLEGORIZATION (vv. 5–6)

In v. 5a, the narrator reports that David becomes angry with the man when he hears the fable. If he thinks this man is Joab, this raises an interesting connection with 11:22, which we should read with the LXX rather than the MT.[33] According to the LXX, David becomes angry with Joab in 11:22. Since the LXX uses the same word for both David's anger toward Joab in this verse and his anger toward the man in 12:5, the narrator subtly suggests that David connects the two characters in his mind.

David introduces his condemnation of the rich man with the oath formula, "As YHWH lives...." David uses the same oath formula when condemning the last reported murder, which benefited him politically. The last occurrence of this formula introduces David's condemnation of Ishbosheth's murderers in 4:9. Verse 5b further supports the idea that David saw the rich man as a murderer since he calls the man a "son of death" (*ben-mawet*). While some take this phrase to mean "one deserving of death" (cf. NRSV), Kyle McCarter argues that "son of..." (*ben*) does not mean "one deserving of..." anywhere else in the Hebrew Bible. He suggests that "son of death" is a derogative title that characterizes the man's actions rather than a statement that condemns him to death.[34]

Pyper extends McCarter's argument. Based on other biblical parallels, he suggests the phrase "son of death" refers to the person responsible for the death.[35] He writes, "David's phrase... may be a description of the man as a murdering, death-dealing scoundrel, one who brings death in his train."[36] While Pyper takes the phrase as an implicit description of David, as noted previously the king repeatedly and explicitly describes Joab as a murderer. For David, if there is one person whom he would see as "bringing death in his train," it would be Joab.

David's identification of the rich man as a murderer in v. 5 suggests that he does not interpret the story as a legal case about a stolen ewe-lamb but as a parable about Uriah's death. So, why does he call for the restitution of the ewe-lamb in v. 6a? If we read with the MT, the fourfold restitution of a stolen lamb follows the law in Exod 21:37. Yet, the LXX is preferred here.[37] The LXX's reading calls for a sevenfold rather than fourfold restitution. Elsewhere in the Hebrew Bible, the term sevenfold emphasizes the need or desire to punish wrongdoings, including murder (cf. Gen 4:15, 24; Ps 79:12).[38] Thus, rather than referring to a specific case law regarding theft, David's use of the word sevenfold reflects an idiomatic expression emphasizing his desire to punish the murderer.

That David refers to the victim as a ewe-lamb rather than a human in v. 6 does not mean he understands the victim as a ewe-lamb literally.

Rather, he simply uses the vocabulary of the parable in his response as he does when he uses the root *hml* ("to show mercy") when creating his interpretative word play. His use of this root to describe the rich man's actions in v. 6b picks up on Nathan's use of the same root to describe the rich man's actions in the parable (v. 4a). Thus, when David says the man should pay sevenfold restitution for the ewe-lamb, he is not specifying the man's punishment but demanding punishment in strong terms.

As with the man's punishment, David's response never specifies the man's crime either. In v. 6b, the king simply says that the man "did this thing (*hadabar hazeh*) and he was not merciful (*hamal*)." While he never identifies the antecedent of "this thing," we should note that he uses this same term to refer to Uriah's death. As mentioned previously, he tells Joab, "Do not worry about this thing (*hadabar hazeh*) because the sword devours one just like the other" (11:25a). If, in light of Nathan's parable, David is trying to revise his previously calm reaction to Uriah's death (v. 25a), his use of *hadabar hazeh* in v. 6b takes on new significance. It means that, in vv. 5–6, David not only calls the rich man a murderer but describes his crime with the same term he uses to describe Uriah's death due to Joab's battle plan.[39] Not only does this severe condemnation point to Joab as the guilty party, it effectively distances David (the traveler) from the crime, something he failed to do in 11:25–27.

This reading makes sense of several apparent tensions scholars have seen in vv. 1–6 in a way that is in keeping with David's character elsewhere in the David story. As seen elsewhere in 2 Samuel, by the end of v. 6 David dodges yet another bullet. He responds effectively to Nathan's suspicions by revising his initial reaction to Uriah's death by coming down hard on the rich man, Joab. Nathan should have no further reason to suspect that the traveler supported the rich man's slaughter of the ewe-lamb. Once again, David satisfies suspicions through a passionate and convincing display of anger and grief. This old trick works again, and the traveler gets off the hook. Yet, this time there is a catch. David's mistake is that he overinterprets the parable if he thinks that Nathan is accusing him of being the traveler for whom the ewe-lamb is slaughtered. According to Nathan's explanation in vv. 7–12, there is no traveler. Thus, Nathan begins his response in v. 7a by correcting David's misinterpretation. No, David is not the traveler; David is the man.

NATHAN'S RESPONSE (VV. 7–15)

It becomes clear in Nathan's response that he does not intend his parable to become a pure allegory. In his response, each character in the parable does not represent just one of the named characters in chapter 11. In fact, when he tells David, "You are the man," he does not specify whether he means the rich man, the poor man, or the traveling man. In v. 8, Nathan says to David that YHWH gave "the wives of your lord into your bosom (*heq*)." This image connects the wives with the ewe-lamb who lied in the bosom (*heq*) of the poor man (v. 3). This would seem to position David as the poor man in the parable. Yet, in v. 9, Nathan positions David as the rich man when he accuses him of Uriah's murder and says that David "took" (*laqak*) Bathsheba just as the rich man "took" (*laqak*) the ewe-lamb.[40]

Nathan does not seem as concerned with drawing specific connections between the characters in the fable and the characters in chapter 11 as much as building up the theme of the destruction of a family unit and David's failure to recognize his role in this destruction. Although the circumstances of the parable and those of chapter 11 remain different, they both revolve around complex familial dynamics that David mishandles in each case. Throughout chapter 11, terms such as "wife," "daughter," and "husband" accompany Bathsheba and Uriah (vv. 3, 11, 26, 27). After telling a parable about how a rich man ruptured the togetherness of a family unit (12:3; cf. Ps 133:1), Nathan specifies the way David ripped apart a family unit in 12:9–10, which reads:

Why have you despised the word of YHWH by doing evil in YHWH's eyes?!! Uriah the Hittite you struck with the sword and his wife you took for yourself as a wife and killed him with the sword of the Ammonites. Therefore, the sword will never turn away from your house for all eternity because you despised me. You took (*laqak*) the wife of Uriah the Hittite as a wife for yourself.

By repeatedly mentioning David's actions in regard to the murder of Uriah and affair with Bathsheba, Nathan does not focus on one act over the other. Rather, his accusation focuses on how David destroyed Uriah and Bathsheba's family unit.

In part, this helps explain why Nathan employs a fable to create his parable. The use of this fable allows Nathan to frame the king's actions within the familial or household sphere. If Nathan did not contextualize David's actions within the familial sphere, it would seem odd that the punishment would focus on David's family, especially since the punishment reflects the principle of correspondence or *lex talionis* (the law of retribution).⁴¹ Unlike the narration in 2 Samuel 11, the fable in 12:1–4 centers on the destroyed togetherness of a family unit or household. The use of the fable helps highlight the effects of adultery and murder and establish a clearer correspondence between his actions in 2 Samuel 11 and the punishment brought upon his family rather than just himself in 12:7–15. Through his fable, Nathan stresses the notion that David destroyed familial togetherness and moves the discourse away from politics and international war. Comparing David's actions to this fable serves Nathan's rhetorical needs better than simply condemning his actions as depicted in 2 Samuel 11.

As a punishment for David's actions, Nathan declares that the sword, which killed Uriah (12:9) and which David ironically commented "devours one just like the other" (11:25a), will cut apart David's family structure from now on. Over the next several chapters, David's family will spiral into a destructive cycle of rape, betrayal, and murder. What David did to Uriah's and Bathsheba's family will happen to his own family. Far from resolving the conflict, Nathan's parable becomes part of a declaration that much more conflict will come David's way.

In vv. 11–12, Nathan specifies further how YHWH will disrupt David's family structure. The prophet declares, "Thus says YHWH, 'See, I am rising up evil against you from your house. Before your eyes, I will take (*laqak*) your wives and I will give them to your neighbor. He will lay (*shakab*) with your wives in the eyes of this sun. Now you did [this] in secret, but I will do this thing before all Israel and the sun.'" Nathan's prophecy comes to fruition when David's son Absalom rebels against him and temporarily usurps the throne (2 Samuel 15–18). While David remains in exile outside of Jerusalem, Absalom sleeps with his father's concubines as an expression of royal authority. He performs this act to show all Israel he is in charge in place of his father. Picking up on the language of Nathan's prophecy, the narrator notes that "Absalom went into his father's concubines before the eyes of all Israel" (2 Sam 16:22b).

Here, Absalom follows the advice of his counselor Ahithopel. In 16:21, Ahithopel suggests that Absalom perform this act to strengthen his political position and to emphasize that he had broken ties with his father, David. It is important to note that Ahithopel is the father of Eliam (23:34) and Eliam is the father of Bathsheba (11:4). In other words, Bathsheba's grandfather advises a course of action that deepens a rift in David's family structure. David created rifts in Bathsheba's family, and now her family creates one in his family. Nathan's prophecy and its fulfillment center on a complex series of events that continue to destabilize family structures. Over the next several chapters, David's inability to handle family matters with any more wisdom and discernment than he did when faced with the conflicts in chapter 11 or the parable in chapter 12 becomes increasingly clear.[42]

THE PARABLE'S AFTERMATH: JUDGMENT VERSUS REPENTANCE

Upon hearing Nathan pass judgment on the future of his family in 12:11–12, David responds, "I have sinned against YHWH" (v. 13a). Although this statement expresses some conviction on the king's part, we should note that the parable does not produce this confession. Rather, David only admits wrongdoing after Nathan confronts him directly about his actions and lays out plainly what David did and how YHWH will punish him.

Furthermore, it remains unclear if this confession inspires a divine change of plan regarding his punishment. As we have noted, the punishment stated in vv. 10–11 centers around conflict and destruction in David's family. After David's confession, Nathan assures him that YHWH has caused his sin to pass away and that he will not die (v. 13b). Yet he follows this assurance by stating that David and Bathsheba's unnamed son will certainly die because of what David did (v. 14). Despite David's confession, the punishment still focuses on the destruction of David's family beginning with the death of his son.

Initially, the announcement of the death of his son seems to inspire a change of behavior in David. After Nathan leaves and the child grows ill, David seeks God. He fasts and lays (*shakab*) on the ground all night long. When the elders of his house encourage him to get up and eat (*barak*), he refuses (vv. 16–17). Although the narrator uses slightly different vocabulary, the imagery evokes an ironic parallel to Uriah, who slept (*shakab*) in the courtyard and refused to go to his house and eat (11:11–13). This parallel may suggest that now David acts like Uriah, the loyal servant.

At the same time, David's public actions in these verses are similar to his public mourning of Abner's death in 2 Samuel 3. In 3:35, the people encourage David to eat (*barak*), but he refuses. As we noted earlier, many interpreters question the sincerity of David's mourning of Abner since the general's death benefited David politically. This parallel raises questions about the king's sincerity in 12:16–17. Furthermore, this change of behavior in David appears short lived. Once the child dies, he surprises his servants by getting up from the ground, cleaning himself up, worshipping YHWH, going home, and eating food (v. 20). After explaining to his servants that he has no reason to continue fasting and weeping once the child died, he comforts Bathsheba, sleeps with her, and impregnates her again.

His behavior after the child dies parallels his behavior toward Bathsheba at the beginning of chapter 11. The fact that 12:24a contains the same series of verbs (i.e., "to come" [*bo'*], "to lay" [*shakab*], and "to conceive" [*yalad*]) to describe David and Bathsheba's actions in 11:4–5 suggests that his behavior does not change much after his encounter with Nathan.

The aftermath of Nathan's parable does not lead to a proper understanding or change of perspective on David's part that will resolve the conflict. Rather, it intensifies the conflict by highlighting the king's inability to handle conflicts within families. He does not know how to handle or respect family networks in either 2 Samuel 11, his allegorization of the fable in 12:5–6, or his subsequent interactions with his increasingly fractured family unit over the next several chapters. The parable functions to help pass judgment of David's lack of insight regarding the surrounding conflicts; it does not provide him with lasting insight regarding these conflicts. Far from providing a means of conflict resolution, it intensifies Nathan's judgment of David by focusing squarely on the destruction of a family network.

CONCLUSIONS

The use of the fable genre invites David to offer an allegorical interpretation. Yet his interpretation exposes the limits of his discernment when dealing with familial matters. David responds to the fable with an over-allegorized interpretation that aims to clear him of responsibility for his part in the conflict, but his allegorization misunderstands the complex nature of the fable. We should not focus on the individual identity of its characters but on the network of relationships in which they all operate. The focus should remain on how to best negotiate the structures and threats involved in kinship networks and not on parallels in the specific circumstances of the fable and the surrounding conflict. David fails to see how the parable works, and thus it becomes a source of judgment rather than insight for him.

The fable allows Nathan to shift the focus of David's actions away from war and international politics and toward their devastating consequences for familial unity. This shift enables Nathan to create a rhetorical correspondence between David's actions and the judgment he announces against David's family. Second Samuel 13 continues to flesh out Nathan's judgment against David's family when David's children begin to rape and kill each other. Nonetheless, David remains unable to handle these increasingly complex familial matters. In the next chapter, we examine the parable in 2 Samuel 14. Here, the wise woman of Tekoa creates a parable that once again focuses on familial matters. We show how, as with Nathan before her, she uses the parable to expose David's inability to deal with complicated familial matters properly.

4

Changing Face and Saving Face: Parabolic Petitions in 2 Samuel 14

"But by chapter 14 all clarity has dissolved, not only for the king but for us also.... We think Joab will speak to the king, but instead he sends a woman. We are told she is wise, but she does not play the part. We are led to think she will convince the king, but she does not. She prepares to accuse the king, but her accusation floats away in the flotsam and jetsam of unconnected words, and she ends up blessing him."

–Patricia K. Willey, "The Importunate Woman of Tekoa and How She Got Her Way"

"[I]t is unclear that the Tekoite really gives any clear guidance to David in making his decision; in reality her 'instructions' in vv. 13–14 essentially represent a second mashal that forces David to make a decision, but fails to clarify which one he ought to make."

–Larry L. Lyke, *King David with the Wise Woman of Tekoa*

As the epigrams above suggest, scholars have puzzled over the encounter between the unnamed wise woman of Tekoa and David in 2 Samuel 14. According to v. 2, Joab sends her to the king with instructions regarding how to dress and what to say. During her encounter with David, she tells him a story that becomes a parable. This parable applies to David's son Absalom's current situation (see 2 Samuel 13). Nonetheless, in addition to the many textual difficulties in translating the wise woman of Tekoa's speech, it seems unclear what Joab or the wise woman of Tekoa hopes to accomplish or communicate through this parable. Scholars often suggest that she or Joab hopes to instruct or advise David regarding Absalom. This suggestion may rest on the assumption that when we speak in parables, we aim to instruct or advise. Yet, when it comes to 2 Samuel 14, no scholarly consensus exists about the content of this instruction.

In this chapter, we find that we should not assume the parable aims to instruct David. Rather, the parable reveals David's inability to handle Absalom's situation properly on his own. By paying close attention to the genre that the wise woman of Tekoa invokes with her speech, we see that she repeatedly exposes the inadequacy of David's judgments. The wise woman of Tekoa's use of the petitionary narrative genre allows her to frame the situation in a variety of ways, but each time David's response proves inadequate. Finally, he defers to Joab's plan for handling the situation.

We begin by reviewing selected interpretations of Joab and the wise woman of Tekoa's goals to demonstrate the difficulties involved in ascertaining their respective agendas. Then we outline briefly the general features of the petitionary narrative genre and argue that, although Nathan's fable does not qualify as a petitionary narrative, the wise woman of Tekoa's speech does. Finally, we examine how this genre allows Joab and the wise woman of Tekoa to accomplish their goals.

WHAT DO JOAB AND THE WISE WOMAN OF TEKOA HOPE TO ACCOMPLISH?

In the previous chapter, we observed that Nathan's prophecy in 2 Samuel 12 centers around trouble for David's family unit. We do not have to wait long for this trouble to begin. Following the death of his infant son in chapter 12, problems continue to intensify within his family throughout chapter 13. By the end of chapter 13, yet another son of David has died, and one has fled from his father's presence. His eldest son Amnon tricks David and rapes his half-sister Tamar, who is also David's daughter. After David does not punish Amnon, Absalom, David's son and Tamar's full brother, tricks David and avenges Tamar's rape. He invites his half-brother Amnon to a banquet, gets him drunk, and has his servants kill him. Afterward, Absalom flees from Jerusalem.

The first verse of chapter 14 obscures David's emotional state regarding his son Absalom. We may read this verse as, "Now Joab the son of Zuriah knew that the heart of the king was upon (*'al*) Absalom," or as, "Now Joab the son of Zuriah knew that the heart of the king was against (*'al*)

Absalom." Depending on how we translate the preposition *'al*, David's heart may be filled with concern or hostility toward Absalom.[1] In other words, Joab knows what we do not, namely David's feelings toward Absalom.[2] This ambiguity contributes to the suspense of the subsequent narrative since it suggests that we cannot know for sure how David will react if Absalom enters the picture again. More important for the present study, we do not have access to the motivations behind Joab's actions in 2 Samuel 14 since we do not know what Joab perceived David's emotional state to be.

Since we lack a clear picture of Joab's motivations, scholars differ regarding what he hopes to accomplish by orchestrating the interaction between the king and the wise woman of Tekoa. For example, Uriel Simon understands the wise woman of Tekoa's speech as giving David "the opportunity of displaying uninhibited mercy towards a mother of a son who had murdered at a time when he still did not yet dare to show mercy to himself."[3] As with Simon, others suggest her speech illustrates for David that he has an opportunity to show mercy.[4] Nonetheless, if this is the case, it seems odd that the king exercises a fairly limited amount of mercy. He follows the letter of her advice but not the spirit. He has Absalom returned to Jerusalem, but he refuses to see him for another two years (vv. 24, 28). During this time Absalom does not know if David has pardoned him and wonders why he was even bought back to Jerusalem in the first place (v. 32). In other words, David does not seem to capitalize on this opportunity for mercy after hearing the wise woman of Tekoa's parable.

According to George W. Coats, the wise woman of Tekoa tells David an anecdote about the murder of a sibling to illustrate the absurdity of an overly rigid application of the law.[5] If this represents the goal of her story, however, it seems ironic that the king employs a rigid application of her point. He has Absalom brought back and does not allow him to die, but he does not show mercy toward his son beyond those actions. Again, the point or spirit of the parable seems lost on David.

Jean Hoftijzer argues that the parable causes David to swear by YHWH to uphold a ruling that David himself acts against in his handling of Absalom. Thus, he faces divine punishment if he does not accept his own oath as binding.[6] Similarly, Hugh Pyper argues that the wise woman of Tekoa tells an oath-provoking narrative that obligates him to return

Absalom as a fulfillment of his oath.⁷ Yet, as Elizabeth Bellefontaine observes, no legal precedent exists requiring David to make a similar judgment in Absalom's case, especially once David realizes the fictitious nature of the wise woman of Tekoa's story.⁸ Bellefontaine sees the wise woman of Tekoa's speech as allowing David to see that he possesses the political power to return Absalom from exile. Yet this lesson appears unnecessary since David has not shown reluctance to exercise political power throughout his career, even when he may not be legally entitled to it (cf. 1 Samuel 25; 2 Samuel 11).

Others suggest that the wise woman of Tekoa's speech contains either multiple messages or a hopelessly confused one. Larry L. Lyke shows how the wise woman of Tekoa's parable could communicate at least three mutually exclusive messages: (1) kill Absalom, (2) return Absalom from exile, or (3) leave Absalom in exile.⁹ He argues that the wise woman of Tekoa does not clarify for David which of these messages she intends. Patricia K. Willey argues that while the wise woman of Tekoa intends to accuse the king, her words become increasingly unconnected and unintelligible and that in the end, she blesses rather than accuses the king (v. 17).¹⁰ Such interpretations suggest that if Joab or the wise woman of Tekoa intends to instruct David to take a particular course of action regarding Absalom, the parable and its application obscure any instruction or advice they wish to communicate. Furthermore, if they hope to resolve David's conflict with Absalom, the parable and its application do not explain adequately how David may bring about such resolution.

Of course, many of these interpretations assume that Joab and the wise woman of Tekoa use the parable as a means of advice or resolution. Nonetheless, further consideration of the genre that the wise woman of Tekoa invokes to create her parable suggests otherwise. Whatever else we may speculate about Joab and the wise woman of Tekoa's goals, at minimum they want David to grant Joab's request, whatever we understand the goal of that request to be (vv. 21–22). For whatever reason, Joab wants to influence the situation involving Absalom (v. 20).

Based on this observation, we argue that the parable does not instruct David on conflict resolution but allows Joab to take charge of the situation, even if we do not know Joab's motives for doing so. The parable does not work to resolve David's familial conflict but exposes his inability to resolve complex familial conflicts and the need for someone else, such as Joab, to intervene.

2 SAMUEL 14 AND THE "PETITIONARY NARRATIVE" GENRE

In general, scholars have not paid much attention to the genre of the wise woman of Tekoa's speech. Rather, they tend to focus on its function when labeling it. David Gunn sees it as a narrative that elicits a judgment,[11] and as noted earlier, Pyper labels it an "oath-provoking" narrative. By contrast, Coats focuses on the genre of the speech and labels it an "anecdote." For Coats, an anecdote "narrates an event or a sequence of events out of a person's past in order to represent the events as intrinsically interesting, amusing, or otherwise important."[12] Yet, based on this definition, we wonder if the anecdote genre remains too broad to be an effective tool for interpretation.

Other scholars have defined the genre of this episode with greater precision. Lyke argues that vv. 1–11 provide an example of the "woman with a cause" motif. In part, this motif involves "the depiction of a woman's audience with the king, the purpose of which is to save the life of a loved one."[13] Lyke sees parallels to 2 Samuel 14 in 1 Samuel 25 (especially compare 1 Sam 25:24 with 2 Sam 14:9) as well as in 1 Kings 3, 2 Kings 6, and the book of Esther, among others.

Nonetheless, Lyke does not consider parallels to 2 Samuel 14 from other ancient Near Eastern literature. For example, in the Egyptian story of "Horus and Seth," the goddess Isis supports her son Horus' right to succeed his father Osiris by exposing Seth's wrongful claim to Osiris's office. She disguises herself as a widow of a herdsman and tells a fictitious story to Seth about how a stranger threatened her son and tried to claim his father's cattle.[14] After Seth sides with the son against the stranger, she exposes the error of his claim to Osiris' office.

This story contains striking parallels with 2 Samuel 14, including the fact that someone disguised as a widow tells the story and that a threat of harm to her remaining son is compared with the addressee's current situation. These similarities suggest that we should include it among stories representing the woman with a cause motif. Yet in 2 Samuel 14 and several of Lyke's other examples of the biblical woman with a cause motif, a woman presents her story to an authority for his ruling. In the story of "Horus and Seth," however, Isis presents her story to one of the parties involved in the dispute, as Abigail does with David when he has a dispute with Nabal (1 Samuel 25). Thus, when we factor in such extrabiblical parallels, the differences in the examples of the woman with a cause motif become too broad for that rubric to carry much interpretive weight for our current project.

If we look for a more general connection between many of these texts, we see that several contain petitions presented in the form of a narrative. Rather than examining how the woman with a cause motif functioned in the ancient Near East, it appears more fruitful to examine how petitionary narratives functioned. Compelling parallels exist between 2 Sam 14:5–7 and the Mesad Hashavyahu inscription from the seventh century BCE.[15] This fragmented inscription records a message from a field worker to a local officer claiming that a certain Ho-sha'yahu ben Shobay took the field worker's garment while he was bringing in the harvest. The petitioner notes that the officer has no legal obligation to return this garment, but he appeals to the officer's sense of mercy as a reason for him to order its return.[16]

F. W. Dobbs-Allsopp argues that both 2 Sam 14:5–7 and the Mesad Hashavyahu inscription include petitions for justice, although the former appears fictitious. He notes several compelling structural similarities between the two texts including petition formulas, volitional forms, the respective petitioners' repeated references to themselves as "servants," a rehearsal of the circumstances of the unjust act, and an accusation of a third party.[17] Expanding on Dobbs-Allsopp's work, Simon B. Parker gathers a number of biblical narratives as examples of these types of petitions, including several texts that Lyke sees as reflecting the woman with a cause motif. Parker calls this genre of narrative "petitionary narratives" and includes 2 Samuel 14 among his examples.[18]

In such cases, the petitioner appeals for justice in the face of an abuse of power that, technically speaking, remains legal. These petitions represent extrajudicial appeals by parties that seek relief from legal but oppressive conditions.[19] The petition does not question the fairness or legality of these conditions. Rather, it suggests that such conditions arise from an abuse of legal power by a superior. Thus, the petition seeks justice outside the normal judicial process. The petitioner may appeal for mercy from a superior (often a king in the Hebrew Bible) as his or her last recourse.[20]

If speakers use petitionary narratives to evoke sympathy from the addressee, the wise woman of Tekoa's appearance seems to work toward that goal. Joab manipulates the wise woman of Tekoa's appearance to make her story appear more convincing. In 14:2, he instructs her to act and dress like a woman who has spent many days mourning the dead (not unlike David, who is mourning his son as well). Since Joab also tells her what to say (v. 3), it seems clear that he wants to create the appearance of a bereaved mother employing a petitionary narrative form of speech when she encounters David. Nonetheless, this observation does not answer the question of why Joab and the wise woman of Tekoa use this particular genre when creating the parable. To do so, we must examine the wise woman of Tekoa's encounter with David in detail.

THE NARRATIVE REPORT AS THE FIRST METHOD OF APPEAL: 2 SAMUEL 14:5–8

The wise woman of Tekoa's petition concerns her two sons. She reports,

Truly, I am a widow. My husband died. Your servant had two sons. The two of them fought in a field and there was no one to come between them. The one struck the other and killed him. Now all of the family rose up against your servant. They said, "Give us the one who struck his brother in order that we might kill him for the life of his brother whom he murdered. Moreover, let us destroy the one who inherits." They would quench my remaining coal and thereby will not place for my husband a name or remainder on the face of the earth (vv. 5b–7).

As with Nathan's parable in 2 Samuel 12, once again the story told to David revolves around the breakdown of a family unit. Yet, as with Nathan's parable, the specific details do not parallel David's current situation very well. For example, if the mourning parent represents David, their respective situations differ considerably. Even if Absalom is killed, which eventually he is (2 Sam 18:14–15), David runs no risk of having his name or remainder removed from the face of the earth. In fact, the narrative emphasizes the fact that every son of David except for Amnon survived Absalom's banquet (13:32–36). It remains possible for David to represent the larger family, which seeks to execute the fratricidal son. Yet, with the possible exception of 14:1, in which David's heart could harbor negative feelings toward Absalom, nothing in the story up to this point suggests that David or any other family member has sought to kill Absalom.

The most obvious connection between this petitionary narrative and David's current circumstances lies in the fact that both concern the unresolved fate of a son who committed fratricide. Like other biblical narratives that function as parables, the comparison does not represent a pure allegory. The story simply creates a more general comparison between two situations to test whether a king can give a prudent response to such complicated conflicts (cf. 1 Kgs 10:1; 2 Chr 9:1).

Parker notes the tragic nature of such familial destruction. He argues that when the wise woman of Tekoa claims that "there was no one to come between [her two sons]," she does not mean that there were no witnesses, but that no one intervened. He writes,

> [B]ut for the absence of [extended family] members, the death might never have occurred. Without implying any direct responsibility on their part, the woman subtly undermines their judgment. They demand blood vengeance for a killing that, but for chance, they themselves might have prevented. This perhaps pertains to David's supervision of his family.[21]

Although we are going beyond Parker's interpretation, if we follow his suggestion here, the wise woman of Tekoa's story may subtly criticize David's handling of his familial situation rather than subtly advising him regarding this situation. The story she tells in vv. 5–7 may simply illustrate David's poor judgment rather than seek to correct it.

If in vv. 5–7 the wise woman of Tekoa is already criticizing the king's poor judgment, her dress and petition may not represent an attempt to disguise the parabolic quality of her speech. After all, the effectiveness of such criticism rests on the ability of its addressee to recognize the intended comparison. Given that the king has encountered parables before (2 Sam 12:1–7) and that he appears to be a highly intelligent character, we should consider the possibility that he would recognize the obvious parallels between the wise woman of Tekoa's story and his current situation involving conflict within his own family. As we will see below, the wording of the subsequent dialogue in vv. 9 and 11 suggests that both the wise woman of Tekoa and David understand the subtext of their conversation even before they state it openly in vv. 19–20. We will find that the petitionary narrative genre does not function as a disguise for its parabolic application in 2 Samuel 14 but as a way of highlighting David's lack of discernment through his repeated failure to resolve familial conflicts. For this reason, Simon's classification of the wise woman of Tekoa's speech as a so-called juridical parable seems inadequate.

David's response to her story in v. 8 seems to further illustrate his poor judgment, and thereby his response plays well into her rhetorical point. His response is a nonjudgment that reveals his inability to handle a complex familial conflict. He instructs her to go home and tells her that he will address her case. David may have good reasons to render a nonjudgment. If he sees the parabolic quality of her story, he may not wish to render a clear judgment because he has been unable to act clearly or decisively with regard to his own children's conflict, due in part to his ambivalence (2 Sam 13:21, 39). He may opt to continue the pattern of noncommittal behavior that he exhibited throughout 2 Samuel 13.

His reply appears ambiguous because he uses the preposition *'al* in his command. Thus, the wise woman of Tekoa could understand his reply as either, "Go home, I will rule concerning (*'al*) you" or "Go home, I will rule against (*'al*) you." Due to this ambiguity in language, his verdict does not clarify how he will handle the petitioner's situation. In either case, both options seem inadequate. If she understands him as saying that he will rule concerning her, then his delayed verdict does not resolve the matter. This response illustrates that he has still not handled the conflict.

If she understands him as saying that he will rule against her, then he seems not to give the response appropriate to a petitionary narrative. As noted earlier, parties employ this genre when seeking mercy or relief from oppressive circumstances. We might expect a king to exercise mercy when a widow in mourning presents such a petition, yet David fails to do so. Instead, he upholds an unreasonable and even cruel application of the principle that requires the life of one who strikes another with a fatal blow (Exod 21:12).[22] His response may illustrate the king's inability to grasp properly the complexities, nuances, and extenuating circumstances of the situation he faces. Generally, petitionary narratives call for consideration of such extrajudicial factors, but instead David simply upholds an absurdly rigid application of the law. In this sense, the petitionary narrative genre helps uncover David's lack of discernment.

ADDITIONAL METHODS OF APPEAL: 2 SAMUEL 14:9–17

Additional reasons exist for the use of the petitionary narrative genre in 2 Samuel 14. As seen in the Mesad Hashavyahu inscription, the petition does not contain only a rehearsal of the facts of the case but includes other forms of appeal. Beyond the narrative itself, the Mesad Hashavyahu petition includes an oath, evidence regarding the availability of witnesses, royal flattery, a blessing, and a plea for mercy. In other words, the petitionary narrative genre allows the petitioner to employ a variety of rhetorical methods if necessary.[23] The rhetorical flexibility of this genre may explain why David's ambiguous response in v. 8 does not bring his encounter with the wise woman of Tekoa to a close. In fact, after hearing the king's inadequate reaction to her story, she continues the conversation through other forms of appeal.[24] Furthermore, the use of this rather flexible genre may help explain her seemingly convoluted rhetoric (as noted in this chapter's first epigram) as well as how she moves from nearly accusing the king in vv. 13–14 to blessing him in v. 17.

Nevertheless, David fails to respond any better to these other methods of appeal and ends up reinforcing his lack of discernment concerning this matter. In other words, use of the petitionary genre allows multiple opportunities to illustrate and thereby reinforce the notion that David cannot handle complex familial conflicts properly.

Following David's initial response, the wise woman of Tekoa shifts to a different tactic in v. 9. She reassures David that he will not be responsible for any of the guilt for the murder if he grants her petition (cf. 1 Sam 25:24). Yet we should pay close attention to the way she words her reassurance. She tells David, "Upon me, my lord, is the guilt and upon the house of my father (*bet 'abi*), but the king and his throne are innocent (*naqi*)" (v. 9b). Her wording recalls the last time the claim of Davidic innocence was asserted during a discussion of bloodguilt. In 2 Sam 3:28–29, David condemns Joab for the murder of Abner. These verses read, "When David heard of [Abner's murder] he said, 'I and my kingdom are eternally innocent (*naqi*) before YHWH regarding the blood of Abner the son of Ner. May it fall upon the head of Joab and towards the house of his father (*bet 'abiw*)'." David's claim of innocence for himself and his kingdom are similar to the wise woman of Tekoa's claim of innocence for David and his throne. Furthermore, the respective guilt falls upon another party and that party's paternal house.

The wise woman of Tekoa may intend to remind David subtly of his earlier condemnation of Joab. In doing so, her statements in v. 9 provide David with his first clue that she speaks for Joab since the verse sets up a contrast between herself and David. This contrast recalls the contrast that David established between himself and Joab in 3:28–29. She may want David to connect her with Joab and may intend that David recognize that he cannot handle conflicts as Joab does. As he did in 2 Sam 3:39, the king should claim his powerlessness and defer to Joab's more ruthless efficiency.[25]

We should remember that we do not know if Joab wants to bring Absalom back to Jerusalem to reconcile him with his father or to have him executed by his father. At a minimum, we know that Joab wants David to agree to his plan to bring Absalom back. The wording of the wise woman of Tekoa's reassurance may suggest to David that Joab appears ready and willing to take drastic action if David is unable to resolve his familial conflict. Moreover, it hints that Joab appears willing to bear responsibility for such actions if David deems it necessary as he did in 3:28–29, 39.

Nonetheless, David's response to this second tactic fails to address the complexities of the familial conflict. In. v. 10, he instructs the wise woman of Tekoa to have the one who harasses her brought to that king so that "he will never again touch [the wise woman of Tekoa]." Although this instruction provides protection for the wise woman of Tekoa against the avenger of blood, it does not protect her remaining son from the family members seeking to kill him.[26] In fact, it does not address the concern of her petition since she never suggests that the other family members sought to do her physical harm. Her concern focuses on her son and her husband's name. Although both of these factors may relate to her own long-term welfare indirectly, she does not focus on her immediate physical welfare in her speech in vv. 5–7 or v. 9. Thus, David's instructions in v. 10 do not address her concerns and miss the nuances on the case presented to him. Increasingly, David's inability to deal with complex family conflicts surfaces.

In v. 11a, the wise woman of Tekoa provides the king with another approach to resolving the matter. She redirects the focus of her petition toward the preservation of her son. She requests that David swear an oath to YHWH that he will protect her son and not allow the avenger of blood to kill him (cf. Num 35:21). The need for this explicit request suggests that she feels David has not grasped her concerns up to this point. The mere continuation of their exchange means that he has left certain factors unresolved despite the wise woman of Tekoa's continued efforts to reformulate the matter through different approaches, thanks to her use of the petitionary narrative genre.

David responds by swearing an oath to protect her son in v. 11b. Once again, we should note the particular wording used. He swears by YHWH that "not a single hair of your son (*missa'arat benek*) will fall to the ground." He may simply be reciting an idiomatic oath of protection since Israelite troops use a similar formula when swearing to protect Jonathan in 1 Sam 14:45. On the other hand, his use of hair imagery may provide a subtle signal that he understands that the petition actually concerns his son Absalom. Often, commentators note the ironic connection between David's oath to protect the hair of a son and the fact that Absalom's leading physical characteristic is his impressive head of hair.[27] As 14:26b notes, "Now at the end of the year [Absalom] would shave it. When it was heavy upon him, he would shave it. He weighed the hair on his head (*se'ar ro'sho*) – two hundred shekels according to the king's weight" (cf. 18:9).

This connection to Absalom may be more than a case of dramatic irony. David's word choice may hint at the fact that he understands that the conversation actually involves Absalom. He may be subtly acknowledging that he knows the intended topic of conversation does not involve the wise woman of Tekoa's family but rather his own family. Just as the wise woman of Tekoa's words in v. 9 hint that Joab stands ready to handle the situation, David's words may hint that he recognizes that the situation actually involves Absalom. It is possible that David has already connected the wise woman of Tekoa's petitionary narrative to his own familial conflict.

Although neither of the characters mentions Absalom directly during their exchange, the references to him become increasingly obvious as the conversation continues. For example, in v. 13b, the wise woman of

Tekoa accuses David of bringing harm on his people because "the king does not restore his banished one" (v. 13b). This thinly veiled although inexact reference to Absalom (technically he is not banished) does not come as a surprise twist or a sudden trap sprung for David once he has sworn to protect her son. Rather, it simply continues to build up the connections between the wise woman of Tekoa's speech and David's family conflict.

Yet David still cannot find an adequate solution to the situation no matter how many different forms of appeal or rhetorical methods the wise woman of Tekoa presents to him. She accuses him of harming the people of God through his plan and thereby bringing a divine punishment upon them (vv. 13–14a).[28] Then, she moves from accusation to a statement of faith that God's plan will handle the situation properly by not requiring life but rather prohibiting the banished one to remain banished forever (v. 14b). We should note that this statement of faith implies that others (in this case God) can formulate better plans than David has for resolving the present conflict. Nevertheless, David does not respond to any of these methods of appeal with an adequate solution. As the comparison between the petition and David's family becomes increasingly obvious, so does the fact that the king has not found a way to deal with this complicated family matter.

Since the wise woman of Tekoa returns to the story of her son and those seeking his life in vv. 15–17, several scholars emend the text so that these verses appear after vv. 5–7 and thus continue her initial report of her crisis to David.[29] This emendation is not supported by any textual evidence in the various witnesses. Rather, it addresses the scholarly assumption that she intends to surprise David with her connection between Absalom and the story of her son in v. 13. Thus, once she reveals this connection and exposes her story as a ruse, it would appear absurd to maintain her fictitious story as she does in vv. 15–17.

We do not need to emend the text, however, if we do not assume that Joab and the wise woman of Tekoa intend to trick David through the use of the petition. The use of the petitionary narrative genre is not meant to fool David. Unlike the unnamed prophet in 1 Kings 20 (see chapter 5 of this book), the wise woman of Tekoa never creates a moment of surprise by revealing her secret identity or her true intention. Instead, she speaks with enough transparency that David figures out the subtext of their conversation himself (v. 19). As we noted earlier, throughout their interaction, both parties subtly acknowledge that the petition invites comparison with the present conflict within David's family. The petition allows the wise woman of Tekoa to highlight the lack of an adequate solution by piling up different methods of appeal that do not lead to a resolution of the conflict. It provides the context for an extended conversation that challenges David to find a proper solution to complex conflicts with extrajudicial factors and demonstrates that he cannot do so, regardless of the way the wise woman of Tekoa frames the issue for him.

If we understand the wise woman of Tekoa's petitionary narrative as setting up multiple methods of appeal rather than a surprise twist, then we need not resort to unsupported textual emendations. Instead, we can make sense of vv. 15–17 in their present location. As the wise woman of Tekoa's speech continues in vv. 15–17, she relies heavily on royal flattery. At one point, she compares the king to "an angel of God, discerning good and evil" (v. 17b). Ironically, David appeared unsuccessful in discerning the difference between good and evil throughout 2 Samuel 13. Nonetheless, the flattery culminates in a final divine blessing in v. 17c: "May your God be with you!" Although she compliments the king's discernment in vv. 15–17, she offers no real advice on how he should discern what to do in this situation. Instruction or advice does not seem to be her primary concern at this point. Instead, these verses emphasize that the king's words have not provided the anticipated source of "rest" that she had hoped for before their meeting (v. 17). Ironically, her closing appeals for mercy through heavy flattery help expose the fact that David has not fully resolved her problem (cf. the Mesad Hashavyahu inscription). Of course, this may represent her intention all along – not to instruct David through a veiled parable but to show that he has not handled his familial conflict wisely through a nuanced comparison.

TURNING FACES AND SAVING FACE: 2 SAMUEL 14:18–23

David offers no direct response to her final methods of appeal. Instead, he drops the comparative language and asks the wise woman of Tekoa to withhold nothing from him (vv. 18–19). Instead of attempting to offer another solution, he urges her to confirm his suspicions. He asks, "Is the hand of Joab with you in all of this?" (v. 19a). The text does not indicate why David decides to stop offering unsatisfactory responses to the wise woman of Tekoa's appeals at this point. We may reasonably speculate that she has worn him down. Her petition has illustrated that none of his proposals measure up to the complexity of such situations. This fictitious test case has betrayed his lack of discernment in these familial conflicts, hypothetical or otherwise. Perhaps he is now ready to defer to Joab's better judgment and to allow his general to take charge of the situation.

The wise woman of Tekoa does not gloat when David acknowledges that Joab lies behind the petition. Nor does she point out David's failure to find an adequate solution to the problems facing him. By contrast, she continues her seemingly hyperbolic flattery of the king. Even though he does not appear particularly wise in 2 Samuel 13–14, she insists that "my lord possesses wisdom like the wisdom of the angel of God, to know everything that is on the earth" (v. 20b). The wise woman of Tekoa may employ such flattery to provide David with an opportunity to save face while still deferring to Joab's plan.

Presenting the issue as a petition requiring extrajudicial considerations allows David to agree to this extrajudicial option, namely deferring to Joab, without undue embarrassment. David can still maintain a posture of authority by authorizing Joab to take control of the situation. He grants the petition even though we have no basis to suppose that the king understands Joab's reasoning behind it. In v. 21, he says to Joab, "Hereby, I have done according to your advice: Go, return the lad Absalom."[30] Like the wise woman of Tekoa did in v. 20, Joab responds with very flattering speech and a very obsequious gesture (v. 22). He praises David for granting his petition and claims to have found favor in the eyes of the king before he executes this order in v. 23.

This technique fits with Joab's previous manipulations of situations involving David. When Joab acted on his own in murdering Abner without ostensible Davidic support of his actions, David cursed him (2 Sam 3:6–39; cf. 1 Kgs 2:5–6). Joab appears savvier in some of his subsequent dealings with David when he convinces David to endorse his involvement in other matters. When he could upstage the king by capturing the city of Rabbah and associating it with his name, he defers to David instead. He informs David that he has campaigned against the city and invites David to wrap up the campaign and claim the city for himself (2 Sam 12:26–31). Similarly, in 2 Samuel 14, Joab may try to provide the king with a way to take public credit for allowing his general to take charge of a situation for a second time. He orchestrates the encounter between David and the wise woman of Tekoa to once again "change the face of the matter," as she puts it (v. 20a). By presenting the matter as a petition rather than as a direct challenge to David's handling of the situation, Joab leaves room for David to decide *who will* handle the matter after exposing that the king cannot decide *how to* handle the matter.

CONCLUSIONS

As we stress throughout this chapter, we do not know why Joab wants to bring Absalom back. We know only that he wants to manipulate the situation ("change the face of the matter"). Likewise, the text gives no reason to suppose that David understands Joab's motivations for wanting Absalom's return any better than we do. The stories throughout 2 Samuel 14 show that David does not anticipate the serious ramifications of this decision. Rather, he simply allows Joab to take charge of the situation. David's encounter with the wise woman of Tekoa does not clarify the proper course of action or even what Joab intends to do. Instead, it demonstrates that David cannot find a proper solution to the situation other than letting Joab take action.

As with several other parables in the Hebrew Bible, we cannot conclude that this parable aims to instruct its addressee or bring conflicts to resolution. We cannot even say for certain that Joab hopes to reconcile David and Absalom through this episode. Joab could have just as easily been trying to intensify their conflict, based on what only he knows regarding David's feelings toward Absalom (v. 1). Ultimately, his actions result in an intensification of conflict in the subsequent narrative. It remains possible that this represents his intention all along. It would certainly not be out of character for him (cf. 2 Sam 3:39). Whatever his intentions, the parable exposes David's lack of discernment and highlights the need for Joab to step in.

The story of the wise woman of Tekoa is not the only biblical text in which a character creates a parable from a petitionary narrative to expose a king's lack of discernment in handling a complex conflict. Although the strategic goals are different, we see a petitionary narrative used to create a parable once again in 1 Kings 20. In the next chapter, we will examine how an unnamed prophet uses this genre to communicate his judgment against King Ahab.

5

Grasping the Conflict: Ahab's Negotiation of Conflicts and Parables in 1 Kings 20

"Whereas the judicial dilemma posed by the petitionary narrative in 1 Kings 3 is used to demonstrate one king's wisdom, that of the petitionary narrative in 2 Kings 6 is used to demonstrate another king's helplessness. In both cases the petitionary narrative is the focal point of the initial exposition of a larger story."

–Simon B. Parker, *Stories in Scripture and Inscriptions*

"Ahab has shown himself to be a king of *hesed* toward Ben-Hadad; he can exercise similar mercy toward a soldier wounded in his service. Or he can judge that the soldier's inattentiveness is blameworthy and hold him fully responsible."

–Jerome T. Walsh, *1 Kings*

In the last chapter, we examined how the wise woman of Tekoa creates a parable out of her fictitious petitionary narrative in 2 Samuel 14.[1] We encounter this use of the petitionary narrative genre again when an unnamed prophet confronts the Israelite king Ahab in the closing verses of 1 Kings 20:

38. Then [the prophet] went and stood before the king alongside the road. He disguised himself with a bandage upon his eyes.[2] 39. When the king was passing by, he cried out to the king and said, "Your servant went out in the midst of the battle. Look, a man turned aside and brought [another] man to me. He said, 'Guard this man! If he goes missing, then it will be your life in place of his life or you will pay a talent of silver.' 40. Now your servant was doing this and that and he [the guarded man] was no more!" The king of Israel said to him, "Thus is your judgment. You yourself decided it."

41. [The prophet] acted quickly and removed his bandage from his eyes. The king of Israel recognized him because he was from among the prophets. 42. [The prophet] said to him, "Thus says YHWH, 'Since you sent from your hand the man whom I trapped,³ it will be your life in place of his life and your people in place of his people'." 43. Then the king of Israel went to his house, towards Samaria, resentful and displeased.

Prior to these closing verses, 1 Kings 20 tells the story of a conflict between Ahab and the Syrian king Ben-Hadad. After verbal negotiations break down at the beginning of the chapter (vv. 1–12), the Israelites and the Syrians fight two vicious battles (vv. 15–21, 29–30). Before each battle, Ahab receives a prophetic assurance that YHWH will deliver Ben-Hadad into his hand (vv. 13–14, 28). Ahab and his army interpret this assurance as sanctioning their massacre of Ben-Hadad's forces in both battles. After they wipe out Ben-Hadad's forces in the first battle, Ben-Hadad regroups his army (vv. 23–27) only to face defeat again. Nonetheless, Ben-Hadad escapes with his life after both battles.

Following the second battle, Ben-Hadad's servants approach Ahab and plead for their king's life. When Ahab learns that Ben-Hadad survived both battles, he brokers a treaty with him and sends him home rather than killing him. Thus, Ahab seems to resolve his conflict with Ben-Hadad through words rather than weapons. He shows a willingness to end further conflict with Ben-Hadad by resuming verbal negotiations. Since the conflict begins and ends with negotiations, they provide a sense of closure to the passage at v. 34.⁴ If the story ended at v. 34, it would seem to demonstrate that words have a greater power than weapons to end conflicts and bring about peace.

Nevertheless, the chapter continues for another nine verses. In v. 35, both Ahab and Ben-Hadad disappear from the story for the first time in the chapter. Suddenly, the scene shifts to an unnamed prophet who speaks to his colleagues through the word of YHWH. Following these conversations, the prophet disguises himself as a wounded soldier and presents Ahab with a fictitious petitionary narrative. Like the wise woman of Tekoa, he disguises himself as a party seeking royal mercy.

After presenting this petitionary narrative, the prophet creates a parable out of his petition. The king takes the petition at face value and delivers a judgment. Rather than releasing the soldier from his punishment, Ahab upholds the punishment when he responds, "Thus is your judgment. You yourself decided it." Following this ruling, the prophet removes his disguise and confronts the king directly. In v. 42, the prophet declares a divinely endorsed death sentence on the king based on a comparison between Ahab's punishment and the punishment of the wounded soldier. In this sense, the prophet creates a parable out of his petition.

In the first section of this chapter, we discuss problems in discerning the function of the petitionary narrative within the context of 1 Kings 20. The situation in the prophet's petition does not share many similarities with Ahab's actions earlier in the chapter and appears to work against the prophet's rhetorical goals. Thus, we may ask why the prophet uses a petitionary narrative rather than a different speech genre as the basis for his parable. Second, we argue that the use of this genre does not function simply to disguise the prophet's message. Rather, in the context of the surrounding conflict in 1 Kings 20, Ahab's response to the petition helps show that he does not know when it is appropriate to extend mercy. Thus, the prophet condemns the king for this lack of discernment. Third, we show how this episode builds on the theme of Ahab's interpretative (in)ability, which runs throughout the conflicts in 1 Kings 20 that lead up to his encounter with the prophet. Fourth, we consider how his decision to release Ben-Hadad breaks with YHWH and Israel's battle plan.

PROBLEMS IN DISCERNING THE FUNCTION OF THE PETITION AS THE BASIS OF THE PARABLE

Several commentators see the primary function of the petition as providing a disguise for the prophet's condemnation.[5] They argue that the disguise induces the king into a self-judgment once the prophet creates a parable out of the petition. The parable reveals that Ahab pronounces a judgment on himself when he rules against the soldier. Since declaring a death sentence on the king directly may involve a great deal of personal danger for the prophet, he tricks the king into passing a judgment on his own actions. Additionally, the parabolic presentation could provide the prophet with a rhetorical technique aimed at convincing Ahab of his wrongdoing.

Nonetheless, such interpretations contain difficulties. Elsewhere in the Hebrew Bible, prophets declare death sentences on kings, including

Ahab, directly, without disguising their message (1 Kgs 21:17–29; 2 Kgs 1:1–17; Amos 7:11). Thus, the prophet's efforts to disguise his message here seem unnecessary. Furthermore, the narrator notes that Ahab becomes "resentful and displeased" after hearing his death sentence (20:43). Yet Ahab goes home "resentful and displeased" (21:4) after Naboth refuses to sell him his vineyard four verses later. In other words, Ahab has the same emotional reaction to his own death sentence as he does to his failed real estate transaction. This reaction suggests that either (1) he does not understand the gravity of the death sentence, or (2) he does not take it seriously. In either case, the prophet's parable does not seem to evoke any sustained self-conviction on Ahab's part.

If the petition is an unnecessary disguise for the parable and an ineffective rhetorical technique, we may ask why the prophet uses a petitionary narrative rather than one of the many other genres at his disposal. Although he could have created his parable out of a song (Isa 5:1–7) or a fable (Judg 9:8–15; 2 Sam 12:1b–4; 2 Kgs 14:9–10; "The Teachings of Ahiqar" [*ANET* 427–30]; Ezek 17:2–10; 19:1–14), the prophet uses the petitionary narrative genre.

Another problem arises when we compare the prophet's petition to Ahab's conflict with Ben-Hadad. The content of the petition does not provide much material for a comparison with Ahab's situation. Although some scholars connect Ahab with the soldier in the petition, their circumstances differ in striking ways. While the Syrian war provides the backdrop for both of their situations, the soldier lets his prisoner go inadvertently during the battle itself, whereas Ahab personally facilitates Ben-Hadad's release after the battle.[6] In fact, based on the wording of the petition, it remains unclear whether the soldier's prisoner escapes or dies. In v. 40, the prophet reports that the prisoner "was no more (*'enennu*)." Although this term *'enennu* could mean that the captive escaped, several other texts in the Hebrew Bible use it to describe someone presumed to be dead (Gen 37:30; 42:13, 32, 36; Isa 17:14; Jer 31:15; Ps 37:36). If we presume the prisoner's death in the petition (cf. Ahab's reaction in v. 41 [LXX][7]), his fate differs markedly from that of Ben-Hadad, who returns home with his life.

Furthermore, the man who delivers the prisoner into the soldier's care warns the soldier about the consequences he faces should the prisoner go missing. By contrast, Ahab receives no instructions about what to do with

Ben-Hadad. Nor does he receive any warning about the consequences of releasing him. In addition, the petition contrasts, rather than compares, the soldier's actions with those of Ahab. The soldier ignores the warning not to let the prisoner "go missing" (*pqr*). A related form of the root *pqr* appears earlier in the chapter as the verb "to gather." Before the first battle, Ahab follows YHWH's instructions very closely when he "gathers" (*pqr*) troops together (v. 15; cf. v. 27). The soldier in the petition cannot account for one prisoner, whereas Ahab keeps track of thousands of troops. Overall, the circumstances and actions of the soldier and Ahab seem very different.

Moving beyond the content of the petition, the very genre of petitionary narrative seems to work against the parable's goals. If the prophet uses the petition to compare the wrongdoings of Ahab and the soldier, he might emphasize the soldier's guilt to make his punishment seem reasonable. Yet, as we saw in the previous chapter, usually one tells a petitionary narrative as an appeal for mercy rather than to emphasize one's guilt. The prophet presents himself as a soldier appealing for mercy. Not only does he disguise himself as a wounded soldier, but when the king passes by in v. 39, he "cries out" (*sa'aq*) to him. Often, the verb *sa'aq* introduces or indicates an oppressed person's appeal for mercy or justice (e.g., Gen 41:55; Exod 5:15; 22:23, 26; 2 Kgs 4:1; 6:26; 8:3; Job 19:7). As a petitionary narrative, the prophet's story has the appearance of a request for relief from some oppressive circumstance.

In this particular case, the soldier appears concerned that he faces a death sentence. Under the terms specified by the man who brought the prisoner to the soldier, if the prisoner went missing, the soldier would pay with a talent of silver or with his life. A talent of silver had the value of roughly 3,000 shekels.[8] Since a slave cost 30 shekels (cf. Exod 21:32), this meant that the fine ran about 100 times the value of a slave. Practically speaking, a common soldier could not afford to pay this fine. Thus, the soldier would have to pay with his life.

The petition does not question the fairness or legality of the conditions. Rather, as with many petitionary narratives, it appeals for mercy from the king as the petitioner's last recourse.[9] Although the death sentence may appear to be a severe punishment for not guarding a detainee properly, we find such conditions attached to the guarding of important detainees elsewhere in the books of Kings (2 Kgs 10:24). Overall, the soldier's physical appearance and his story seem crafted to evoke sympathy instead of condemnation from the king. As Simon B. Parker observes, the prophet "must convince the king that he is at the same time *seeking* a favorable judgment and *deserving* of an unfavorable judgment."¹⁰ In this sense, the prophet's use of the petitionary narrative genre does not represent an effective rhetorical strategy.

THE PETITIONARY NARRATIVE AND ISSUES OF MERCY

Of course, this conclusion assumes that the prophet intends to compare the soldier's and Ahab's actions. Nonetheless, this assumption misrepresents the prophet's intentions. The prophet never directly compares the two characters as Nathan does with David when he says to the king, "You are the man" (2 Sam 12:7a). In fact, not only does the prophet present the soldier's story as different from Ahab's situation, he does not make direct parallels in vocabulary when describing their respective actions. Rather, his indictment of Ahab parallels Ahab's own words to Ben-Hadad more directly than it parallels the soldier's words or actions. In v. 34, after Ahab makes a treaty with Ben-Hadad, Ahab says to him, "According to the terms of this treaty, I myself will send (*shalah*) you away." In v. 42a, the prophet specifies the charge Ahab faces when he says to him, "Since you sent (*shalah*) from your hand the man whom I trapped...."

The use of the verb "to send" (*shalah*) picks up on a major theme that runs throughout 1 Kings 20. The act of "sending" people and messages provides the kings with their central task in vv. 1–34. The prophet's indictment accuses Ahab of failing at this task when he sends away the one person he should not have. Throughout the chapter's opening verses, the two kings "send" messages back and forth (vv. 2, 5, 6, 7, 9). These messages escalate hostilities until Ben-Hadad "sends" what amounts to a declaration of war (v. 10) and Ahab "sends" out his troops from Samaria (v. 17). In addition, the verb helps narrate the release of Ben-Hadad when Ahab sends him away in v. 34. In v. 42, the prophet repeats this verb to connect his criticism to Ahab's handling of the conflict. Nonetheless, the prophet could have made this connection without ever telling the petitionary narrative. The soldier's petition in vv. 39–40 does not contain any of the key vocabulary used in the prophet's indictment of Ahab in

v. 42a. Instead, the petitionary narrative seems to interrupt and muddle this connection built around the verb "send."

In this section, we find that, ultimately, similar presentation styles rather than similar circumstances connect the prophet's petitionary narrative with Ahab's release of Ben-Hadad (vv. 31–34). Although technically speaking the Syrians do not use the petitionary narrative genre, they do plead for Ahab's mercy as a last resort to save Ben-Hadad's life. They even claim that Israelite kings are "kings of mercy" (*hesed*) (v. 31). This claim helps focus the reader's attention on mercy as a key issue in 1 Kings 20. The prophet's use of the petitionary narrative genre foregrounds the issue of mercy once again. Previously, Ahab had shown mercy to Ben-Hadad by letting him live. The prophet's petition tests whether Ahab will extend this same mercy to one of his own soldiers.

Several similarities exist between the two pleas presented to Ahab, including the petitioners' appearance, vocabulary, and response to Ahab's judgment. Both Ben-Hadad's messengers and the prophet manipulate their appearance to gain Ahab's sympathy for their respective requests. After their second defeat, the servants of Ben-Hadad inform their king, "We have heard that the kings of the house of Israel are kings of mercy. Please let us put sackcloth on our loins and cords around our heads and let us go out to the king of Israel. Perhaps he will preserve your life" (v. 31).[11] In the following verse, they "gird" (*hagar*) their loins with sackcloth and tie cords around their heads and go to Ahab. Based on Near Eastern parallels, the servants' appearance in v. 32 (sackcloth with a cord around their head) may signal their desire for clemency from Ahab.[12] Elsewhere in the Hebrew Bible, characters may "gird" (*hagar*) themselves with sackcloth as a sign of mourning (Jer 4:8; Lam 2:10). This mode of dress functions as a strategic move aimed to gain Ahab's sympathy and influence his decision regarding their request. Similarly, the prophet wraps a bandage around his eyes (presumably to cover the wounds he received in v. 37) before he goes out to meet Ahab.

In addition, the prophet presents his petitionary narrative with vocabulary recalling that used by Ben-Hadad's messengers (vv. 31–32). The messengers refer to Ben-Hadad as "your [Ahab's] servant" just as the prophet refers to himself as "your servant." This language reflects an expression of royal etiquette that appears often when a subordinate makes a request of a king (1 Sam 22:15; 2 Sam 19:27, 29; 2 Kgs 16:7; Neh 2:5). Yet a more specific parallel occurs when only the messengers and the prophet use the word "life" (*nefesh*) in this chapter (vv. 31, 32, 39, 42). In v. 32, Ben-Hadad's messengers report to Ahab, "Your servant Ben-Hadad said, 'Please, may my life (*nefesh*) continue'." In his petition, the prophet, disguised as the soldier, informs Ahab that the soldier faces a death sentence. The soldier reports that the man warned him, "It will be your life (*nefesh*) in place of his life (*nefesh*)." The repetition of this word focuses the two petitions around a plea for life since it seems that both Ben-Hadad and the soldier face certain death unless Ahab spares them.

A final connection between the two requests appears after Ahab delivers his respective response to each party. In both cases, he gives a rash response without taking time to consult with anyone else or ask for clarification. (This contrasts with his earlier actions in vv. 7–8 and 14.) The narrator describes both Ben-Hadad's messengers and the prophet as acting "quickly" (*mahar*) in reaction to Ahab's response (vv. 33, 41). Not only does the prophet present his petition in a similar style to that of Ben-Hadad's messengers, but also his reaction seems similar to their reaction.

Similarities between the messengers' and the prophet's encounters with Ahab may help explain why the prophet uses a petitionary narrative as the basis for his parable. The petitionary narrative frames the prophet's story as an appeal for mercy. In other words, the prophet does not employ this genre only to disguise his judgment but also to foreground the issue of mercy. We would think the sight of a wounded soldier may evoke Ahab's sympathy and make him more responsive to the soldier's petition. Indeed, the prophet works hard to make the soldier seem like a sympathetic character through both his words and appearance. This case represents one in which the king should exercise mercy. Yet, he does not do so. Rather, he upholds the punishment. This decision is in stark contrast with his earlier treatment of Ben-Hadad, whom he releases alive after making a treaty with him. When the Syrians plead for Ben-Hadad's life, Ahab shows mercy. When one of his own soldiers pleads for his life in similar terms, Ahab shows no mercy.

Ultimately, Ahab does not understand when it is appropriate to exercise mercy. The petitionary narrative presents him with a fictitious case that tests this claim. It exposes his lack of interpretative skill in that he cannot discern the appropriate action for the appropriate moment.

The prophet does not use his petition to create a comparison between Ahab and the soldier's actions or situations. Rather, he uses it to contrast Ahab's responses to two appeals for mercy.

After the prophet reveals his identity to Ahab, he condemns the king to death. First, he indicts the king for releasing Ben-Hadad (v. 42a). Second, he pronounces a death sentence on Ahab and his people (v. 42b). Repetition of the phrase "your life in place of his life" represents a significant parallel between the respective punishments that the soldier and Ahab face. According to the petitionary narrative, the man warns the soldier that if the prisoner escapes, "It will be your life in place of his life or you will pay a talent of silver." When the prophet passes judgment on Ahab, he says, "It will be your life in place of his life and your people in place of his people." The prophet's judgment of Ahab does not include the option of paying a talent of silver, but this difference may simply ensure that the king does not buy his freedom. Unlike the soldier in the petition, Ahab could afford a talent of silver. This difference ensures that now both punishments entail a death sentence. The soldier's and Ahab's respective punishments form the actual basis for the comparison or parable. The prophet draws a comparison between their punishments rather than between their characters or their actions. As we noted earlier, their actions differ significantly.

In v. 42, the prophet's response to Ahab's judgment of the soldier's petition does not necessarily mean that the prophet endorses the king's handling of the petition. Rather, Ahab's inappropriate judgment of the petitionary narrative provides further evidence of his inappropriate judgment throughout 1 Kings 20–21. Indeed, in the next chapter, Ahab allows another one of his fellow Israelites to face a death sentence (Naboth in 1 Kgs 21:8–16) and is once again himself condemned to death by a prophet (1 Kgs 21:17–19). The king has reacted to the soldier's petition inappropriately, so in v. 42 the prophet turns the death sentence that Ahab chooses to uphold against the king. The king did not spare the soldier's life, and now YHWH will not spare the king's life. Ben-Hadad's messengers, the "soldier," and then the prophet all repeat the word "life" (*nefesh*) throughout their various pleas and judgments. These repetitions focus the story on the appropriate conditions under which to spare life and to respond positively to pleas for mercy.

Although the prophet's confrontation with Ahab highlights concerns over the king's interpretative ability, it is not the first time this issue arises in 1 Kings 20. Rather, the chapter subtly addresses Ahab's interpretative ability throughout his conflict with Ben-Hadad. In the following sections, we review the scenes in which Ahab must act as an interpreter in vv. 1–34. We show how vv. 35–43 build on these scenes and connect with Ahab's (mis)handling of the conflict.

AHAB AS INTERPRETER OF THE CONFLICT

The petitionary narrative in vv. 39b–40a is embedded in a larger narrative. It does not represent an actual petition like the Mesad Hashavyahu inscription (see chapter 4 in this book). As such, the prophet's petition does not function solely to provide relief of the soldier's oppressive circumstances. Instead, it serves larger rhetorical goals. In the context of 1 Kings 20, it serves the prophet's goal of exposing Ahab's lack of discernment and bringing judgment upon him. In the larger context of the books of Kings, it serves the author's goal of royal characterization. Often, Hebrew Bible texts that include petitionary narratives concern themselves primarily with the reaction of the king rather than the fate of the petitioner (see our discussion of David's reaction in 2 Samuel 14 in the previous chapter). The king's reaction tells the reader a great deal about his character, as in the cases of Solomon (1 Kgs 3:16–30) and another unnamed king (2 Kgs 6:24–30). Following Parker's observation in the first epigraph for this chapter, the petitionary narratives are focal points for the exposition of Solomon's wisdom and for the unnamed king's helplessness within a larger narrative crisis. The authors or editors of the books of Kings use a similar narrative technique in 1 Kings 20. Once again, a petitionary narrative becomes the focal point for the exposition of the leadership qualities of a king within the larger narrative. In this case, it highlights Ahab's lack of discernment.

The story introduces the theme of Ahab's interpretations of the conflict in the opening verses of 1 Kings 20. According to v. 1, Ben-Hadad gathers a large military force, which includes his own army, 32 other kings, as well as horses and chariots to besiege Ahab's capital city, Samaria. As in 2 Samuel 11–12, a military conflict provides the backdrop for the story (see chapter 3). In v. 2, communications begin between Ben-Hadad and Ahab when the former sends messengers to the latter. As in 2 Samuel 11–12, much of the action throughout the chapter involves the "sending" (*shalah*) of messages and people back and forth (vv. 2, 5, 6, 7, 9, 10, 17, 34, 42). The two kings will have to interpret the intentions behind these sent messages. The repetition of this verb helps develop an episode that foregrounds the issue of royal interpretative (in)ability.

In vv. 3–4, Ben-Hadad informs Ahab through his messengers that he lays claim to all Ahab's silver and gold as well as his fairest wives and children. Ahab agrees to these demands and is willing to part with his wealth and family, both of which can represent his royal power (cf. Deut 17:17). Although these demands contain political overtones (cf. 2 Kgs 18:15; 20:12–19), they also introduce the motif of familial terms into the narrative. Later in the story, Ahab refers to Ben-Hadad as "my brother" when he learns that Ben-Hadad survived their second battle (v. 32). Familial terms were a standard means of addressing others in ancient Near Eastern political rhetoric.[13] For example, a king would typically refer to another ruler of equal political standing as "my brother" (1 Kgs 9:13; *KAI* 216:14).[14] At the same time, this use of familial rhetoric within political negotiations introduces a subtle criticism of Ahab. He easily agrees to relinquish his wives and children, which involve relationships that he should protect. Yet, in vv. 32–34, he strives to preserve a relationship with his so-called brother Ben-Hadad, a relationship that the prophet suggests he should not preserve.

In vv. 6–7, Ben-Hadad's messengers return and report that Ben-Hadad will not only claim Ahab's wealth and family members, but that the next day he will "send" his servants to search Ahab's palace and take Ahab's most prized possession. Ahab interprets this second demand as an attempt to establish a pretext for war.[15] In v. 7, Ahab calls together the elders of the land and tells them, "See and understand that [Ben-Hadad] is seeking evil because he sent [word] to me [demanding] my wives, my children, my silver, and my gold and I did not withhold them." Ahab does not just repeat Ben-Hadad's demands to the elders of the land but interprets the demands for them. He sees aggressive intentions behind Ben-Hadad's message.

After the elders of the land advise Ahab not to give in to Ben-Hadad's demands, he informs Ben-Hadad's messengers that although he agreed to Ben-Hadad's first set of demands, he cannot agree to his additional demands (v. 9). Since antiquity, interpreters have puzzled over why Ahab would agree to the first demands but not the second.[16] In comparative ancient Near Eastern texts, a ruler could search a vassal's home when the ruler suspected the vassal of holding out on the ruler, even after the vassal had paid a substantial tribute. In his second demand, Ben-Hadad says his servants will "search" (*hapash*) Ahab's palace. Elsewhere, the Hebrew Bible uses similar forms of this verb when describing searches for stolen or concealed property or fugitives (Gen 31:35; 44:12; 1 Sam 23:23; Amos 9:3; Zeph 1:12). Ahab may object to Ben-Hadad's second demand because he interprets it as accusing him of "holding out" on Ben-Hadad and such an accusation insults Ahab.[17] Here, Ahab seems to consider the intentions behind Ben-Hadad's messages carefully. He takes time to consult with the elders of the land rather than rushing to a decision as he does when approached with pleas for mercy later in the chapter (vv. 31–34, 38–43).

Upon hearing Ahab's response, Ben-Hadad becomes much more explicit with his insults. In v. 10, he sends his messengers back to Ahab with a direct taunt. He says, "May the gods do this and even more to me if there remains sufficient dust of Samaria for a handful for every one of the people that follow me [i.e., Ben-Hadad's soldiers]." By vv. 10 and 11, the sending of messages back and forth has degenerated into declarations of war. Ahab responds with a taunt-*mashal* (see chapters 1 and 6 of this book) in v. 11. He quotes a proverb: "The one who puts on [armor] should not boast like one who takes off [one's armor]." This proverb advises that one should boast about a victory only after one achieves said victory. Ahab taunts Ben-Hadad by defying his guarantee of victory.

Ahab's *mashal* contains dramatic irony, however, when read within the context of the entire chapter. Just as his proverb questions Ben-Hadad's assurance regarding the outcome of the coming conflict, the prophet's parable (another type of *mashal*) illustrates that Ahab has not understood the outcome of the conflict either. In addition, Ahab's proverb does not function as an attempt at diplomacy but as a taunt that provokes greater conflict. Likewise, the prophet's parable will function to announce greater conflict rather than the resolution of the present conflict.

Beginning with v. 13, the scene shifts to an unnamed prophet who approaches Ahab and declares that YHWH will give the great army assembled against Ahab into his hand. Ahab responds to this prophetic assurance of victory by requesting more specific information. Once again, Ahab holds the position of interpreter. In the previous episode, he had to interpret Ben-Hadad's words as conveyed through his messengers. Now he must interpret YHWH's words as conveyed through a prophet. Ahab understands the prophet's declaration as a typical oracle regarding the outcome of a battle (cf. Num 21:34; Josh 6:2; 8:1; Judg 4:6–7; 1 Sam 23:4). Often, when presented with such an oracle, those going into battle will ask specific questions about whether the deity will bless their war efforts or how they should conduct the battle (Judg 1:1–3; 6:36–40; 20:18–28; 2 Sam 2:1; 5:19). In this case, Ahab takes the time to ask for clarification regarding exactly who will serve as the means of God's victory. Likewise, when interpreting Ben-Hadad's words, he took the time to consult with the elders of the land. Again, this thoughtful consideration contrasts with his rash judgments regarding pleas for mercy toward the end of the chapter.

After the prophet tells him that YHWH will accomplish this victory through the young men of the princes of the provinces, Ahab asks, "Who shall bind the battle?" (v. 14b). Based on an Akkadian parallel (*tahaza kasaru*, "to bind up a battle, to prepare a battle" [CAD K, 260]), the verb "bind" in this verse carries the sense of "prepare" as in, "Who shall prepare for battle?" Some scholars understand bind as clinch or wrap up, but they derive this understanding from an idiom in English.[18] The only other use of this idiom in the Hebrew Bible does not support the understanding of wrapping up the battle but rather preparing for the battle (2 Chr 13:3).

The prophet offers a one-word answer to Ahab's second question: "you." Ahab will prepare for the battle. After pressing the prophet for more information, Ahab seems to follow YHWH's instructions closely. He gathers the young men of the princes of the provinces, who number 230. After gathering these young men, he gathers an additional 7,000 from among all the Israelites. The Israelites score a decisive victory in this first battle (vv. 20–21). Yet Ben-Hadad escapes on horseback.

Following Ahab's first victory, an unnamed prophet approaches him again. The prophet delivers a cryptic message. He warns Ahab that Ben-Hadad will return the following year and that Ahab should strengthen himself and consider carefully what he should do. Yet he does not communicate any further word from YHWH regarding how to prepare for the upcoming battle. After stating the situation in v. 22, the prophet does not provide Ahab with any additional guidance as we might expect. Rather, he focuses attention on Ahab's own interpretative ability. As the conflict continues to escalate, the prophet tells the king that his ability to understand the conflict is of paramount importance. The prophet uses the same idiom for "consider carefully" (literally "see and understand") that Ahab used in v. 7. In v. 7, Ahab informed the elders of the land that Ben-Hadad sought a pretext for war and told them to consider carefully the situation ("see and understand"). The elders advised Ahab to resist Ben-Hadad rather than accommodate his wishes. In v. 22, the prophet tells Ahab to consider the situation with Ben-Hadad carefully. Yet, whereas the elders of the land encourage resistance to Ben-Hadad, ultimately Ahab opts for accommodation when he makes a treaty with Ben-Hadad and sends him home in vv. 31–34.

The scenes in vv. 35–43 suggest that Ahab has not considered the conflict carefully enough. Repeatedly, Ahab's interpretative (in)ability appears as an important element in his conflict with Ben-Hadad. The prophet's petitionary narrative provides a final test of his discernment. His negative reaction to his own soldier's plea for mercy calls into question his ability to read complex situations properly. The prophet uses his reaction as a springboard to criticize his handling of Ben-Hadad's release.

Based on the prophet's indictment in v. 42a, Ahab seems to have overlooked YHWH's involvement in the battle. In fact, his decision to let Ben-Hadad live seems to follow the Syrians' battle plan more closely than the Israelites' interpretation of YHWH's battle plan. The petitionary narrative helps bring his confusion of party lines into focus. It demonstrates his confusion by contrasting his treatment of the Syrian king (vv. 31–34) with that of an Israelite soldier (vv. 38–43). In the following section, we examine the contrast between Ben-Hadad's battle plan and YHWH's battle plan as interpreted by Israel. We show how Ahab's release of Ben-Hadad reflects the Syrian strategy as opposed to the Israelite strategy.

AHAB'S ACTIONS IN LIGHT OF SYRIAN AND ISRAELITE BATTLE PLANS

Although Ahab's troops set out at noon for a bold midday attack on Ben-Hadad and his military coalition in v. 16, they possess a distinct advantage since Ben-Hadad and his fellow kings are drinking themselves into a stupor (v. 12). Following YHWH's instructions, the young men of the princes of the provinces go out to battle first (v. 14). At this point, Ahab seems to have fulfilled his part in the battle plan just as YHWH had specified. When Ben-Hadad hears about the approaching Israelite troops, the drunken king tells his servants his own battle plan. He says, "If they have come out for peace, capture them alive (*ha*) and if they have come out for war, capture them alive (*ha*)" (v. 18). Although he does not specify a reason, Ben-Hadad's plan focuses on preserving the lives of the enemy. The narrator contrasts the manner in which the two parties approach the battle by reporting that the Israelites came out of the city and each one killed (*nakah*) a Syrian soldier (v. 20). Far from preserving life, the Israelites interpret YHWH's promise of victory as a sanction to massacre the Syrian coalition. The Israelite battle plan resolves around killing the enemy. In fact, the root translated as "kill" (*nakah*) appears four times between vv. 20 and 29 in reference to Israel's actions during the two battles.

Several factors support the Israelites' interpretation of YHWH's promise. Before the second battle, the two armies remain in a standoff for seven days (v. 29). Although the narrator never mentions YHWH's involvement in the battle directly, several commentators compare this seven-day period to the seven days of preparation the Israelites engaged in before YHWH destroyed the walls of Jericho (cf. Josh 6:12–21).[19] Before the first battle, a prophet specifies that as a result of this divinely endorsed victory, Ahab "will know that I am YHWH" (v. 13). The formula, "X will know that I am YHWH," appears at several points elsewhere in the Hebrew Bible, most often in the book of Ezekiel in contexts of a divine destruction or restoration (e.g., Ezek 6:7; 7:4; 11:10; 20:42; 36:11; 37:6). In these cases, the formula draws attention to the overwhelming power of YHWH and the deity's control over human conflicts. At other points, it appears when YHWH fights for Israel against a military foe, similar to the situation in 1 Kings 20. For example, the formula appears often in the Exodus narrative, where increasingly the narrator depicts the conflict as one between the Egyptians, who claim not to "know" YHWH (Exod 5:2), and YHWH (cf. Exod 6:7; 7:5; 10:2; 14:4, 18). In 1 Kings 20, the formula appears again in v. 28 after the Syrians recognize that their conflict with Ahab actually involves the Israelite deity as their principal opponent (v. 23; cf. Exod 14:25).

Furthermore, when the second battle begins, the Israelites kill 100,000 members of Ben-Hadad's coalition. After 27,000 survivors of Ben-Hadad's forces retreat into the city in v. 30a, the city's wall suddenly collapses upon them. Although the narrator does not explain why the wall collapses, in the Hebrew Bible the phrase "and the wall fell down" (*wattippol hahomah*) occurs only in v. 30 and Josh 6:20. Thus, several commentators suggest that YHWH may have caused the wall to collapse just as YHWH did in Josh 6:20. Although the parallels between the two battles remain far from exact,[20] the notion that YHWH caused the wall to fall appears suggestive given the focus on divine intervention in the verses leading up to the battle. Also, this interpretation fits with Israel's battle plan elsewhere in 1 Kings 20; a plan that seems to focus on complete destruction of the enemy. In v. 30, the narrator hints that the wall's collapse assured that all the remaining enemy forces died after the Israelites had killed the first 100,000. If in fact YHWH had knocked down the wall, then YHWH facilitated the death of any troops that may have escaped into the city. By contrast, after Ben-Hadad escapes into the city (v. 30b), Ahab allows him to live.

After the second battle, the Syrian strategy aims again for the preservation of life, although this time it is Ben-Hadad's life that needs preserving. In v. 32, Ben-Hadad's messengers report to Ahab that "your servant Ben-Hadad said, 'Please, may my life (*nefesh*) continue'." Ahab responds, "He is still alive (*ha*)? He is my brother!" In v. 18, Ben-Hadad used the same vocabulary when he ordered his troops to take the Israelite forces "alive" (*ha*). As we know by v. 32, Ben-Hadad had greatly miscalculated the outcome of the first battle. Likewise, Ahab's decision to allow Ben-Hadad to live represents a grave miscalculation regarding the outcome of the second battle.

Immediately following Ahab's release of Ben-Hadad, the scene shifts to the prophet's conversations with his colleagues. Since at least the time of Rashi, a number of interpreters have understood this exchange between the prophet and his colleague as a symbolic enactment (or sign-act) of YHWH's judgment on Ahab (vv. 35–37).[21] Frequently, the prophets performed sign-acts of divine judgment to communicate their message (cf. Jer 19:1–15; 27:1–22; Ezek 3:22–5:17). YHWH's judgment as portrayed in vv. 35–37 moves the focus away from the preservation of life and back to the taking of life. Earlier, the narration of the Israelites' battle plan revolved around the word "kill" (*nakah*). Now, the sign-act of YHWH's judgment does the same. Various forms of the word "kill" (*nakah*) appear seven times in vv. 35–37 alone.

In v. 35, the prophet commands his colleague to *nakah* him. The colleague refuses to follow the command, possibly because he interprets the command as instructing him to kill the prophet. Although the verb *nakah* may carry the meaning "to strike" here, it has meant "to kill" in its previous uses throughout chapter 20 when it characterized the Israelites' slaughter of Ben-Hadad's forces. In addition, it carries the sense of "to kill" when it appears twice more in v. 36. Following the colleague's refusal to obey the prophet's command, the prophet declares that a lion will kill (*nakah*) his disobedient colleague (v. 36a). Indeed, a lion promptly kills (*nakah*) the colleague (v. 36b). In v. 37, the prophet gives a second colleague the same command. The second colleague interprets the command as "strike me" rather than "kill me." He carries out the command promptly and beats the prophet to the point of wounding him.

As a sign-act, vv. 35–37 draw parallels between Ahab and the prophet's first colleague. Just as Ahab refuses to act against Ben-Hadad, the first colleague refuses to act against the prophet. The divine judgment comes regardless of the fact that a prophet does not tell either party explicitly that YHWH wants them to kill/strike anyone. Before the second battle with Ben-Hadad, a prophet tells Ahab to consider carefully what to do but gives no further instruction (v. 22). In v. 35, a prophet tells his colleague to strike/kill him but gives no indication that YHWH inspires this command. According to this interpretation, the prophet represents Ben-Hadad, his colleague represents Ahab, and the lion represents the instrument of YHWH's punishment (cf. 1 Kgs 13:20–26).

Whereas Ahab's negotiations with the Syrians focused on the preservation of Ben-Hadad's life (vv. 31–34), the word of YHWH brings the focus back to the killing of Ben-Hadad. If we understand *nakah* as meaning "to kill" throughout vv. 35–36, the prophet says essentially, "Since you did not kill me, the lion will kill you." A few verses later, the prophet uses his parable to reiterate this message when he repeats the phrase "your life in place of his life" to Ahab in vv. 39 and 42. We see this technique of juxtaposing a sign-act and parable to intensify a judgment elsewhere in prophetic literature (cf. Ezekiel 24).

CONCLUSIONS

In 1 Kings 21, an Israelite named Naboth refuses to sell Ahab his family vineyard. A disgruntled Ahab supports a conspiracy to kill Naboth and claim his vineyard (21:1–16). As in 1 Kings 20, a prophet confronts Ahab once again and announces the destruction of his lineage. After noting parallels between chapters 20 and 21, Larry L. Lyke observes that the prophet in chapter 21 "indicts Ahab for almost the opposite misconduct [as in chapter 20]: here he kills when he should not!... perhaps the real message [of 1 Kings 20 and 21] is that one needs to come to know one's true enemies. Ben-Hadad deserves to be killed while Naboth does not."[22] The petitionary narrative foregrounds an issue that the narrative develops throughout 1 Kings 20 and 21: Ahab does not understand the network of relationships that involve him.

He does nothing to protect his "fairest wives and children" (20:3–4) but works to protect "his brother" Ben-Hadad (vv. 31–34). YHWH promises repeatedly to deliver the Syrians into Ahab's hand (vv. 13, 28). In fact, the prophetic messages in vv. 13 and 28 frame the conflict in chapter 20 as a conflict between YHWH and the Syrians. Even the Syrians recognize this fact (v. 23). Nevertheless, Ahab works against YHWH's promise by releasing the Syrian king from his hand (v. 42a). Ahab preserves Ben-Hadad's life but twice allows his fellow Israelite (the soldier in chapter 20 and Naboth in chapter 21) to face a death sentence. As the prophet's parable demonstrates, Ahab does not discern properly to whom his loyalties belong. His inappropriate judgment of the petitionary narrative highlights his inappropriate judgment of the conflicts throughout the surrounding narrative.

When the prophet creates a parable out of his petition, it helps intensify and justify his condemnation of the king. As with other parables in the Hebrew Bible, the prophet does not use this parable to convince his addressee to change his ways. Rather, the prophet exposes Ahab's interpretative inadequacies and condemns his handling of a larger conflict in the surrounding narrative. Once again, the condemnation involves further conflict and violence for its addressee rather than resolution of the conflict.

We observed toward the beginning of this chapter that if 1 Kings 20 ended at v. 34, it would appear that Ahab resolved the conflict through words rather than weapons. In other words, he assesses wisely that violence will not resolve anything and seeks other means of resolution. Yet the prophet reframes and extends the conflict by telling a parable to Ahab and passing judgment on him. The parable and judgment announce further conflict and even greater loss of life for the king. Ultimately, Ahab dies in another battle with the Syrians in 1 Kings 22. Thus, although Ahab seems to resolve the conflict with the Syrians by v. 34, the parable helps continue it rather than provide closure to it. Ironically, through the parable, the prophet uses words to extend the conflict for Ahab. At the end of 1 Kings 20, words help reopen the conflict rather than resolve it.

6

Intellectual Weapons: The Parable's Function in 2 Kings 14 and 2 Chronicles 25

"What a period, when kings, in diplomatic communications, wielded the intellectual weapon of the fable!"

—Gerhard von Rad, *Wisdom in Israel*

"The point of this homely fable cf. that of Jotham, also of trees (Judg. 9.7–15), needs no elaboration. It may be matched by a homely saying as pregnant and even more brief among the Arabs, e.g. 'The mule says the horse was his father'."

—John Gray, *I and II Kings: A Commentary*

Of all the parables we have discussed so far, the one appearing in 2 Kings 14 and 2 Chronicles 25 has received the least amount of scholarly attention. Many commentators seem to agree implicitly with John Gray's assessment in this chapter's second epigraph, namely, they see the parable's interpretation as self-evident. As with Gray, they seem content to go no further than labeling it as a fable and noting that it shares arboreal imagery with Judges 9. Occasionally, they cite similar imagery in other ancient Near Eastern fables.[1] This dearth of scholarly attention means that relatively few have considered how it addresses the conflict in the surrounding narrative in much detail.

As in 1 Kings 20, the parable in 2 Kings 14 and 2 Chronicles 25 addresses an international conflict. In this case, the conflict involves the northern kingdom of Israel, the southern kingdom of Judah, and their neighbor Edom. The Judean king Amaziah trounces the Edomites, killing thousands (2 Kgs 14:7; 2 Chr 25:5–16). Then, he turns his attention to the Israelite king Jehoash. (The Chronicler provides a much longer version of these events.) During the dialogue between the two kings prior to their battle, Jehoash tells Amaziah a fictional story involving personified plants (a fable) that Jehoash turns into a parable in both Kings and Chronicles. The shorter version of their dialogue and ensuing conflict appears in 2 Kgs 14:8–15, which reads:

> 8. Then Amaziah sent messengers to Jehoash son of Jehoahaz, son of Jehu, king of Israel saying, "Come, let us look each other in the face!" 9. Jehoash king of Israel sent [a message] to Amaziah king of Judah saying, "A bramble that was in Lebanon sent [a message] to the cedar that was in Lebanon saying, 'Give your daughter to my son as a wife.' Yet an animal of the field that was in Lebanon passed by and trampled the bramble. 10. You have severely defeated Edom and your heart has lifted you up. Be honored and dwell in your house. Why engage in strife against evil so that you fall, yourself and Judah with you?" 11. Amaziah did not listen (*lo'-shama'*). Jehoash king of Israel went up and they looked each other in the face, he and Amaziah king of Judah, in the house of Shemesh, belonging to Judah. 12. Judah was smitten before Israel and everyone fled to their tent. 13. But Jehoash king of Israel captured Amaziah king of Judah, son of Jehoash, son of Ahaziah, in the house of Shemesh. [Jehoash] came to Jerusalem, and broke through the wall of Jerusalem at the Ephraim Gate to the Corner Gate, a four hundred cubit distance. 14. He took all the gold and silver and the vessels that were found in the house of YHWH and in the treasuries of the house of the king and hostages and returned to Samaria. 15. The remainder of the acts of Jehoash that he performed and his valor and that he waged war with Amaziah king of Judah are they not written on the document of the Annals of the Kings of Israel?

In v. 15, the narrative suggests that other, possibly more detailed, accounts about the conflict between Jehoash and Amaziah existed at one point. Another extant account to this story appears in 2 Chronicles 25. Jehoash's fable, which he turns into a parable (2 Kgs 14:8), is worded the same in 2 Chr 25:18, and only minor differences exist between the accounts of their battle in 2 Kgs 14:11b–14 and 2 Chr 25:20b–24.[2]

As with the parables considered in previous chapters, this parable does little to resolve the conflict in the surrounding narrative. Furthermore, in keeping with the addressees' reactions to other parables, it is not clear that Amaziah understands the parable or interprets it correctly since the verb *shama'* in v. 11 can mean "to listen" in the sense of obey, or "to understand" in the sense of comprehend. For example, Gen 42:21–23 uses *shama'* repeatedly and employs both senses of the verb. As seen below, the parable does not fit Amaziah's situation easily, and thus its potential lesson (if it contains one at all) may appear less than obvious. Thus, it is possible that Amaziah does not properly grasp the sense of Jehoash's parable. At any rate, the violence does not subside even after v. 15. The following verses report the deaths of both kings, noting that Amaziah falls victim to a murder conspiracy. He is killed in Lachish and then brought back to Jerusalem (vv. 19–20).

In this chapter, we focus mainly on 2 Kings' account to make the following arguments: (1) Contrary to the general consensus, Jehoash does not try to defuse his conflict with Amaziah by advising or warning him through his parable. In fact, whereas Amaziah's intentions in sending a message to Jehoash remain unclear, Jehoash is clearly the conflict's primary military aggressor. (2) The parable has little correspondence with the conflict in the surrounding narrative in both the Kings and Chronicles' accounts. This lack of correspondence seems to muddle any potential warning or lesson for Amaziah rather than bring it into sharper focus. (3) Thus, we reconsider the parable's function by turning to matters of genre. After examining taunt comparisons in both the Bible and comparative ancient Near Eastern literature, we argue that the Israelite king does not use his parable to intensify his warning. Rather, he uses it to intensify his taunt of the Judean king. Rather than defusing tensions, the parable helps escalate them and thereby provides a pretext for the speaker (Jehoash) to take hostile action against its addressee (Amaziah) in the following verses. (4) We show how Chronicles presents Jehoash's parable as a means of facilitating a hostile divine action against its addressee rather than as a means of warning the Judean king against excessive pride and a foolish military campaign. Although Chronicles' account is more explicitly theological than Kings' account, its presentation remains in keeping with the function of the parable in the book of Kings.

Jehoash's parable is the last one we will study that appears within the prose portions of the Hebrew Bible. All parables we have studied to this point appear within the so-called Deuteronomistic History, and most of them involve a king in some fashion. Thus, in the conclusion of this chapter, we examine the implications of this book's findings for the study of ideologies toward kingship in the Deuteronomistic History.

WHO PROVOKED THE CONFLICT IN 2 KINGS 14?

In 2 Chronicles 25, Amaziah's intention in sending a message to Jehoash seems to come in reaction to the murder of his people by the disgruntled Israelite troops (v. 13). He wants to avenge the Israelites' actions with a military confrontation. Yet since these details regarding the disgruntled Israelite troops do not appear in 2 Kings 14, Amaziah's intention behind his message remains less clear in 2 Kings. According to both 2 Kgs 14:8b and 2 Chr 25:17b, Amaziah requests that the two kings "look each other in the face (*nitra'eh panim*)." The equivalent Akkadian term *nanmurru* signals a peaceful encounter but occasionally a military confrontation as well.[3] In Jehoash's parable, the bramble tries to enter into a marriage alliance with the cedar rather than a military confrontation. This difference could represent a lack of correspondence with the surrounding narrative or signal that Amaziah does not intend his message to provoke a conflict.

If we consider the latter option, Jehoash could have understood Amaziah as attempting to enter an alliance with him through marriage. Such marriages helped build relations between the two states in the past, as seen in the marriage of Joram of Judah and Athaliah of Israel (2 Kgs 8:26; 2 Chr 22:2). Ann M. Vater Solomon suggests that Jehoash uses a marriage image rather than a military image in his parable to remind Amaziah that he does not really want to battle the Israelites in the first place.[4] Yet, if this represents Jehoash's intention, he could have communicated this point without the insulting comparison between Amaziah and a trampled bramble. Thus, we should consider the possibility that Jehoash is the one who turns the encounter into a hostile one by insulting Amaziah's attempts at forming a marriage alliance.

When the two kings do finally "look each other in the face (*wayyitra'u panim*)" in v. 11 (cf. 2 Chr 25:21), the phrase indicates a military confrontation. This may suggest that the earlier use of the similar phrase in v. 8 indicates that Amaziah means to engage Jehoash in battle.[5] Nonetheless, the context of the encounter in v. 11 is different from the context of the proposed encounter in v. 8. We should note the location of the battle. According to v. 11, Jehoash enters Judean territory. The narrative emphasizes the fact that the encounter occurs in "the house of Shemesh, belonging to Judah." The narrative may have included "belonging to

Judah" to distinguish this "house of Shemesh" from other towns of the same name located in Israel (cf. Josh 19:38; Judg 1:33). Yet, in doing so, this usage makes clear that Jehoash launched an offensive into Judean territory. Although Amaziah positions himself in a northern Judean town near the border with Israel, he does not overtly pursue any further military actions. Whereas Amaziah simply sends messengers into Israelite territory when he requests to look Jehoash in the face, Jehoash brings an army into Judean territory when he looks Amaziah in the face.

The narrative does not indicate that Amaziah intended to engage Israel in a military conflict. It remains just as plausible that Jehoash frowned upon Amaziah's attempts to enter into an alliance through marriage. Thus, Jehoash provokes the military confrontation. If this is the case, we should explore how Jehoash's parable helps him provoke rather than prevent conflict. We begin this task by showing how the parable's ambiguity works against communicating a message that would resolve the growing conflict. Jehoash does not construct his parable as an obvious or easily understandable piece of advice for Amaziah since his parable has little correspondence with the situation in the surrounding narrative.

PROBLEMS OF CORRESPONDENCE BETWEEN THE PARABLE AND THE ROYAL ENCOUNTER

The parable itself does not function as a pure allegory due, most obviously, to the lack of correspondence between the characters in the parable and those in the surrounding narrative. As with Nathan and his parable in 2 Samuel 12, Jehoash does not seem to intend each parabolic character to represent someone in the larger story. Most likely, the bramble represents Amaziah since the bramble "sends" (*shalak*) a message to the cedar tree (v. 9) just as Amaziah "sends" (*shalak*) a message to Jehoash. According to this interpretation, the cedar would represent Jehoash since both characters function as recipients of messages. Yet, unlike Jehoash, the cedar does not respond to the bramble's message in the parable.

It seems more difficult to account for the unnamed animal of the field that tramples the bramble in the parable. This animal cannot represent Edom since Edom does not trample Amaziah. Rather, Amaziah defeats Edom soundly as Jehoash himself acknowledges in v. 10a. Understanding

Amaziah as proposing a battle instead of a marriage, Walter Brueggemann suggests that the animal of the field may represent either Syria or the Assyrian empire.[6] Thus, Jehoash tries to discourage a military conflict with Amaziah in light of the more serious Assyrian threat. Nonetheless, if the animal represents Assyria, it appears more likely that Jehoash is boasting that Amaziah appears outmatched rather than warning against an Israelite-Judean conflict. The Tell al Rimah stele lists Jehoash as a tributary of the Assyrian king Adad Nirari III.[7] Thus, Jehoash would have Assyrian military protection. Furthermore, if Jehoash tries to advise Amaziah against war due to the larger Syrian or Assyrian threat in v. 10, then he acts against his own advice by going on the offensive against Judah in v. 11.

Both the cedar and the animal of the field could represent Jehoash. As seen in chapter 3 of this book, the rich man, the poor man, and the traveling man could all represent David. Likewise, the poor man, the traveler, and the ewe-lamb could all represent Uriah. In 2 Kings 14, Jehoash receives the message of Amaziah just as the cedar receives a message. He also tramples Amaziah just as the animal of the field tramples the bramble. Since the cedar never responds to the bramble's message, the parable never informs Amaziah whether Jehoash responds positively or negatively to his request if Amaziah interprets the cedar as Jehoash. On the other hand, if Amaziah interprets the animal of the field as Jehoash, then the reaction is more explicitly negative. Just as Jehoash moves into Judean territory in v. 11, the animal of the field moves into the bramble's location and attacks the bramble in v. 9. Since we could understand Jehoash as either the cedar or the animal of the field, the parable provides little information regarding Jehoash's reaction to Amaziah's request in v. 8. Amaziah could have interpreted the parable's veiled message(s) in a number of ways.

Jehoash's statements in v. 10 do not help further clarify his intentions. In a rhetorical question, he asks Amaziah, "Why engage in strife against evil?" since such action will lead to Amaziah's downfall. Evil functions as a personified opponent for Amaziah in this verse since "evil" (*ra'ah*) has a *b-* prefix following the hithpael form of the root *grh* (*welamah hitgareh bera'ah*). In other occurrences of this construction in the Hebrew Bible, the object with the *b-* prefix represents the opponent of the verb's subject (Deut 2:5, 9, 19, 24; Jer 50:24). Nonetheless, even if evil represents

Amaziah's opponent, it is unclear whom Jehoash identifies as Amaziah's opponent in this verse. Is his opponent the cedar, the animal of the field, Jehoash himself, or an unnamed enemy such as the Syrians or the Assyrians? Jehoash's elaboration in v. 10 does not reveal whom Amaziah should avoid engaging. In this sense, v. 10 not only fails to clarify the parable but also does not provide much warning regarding Jehoash's oncoming attack on Judah.

Furthermore, Amaziah ostensibly follows the command in v. 10 to stay at home. According to v. 11, it appears he is staying in "the house (*bet*) of Shemesh" near the Judean border. This reference to a house within Judean territory picks up on Jehoash's command that Amaziah should stay in his house (*bet*) in v. 10. Depending on how broadly we interpret Amaziah's "house," he may have tried to follow Jehoash's command rather than provoke a conflict. If so, Amaziah may not anticipate Jehoash's attack. As Marvin A. Sweeney puts it, "The Israelite king *surprised* Amaziah by sending a military expedition."[8]

Based on the lack of correspondence between the parable and the surrounding narrative and the multivalent quality of the parable's symbols, we can see how Amaziah may have misunderstood Jehoash's intention. Contrary to John Gray's position expressed in this chapter's second epigram, the parable is not entirely clear. More accurately, Sara Japhet observes the problems in correspondence among the parable, the surrounding situation, and Jehoash's speech in v. 10 (cf. 2 Chr 25:19). She concludes:

The only relevant lesson which can in reality be derived from this parable is that Joash [Jehoash] sees himself as a cedar, while Amaziah is a presumptuous thistle! Joash's parable is a demonstration of confidence, even arrogance, and the conventions of courtly wisdom are here peppered with a mocking tone.... Amaziah will never retreat from his initiative after such a mocking challenge.[9]

Japhet's conclusion implies that the parable functions more as an insult and a challenge rather than as a lesson. This implication raises the question of whether Jehoash intends to advise Amaziah regarding a particular course of action. If the parable functions to give rhetorical intensity to Jehoash's "demonstration of confidence," it seems better to understand the parable as a taunt rather than a lesson. As with the wise woman of

Tekoa's parable in 2 Samuel 14 (see chapter 4), Jehoash's parable's allegorical possibilities remain too broad to serve as endorsing a specific course of action.[10] Nonetheless, however we interpret its message(s), the comparison stands between Amaziah and a crushed bramble, and this comparison appears less than flattering. Whatever else it may do, the parable communicates an insult.

Insults or taunts were not uncommon in ancient Near Eastern diplomatic exchanges, especially those exchanges that preceded military conflicts. For example, Ahab taunts Ben-Hadad with a popular proverb (proverbial *mashal*) in 1 Kgs 20:11: "The one who puts on [armor] should not boast like one who takes off [one's armor]." This taunt is a direct catalyst for the military conflict that unfolds in the remainder of 1 Kings 20 (see chapter 5). As noted in chapter 1, *meshalim* or comparisons within the Hebrew Bible may function as insults or bywords in a variety of forms (e.g., Isa 14:4; Deut 28:37; Jer 24:9). Nonetheless, the question remains as to why Jehoash creates his parable out of a fable involving plants and animals rather than a pithier proverb or some other type of narrative that relates to the surrounding situation more clearly. As with the parables studied in this book's previous chapters, to answer this question we must examine the genre of the narrative, which becomes Jehoash's parable, in more detail.

JEHOASH'S PARABLE AND ANCIENT NEAR EASTERN DISPUTATION TEXTS

A number of recent commentators show some ambivalence regarding the function of Jehoash's parable. Although most of them see its primary function as trying to dissuade Amaziah from his present course of action, they often acknowledge that it insults or mocks Amaziah as well. For example, Solomon interprets Jehoash's speech as trying to "warn" Amaziah of his inevitable defeat and to "persuade Amaziah that he really does not want a war."[11] Elsewhere, however, she observes, "Jehoash's fable in 2 Kgs 14 hurls an insulting challenge at the rival to his kingship, Amaziah."[12] Richard Nelson writes, "Conflict arises with Jehoash's insulting fable."[13] According to Gina Hens-Piazza, "Jehoash insults the southern king with a parable (v. 9)."[14] Brueggemann claims that "the parable ... answers Amaziah with dismissive contempt."[15] In light of such comments, it seems odd that Jehoash's parable would dissuade Amaziah from conflict by using rhetoric that appears to encourage conflict.

The previous section addressed this tension by showing that the comparison Jehoash creates functions most clearly as an insult (Amaziah is a crushed bramble) instead of a warning or piece of advice. This conclusion remains in keeping with the use of other types of *meshalim* that appear during diplomatic exchanges in the Hebrew Bible. Although on occasion stronger opponents try to warn or dissuade their weaker counterparts from engaging them (e.g., 2 Sam 2:22–23; 2 Chr 35:21–22), they tend not to use parables as a means of persuasion. Rather, within the context of diplomacy, the parable serves as a means of provoking conflict.

To say that Jehoash's parable is a taunt rather than a warning, however, reflects a statement about the parable's function rather than its genre. As with its various types of comparisons, the Hebrew Bible does not limit taunts and insults to a particular genre or form. Taunts and insults may come in a variety of forms including, but not limited to, comparisons. For example, the Philistine warrior Goliath taunts (*harep*) the armies of Israel before his battle with David (1 Sam 17:10, 25, 26, 36, 45; cf. 2 Sam 21:21). He taunts David by saying, "Come to me so that I may give your flesh to the birds of the air and the beasts of the field" (1 Sam 17:44). When David tries to invade Jerusalem in 2 Samuel 5, the Jebusites mock his efforts. They claim, "Even the blind and the lame would turn you away saying 'David may not come in here'" (2 Sam 5:6b).[16] In the Babylonian creation epic *Enuma Elish*, the deities Marduk and Tiamat exchange taunts and retorts prior to their battle (*COS* 1.111:397–98). Yet none of the speakers in these examples constructs his or her taunts from a narrative comparison (a parable), even though they function as pre-battle taunts just as Jehoash's parable does. If Jehoash could have used a range of forms of speech to taunt Amaziah, we may ask if the fact that he uses a fable involving plants and animals holds particular significance.[17]

As noted in the first chapter of this book, many scholars distinguish between a parable and a fable. Often, they understand a fable as a short story that employs animals and plants as central characters rather than humans. Although this definition describes these narratives in a general sense, it reveals little about their rhetorical function or why Jehoash would employ this genre in this situation. A few scholars provide a more nuanced discussion of the fable genre. Following Solomon, Burke O. Long refers to Jehoash's speech as "an attenuated political FABLE (14:9b), a short tale that renders plants or animals as talking characters and expresses a moral principle or judgment."[18] Yet, labeling 2 Kgs 14:9 as an "attenuated political fable" does not provide much explanatory force for the present text since the verse expresses a prebattle taunt or insult more clearly than any "moral principle or judgment."

We may better understand the rhetorical function of Jehoash's parable if we define the genre of the narrative that becomes a comparison with greater precision. In his classic work *Babylonian Wisdom Literature*, Wilfred G. Lambert provides six examples of a type of fable he labels "contest literature" (adaman.dug4.ga). Lambert distinguishes between these types of fables that recount "verbal contests between creatures, substances, or other personifications ... written in several cases expressly for kings of the Third Dynasty of Ur" (2000–1900 BCE) and more popular fables or proverbs.[19] According to Lambert, "contest literature" usually follows a general pattern: "a mythological introduction leads up to the meeting of the two contestants, who proceed to the cut and parry of debate. The session is wound up with a judgment scene before a god, who settles the question."[20] Lambert's six extant examples, some more fragmentary than others, include disputes between the "Tamarisk and the Palm," "The Fable of the Willow," "Nisaba and Wheat," "The Fable of the Fox," and "The Fable of the Riding-donkey."[21] As with Jehoash's parable, these extant examples focus on interactions between plants and animals rather than humans.

The exact form of the contest literature genre is not overly rigid. For example, the text of the contest between the deity of grain Nisaba and personified wheat is too fragmented to know for certain whether it contains a judgment scene.[22] The Fable of the Fox involves several animals (a fox, a dog, a lion, and a wolf) rather than two parties in a dispute. Lambert suggests that the Fable of the Fox does not represent Sumerian contest literature but a later development from this type of literature.[23] In this sense, a text may draw on elements that reflect the genre of contest literature rather than provide a pure example of this genre. In keeping with the discussion of genre in chapter 1, texts do not belong to genres; texts invoke genres.

Herman L. J. Vanstiphout helps examine this phenomenon by giving nuance to Lambert's presentation of "fable" and "contest literature." He suggests that Lambert should not classify the disputation texts as fables. Regarding "Disputation between the Bird and the Fish," Vanstiphout writes:

It intentionally mixes the generic features of the disputation with those of a fable.... There should be no longer a misunderstanding about the difference between a fable, which is essentially a *narrative* form, and a disputation, which is essentially a *rhetorical* form. Therefore the chapter heading 'Fables or Contest Literature' in Lambert (1960) is misleading (*COS* 1.182:581, 581 n. 2).

Following this distinction between fable and disputation, we see features of the disputation in various types of narratives, especially those involving animals and plants. Yet, if genres provide a rhetorical orientation for texts, as we proposed in chapter 1, Jehoash's use of fable allows him to invoke a sense of disputation within his discourse.

In general, the disputes among the plants or animals revolve around matters of prestige, abilities, and usefulness to humans (as seen in chapter 2, the issue of usefulness to humans surfaces at several points in Jotham's parable in Judges 9 as well). Such disputes aim to settle contested matters of status between the animals or plants. As with Japhet's observation regarding Jehoash's parable (see below), these disputes function as a "demonstration of confidence, even arrogance." To be sure, Jehoash's parable lacks the mythological introduction of other contest literature because of its terse presentation. In addition, an animal of the field rather than a deity is the third party that settles the potential dispute between the bramble and the cedar. These differences may result simply from stylistic differences between Sumerian literature and biblical Hebrew prose. Nevertheless, the narrative that Jehoash turns into a parable invokes key themes (confidence/arrogance) and imagery (plant/animal) found in Sumerian contest literature even if it does not represent a fully developed example of such literature. In his parable, Jehoash compares Amaziah to a character (the bramble) that recalls the disgraced party in a disputation text.

Although the narratives in 2 Kings 14 and 2 Chronicles 25 differ significantly in content and style from these Sumerian texts, certain Sumerian texts suggest that the rhetorical elements reflecting disputations may appear in a variety of narrative types. Examples of Sumerian texts that weave elements from disputations into a larger narrative include "The Heron and the Turtle" (*COS* 1.178:571–73) and "Etana" (*COS* 1.131:453–57). "The Heron and the Turtle" contains a narrative about a dispute between two animals but does not actually provide a record of the dispute (*COS* 1.131:453–57). By contrast, the legend of Etana incorporates elements of Sumerian contest literature into a larger narrative that details the dispute. In "Etana," the first human king builds a temple for the deity Adad, and a tree grows there. Eventually, a dispute arises among the tree's residents: an eagle and a snake. After the snake presents his case that the eagle violated their oath to the deity Shamash, Shamash sets in motion a plot to punish the eagle, ultimately leaving the eagle to die in a pit. Meanwhile, Etana learns of a "plant of birth" in his efforts to secure an heir. He saves the eagle in order that the eagle may help him obtain the plant. Together, they attempt to ascend to heaven and reach Ishtar, the goddess of procreation.[24] Like the legend of Etana, Jehoash's fable incorporates elements of contest literature into a larger narrative that details the dispute.

Creating a parable from a narrative incorporating elements of contest literature allows Jehoash to intensify his taunt of Amaziah. He could have used another form of speech to convey his taunt as Goliath, the Jebusites, or Marduk do in their prebattle taunts. Yet, by employing narrative elements found in Sumerian disputation texts, he emphasizes the insulting nature of his reply to Amaziah's request. When this type of narrative becomes a parable applied to the speaker's perceived opponent, it promotes rather than avoids conflict. It represents a claim of superiority over one's addressee rather than a word of advice toward one's addressee.

The imagery drawn from the disputation genre helps strengthen the offensive tone of his taunt. Whatever Amaziah's original intentions may have been in contacting Jehoash, Jehoash has turned their exchange into a pretext for military aggression. He does not create his parable to warn or change Amaziah's mind but to help set the tone for the hostile actions he will take toward Judah in the following verses. If comparisons help intensify the speaker's point(s), the use of animal and arboreal imagery common to disputation texts in Jehoash's comparison helps intensify his taunt.

THE FUNCTION OF THE PARABLE IN 2 CHRONICLES 25

Up to this point, we have concentrated on the book of Kings' account of the parable and conflicts under discussion. Before concluding this chapter, we will show that, though Chronicles' account is more expansive, like Kings it does not present Jehoash as using his parable to warn or advise Amaziah against a particular course of action. Rather, the Chronicler places the parable and related conflicts in a more obviously theological context. This enables the Chronicler to present the parable's relationship to a hostile divine action in a more explicit manner. Nonetheless, this presentation remains in keeping with the general function of the parable in 2 Kings 14 even if this function seems more implicit in Kings because of its less detailed and less overtly theological narrative.

Both 2 Kings 14 and 2 Chronicles 25 begin with qualified praise of the Judean king Amaziah, noting that he "did the right thing in the eyes of YHWH." Yet, 2 Kgs 14:3 observes that although he did as well as his father did, he did not do as well as David did. Second Chronicles 25:2 comments that he did not act with a perfect heart. As with Ahab in 1 Kings 20, initially, Amaziah seems to resolve conflicts well according to both Kings and Chronicles. Once he establishes his reign, he avenges the death of his father, who fell victim to his servants' murder conspiracy (cf. 2 Kgs 12:21; 2 Chr 24:25). Yet both Kings and Chronicles note that Amaziah did not execute the conspirators' children in accordance with the Mosaic law that prohibits the execution of children for the sins of their parents and vice-versa (Deut 24:16; cf. Jer 31:29–30; Ezek 18:4, 20).[25]

The largest difference between the two accounts concerns the reasons why Amaziah confronts Jehoash and why Amaziah does not listen to Jehoash's parable. Unlike 2 Kgs 14:7, the narrative in 2 Chronicles 25 reports that Amaziah hired Israelite warriors to help him fight the Edomites, but then he did not let these warriors fight after hearing a prophetic warning. The disgruntled Israelite warriors raided Judean cities, killing 3,000 people (v. 13). In vv. 14–15, a prophet declares that Amaziah had angered YHWH by confiscating the Edomite gods and worshipping them. When Amaziah rebukes the prophet, the prophet declares that YHWH has determined to destroy Amaziah because "you did not listen (*lo'-shama'ta*) to my counsel" (v. 16b). Despite this prophetic announcement, Amaziah confronts Jehoash (v. 17).

Unlike 2 Kgs 14:11a, 2 Chr 25:20 provides the reason Amaziah did not listen to Jehoash's parable. The narrator explains, "But Amaziah did not listen (*lo'-shamaʿ*) because it was from God in order to give them into the hand [of Jehoash] because they sought the gods of Edom." In 2 Chronicles 25, God prevents Amaziah from listening to the parable in order to begin the king's foretold destruction because he did not listen to God's prophet. Here, Amaziah's disregard of the parable relates to his disregard of the prophetic word. Jehoash's parable provides Amaziah with another opportunity not to listen and thereby emphasize his lack of discernment. Through the repetition of the phrase "did not listen," the Chronicler reinforces the notion that Amaziah did not act wisely in the aftermath of his Edomite victory according to both the prophet and Jehoash. He had no business worshipping Edomite gods according to the prophet, and he had no business confronting Israel according to Jehoash. The Chronicler uses Jehoash's parable to emphasize the point that Amaziah could not handle his conflicts properly with either Edom or Israel.

In v. 19, when Jehoash uses a more straightforward mode of speech than a fable (cf. 2 Kgs 14:10), he draws out the point regarding the aftermath of the Edomite conflict more directly. Due to Amaziah's Edomite victory, Amaziah's heart has lifted him up and he has overstepped his limits. According to Jehoash, this reaction is not an appropriate way of handling his victory. Neither the bramble in the parable nor Amaziah in the surrounding narrative have handled their respective encounters properly.

The narrative in 2 Chronicles 25 provides a more detailed and theologically motivated account of the conflicts involving Judah, Israel, and Edom than 2 Kings 14. This longer account resonates well with the function of the parables studied in previous chapters. Far from presenting Jehoash's parable as a lesson aimed at changing Amaziah's course of action, the Chronicler presents the parable as a means of facilitating a hostile divine action against Amaziah. God causes Amaziah to disregard the parable or possibly even not understand or interpret it correctly, depending on how we take the sense of *shamaʿ*.

In v. 19, Jehoash hints at the reason Amaziah disregards or cannot understand his parable. Whereas 2 Kgs 14:10 reads the verbal root *kbd* as a niphal imperative ("your heart has lifted you up. Be honored [*hikkabed*] and dwell in your house"), 2 Chr 25:19 reads it as a hiphil, rendering the phrase as "your heart has lifted you up for hardness (*lehakbid*)." The reading in v. 19 recalls the repeated use of various forms of the hiphil of *kbd* in Exodus to describe the hardening of Pharaoh's heart "so that he would not listen (*lo'-shamaʿ*) to [Moses and Aaron] just as YHWH said" (Exod 8:11b; cf. 8:28; 9:34; 10:1).[26] The account in Chronicles invokes imagery from Exodus that recalls how God caused Pharaoh to disregard Moses' message in order to facilitate hostile divine actions against Pharaoh. If this is the case, the Chronicler does not present the parable as a tool that could change Amaziah's mind. Rather, the parable functions to announce and highlight Amaziah's downfall and his inability to prevent it.

Second Chronicles 25 presents the parable's function as helping to facilitate a hostile divine action against Amaziah rather than warning him against a foolish military campaign. Although the version in 2 Kings 14 does not attribute the hostile actions to an act of God explicitly, it nevertheless presents the parable as helping to facilitate a hostile action against its addressee. The function of the parable in Chronicles does not break with its function in Kings. Rather, it provides a more explicit theological understanding for its use than Kings does. In both cases, the parable escalates the conflict in the surrounding narrative because it does not clarify a lesson in foreign policy as much as it epitomizes the height of royal posturing. In 2 Kgs 14:12–14 (cf. 2 Chr 25:22–24), the narrative spends three verses detailing specifics of the conflict's aftermath. By recording the capture of prisoners, the items taken from Jerusalem, and even the size of the hole Jehoash creates in Jerusalem's wall, these verses help highlight the continued violence following the parable.

CONCLUSIONS AND IMPLICATIONS: READING PARABLES WITHIN THE DEUTERONOMISTIC HISTORY

Instead of resolving conflict, Jehoash's parable appears to promote conflict. Although Amaziah may have wanted to enter into a marriage alliance rather than a military conflict, it appears possible that Jehoash turned the encounter into a conflict through his parabolic reply to Amaziah's request. Instead of offering a simple and straightforward reply, he speaks in parables. This mode of communication gives his reply a multivalent quality with a number of interpretive opinions. As with the wise woman of Tekoa in 2 Samuel 14, he does not appear to recommend a clear course of action. It is easy to see how Amaziah could have disregarded or misunderstood it. Nonetheless, his responses suggest he does not discern properly the conflict presented to him in the parable. Furthermore, Jehoash's speech in 2 Kgs 14:10 and 2 Chr 25:19 implies that Amaziah has not handled the aftermath of his conflict with the Edomites properly.

The overall impact of Jehoash's parable in vv. 9–10 condemns Amaziah's ability to handle conflict with discernment. As with other parables in the Hebrew Bible, the parable helps justify further conflict. However we choose to allegorize the specifics of Jehoash's parable, the parable's imagery invokes a genre associated with insults and posturing. In recognizing this imagery as not simply that of a fable, but that of a disputation text, we gain a greater appreciation for the intensity of Jehoash's taunt. We should not be surprised that such language could serve as a catalyst for conflict.

Although Jehoash's parable shares several features with parables studied in previous chapters, we should note a feature distinguishing it from the others. In previous chapters, we found that the speaker of the given parable had a political disadvantage with respect to his or her addressee. Jotham does not have the same political capital as Abimelech or the lords of Shechem (Judges 9). Nor do Nathan and the wise woman of Tekoa with respect to David (2 Samuel 12, 14) or the unnamed prophet with respect to Ahab (1 Kings 20). Based on these texts, it is tempting to conclude that speakers used parables to deliver their criticism indirectly because a more explicit condemnation of their more politically powerful addressees would endanger the speakers.[27] Nonetheless, the fact that the speaker of the parable in 2 Kings 14 and 2 Chronicles 25 holds a major political advantage over his addressee calls into question this theory of why speakers use parables in certain communicative situations. Furthermore, as we observed in chapter 5, prophets such as Jeremiah, Elijah, Elisha, Amos, and others repeatedly announce death sentences and other condemnations of kings directly (e.g., 1 Kgs 21:17–29; 2 Kgs 1:1–17; Jer 21:1–10; 34:1–5; Amos 7:11). As we have reiterated throughout this book, parables do not function to disguise the point(s) of a parable but to intensify the point(s) of a parable. The communicative situation in 2 Kings 14 and 2 Chronicles 25 warns us against trying to understand why speakers used parables based on generalizations about power disparities between speakers and addressees. Furthermore, we should not make much of the fact that kings (David, Ahab, Amaziah) represent most of the addressees of parables discussed thus far. After all, the narratives in the books of Samuel and Kings focus on various kings as their main characters. Thus, kings appear as frequent addressees of most forms of speech, parables or otherwise.

Kingship themes play a major role in the so-called Deuteronomistic History, a section of the Hebrew Bible that includes all the parables we have studied thus far (Judges 9; 2 Samuel 12, 14; 1 Kings 20; 2 Kings 14). Thus, we could ask how the repeated use of parables figures into the ideological investment(s) encoded within the Deuteronomistic History. Nonetheless, we should avoid making anything more than a general observation that the parables would fit in with and help reinforce a negative commentary on the fate of Israel and Judah for exilic or postexilic Deuteronomists. Most likely, the fact that the parables discussed thus far appear mostly within the Deuteronomistic History remains a coincidence and does not indicate intentional editorial activity by the Historian(s). No pattern emerges for the parables' present locations within the Deuteronomistic History that provides evidence of their special redactional use beyond their appropriateness for situations of escalating conflict and destruction.

The repeated presence of parables in the Deuteronomistic History may contribute to negative views on kingship. Yet that contribution comes from the general use of parables to promote conflict instead of a redactor's unique deployment of parables to formulate a particular negative view of kingship. After all, as we saw in this chapter, the Deuteronomistic History includes an example of a king creating a parable himself. Rather than attempting to discern a specific Deuteronomistic use of parables for ideological commentary, we should simply observe that the parables within the Deuteronomistic History function in a manner consistent with their use in other parts of the Hebrew Bible. We have already seen this consistency with the Chronicler's use of Jehoash's parable to promote conflict and condemn Amaziah in 2 Chronicles 25. The following chapter concludes this book by showing that this use of parables also appears within prophetic literature that either predates or appears contemporaneously with various editions of the Deuteronomistic History.

Moving beyond the parables surrounded by biblical prose, we examine Isa 5:1–7 and Ezek 17:1–24 to show that our conclusions regarding the use of parables in Judges, the books of Samuel, and the books of Kings have implications for the study of Hebrew Bible parables beyond the ideological landscape of the Deuteronomistic History.

7

∞

Conclusions and Implications for the Study of Hebrew Bible Parables

"Don't you know what these things mean?"
—Ezekiel 17:12

"Who is like the wise person and who knows the interpretation of a word?"
—Ecclesiastes 8:1a

This final chapter expands on the conclusions of the previous chapters and examines their implications for the study of parables found elsewhere in the Hebrew Bible, especially in the Latter Prophets. The previous chapters built the case that the prose contexts of Hebrew Bible parables call into question scholarly assumptions about their rhetorical function. In short, we found that parables (1) intensify announcements of judgment and condemnation rather than call for a change of behavior or facilitate conflict resolution; and (2) perform this intensifying function by invoking specific genres to address the speaker's specific communicative needs. Moving beyond the prose portions of the Hebrew Bible, this chapter tests this thesis further by briefly examining selected parables from Ezekiel and First Isaiah. We will use Isa 5:1–7 and Ezek 17:1–24 as test cases.

ISAIAH 5:1–7

In v. 1a, Isaiah refers to the following verses as a "song" (*shir*) for his beloved. In the most general sense, we could refer to this passage as a song *mashal* since Isaiah bases his comparison (v. 7) on a song (vv. 1–2). The fact that Isaiah refers to this passage as a song does not mean it does not contain a narrative. Though unlike Ugaritic literature the Hebrew Bible does not contain long narrative poetry, it does contain brief poetic vignettes, as we find in Isaiah's song.[1] The song narrates how a vineyard owner carefully prepares his beloved vineyard on a fertile ridge. He builds a tower for it and prepares a wine press in the hope that the vineyard will yield fruitful grapes. Yet, despite his careful preparations, the vineyard produces only wild grapes (vv. 1–2). In vv. 3–4, the narration shifts from the third person to the first person and depicts the owner calling on the inhabitants of Jerusalem and the men of Judah to judge between him and his vineyard. In vv. 5–6, the owner describes in graphic detail how he plans to decimate his beloved vineyard. In v. 7, Isaiah concludes the passage by comparing the destroyed vineyard to the house of Israel and the people of Judah.

To understand why Isaiah creates his parable out of a song instead of another narrative genre, we must examine the specific genre of the song. Scholars have written a great deal on the genre(s) of this passage. We will not review scholarly opinions on this matter in detail since helpful overviews of these discussions already exist.[2] In general, debate has focused on whether we should classify the passage as a whole as a parable or an allegory. For this book's purposes, however, this choice represents a false dichotomy since every parable requires limited allegorical interpretation to accomplish its role as a comparison (see the discussion of parables and allegories in chapter 1). This passage does not represent a pure allegory since each of the vineyard owner's actions does not correspond to a particular moment in Judah and Israel's history.[3] Rather, v. 7 uses a limited allegory to create a comparison between the vineyard and the house of Israel and the people of Judah. Since the prophet compares Israel and Judah with the narrative involving the vineyard, this passage qualifies as a parable by this book's functional rather than generic definition.

Yet we should note that although a number of scholars label the passage as a parable, they understand this label as representing a genre instead of a function. Influenced by Uriel Simon's work, they often designate the genre of the entire passage as a juridical parable.[4] In keeping with the use of the term genre popular in the early 1980s, these scholars identify a text as a juridical parable based on the presence of certain literary features that represent this genre in its hypothetical or ideal form. Based on this technique, however, it remains difficult to classify Isa 5:1–7 as part of the juridical parable genre because the text does not exhibit key features of this genre in its hypothetical or ideal form. Gerald T. Sheppard has shown that we can only supply these missing features by moving Isa 3:13–15 into the midst of 5:1–7.[5] This emendation, however, finds no support in any of the versions.

Arguments that 5:1–7 represents a juridical parable based on its function rather than its form do not work either. According to Simon, a juridical parable aims to trap its addressee into self-condemnation. We should not assume, however, that Isaiah intends his parable to trap his addressees in this way. As Isaiah does not record his addressees' reaction to his parable, it is a large and unfounded assumption to suggest that Isaiah's addressees would have been surprised when the prophet applied the song of the vineyard to their situation. As we saw in chapter 3, since addressees show enough sophistication to understand when a prophetic sign-act applies to them elsewhere in prophetic literature (Ezek 24:19; cf. Ezek 21:5), little reason exists to assume the use of a metaphor would trap them in this instance.[6]

Nevertheless, based on Hosea's use of the vineyard image for the northern kingdom (Hos 9:8; 10:1; 14:8), Gale A. Yee argues that when Isaiah requests that Jerusalem and Judah "judge" between the owner and the vineyard (v. 3), Isaiah's Judean audience would understand the image of the vineyard as referring to the northern kingdom instead of themselves. Accordingly, Isaiah would trap them into self-condemnation when they judge against the vineyard, only to find out in v. 7 that the vineyard includes Judah as well as Israel. Contrary to this proposal, it is possible that the addressees could associate the vineyard image with Jerusalem as well as the northern kingdom since Isaiah compares Jerusalem to an abandoned booth in a vineyard in 1:8 (cf. 7:23; 16:10).[7] It remains unconvincing that the addressees would believe the obviously personified vineyard refers to the northern kingdom alone and not Judah.

We should also not assume that the addressees would judge in favor of the owner and against the vineyard, even though v. 3 uses the language of a legal petition. Regarding the owner's proposed actions in vv. 5–6, H. G. M. Williamson observes, "The owner might be thought to be acting unreasonably in some respects; most husbandman would try to solve the problem of the production of diseased grapes before moving to destroy the whole vineyard."⁸ Due to the graphic nature of the vineyard's destruction in vv. 5–6, those judging between the owner and the vineyard may view the owner's actions as extreme and not endorse such actions. The switch to first-person narration in vv. 3–6 reinforces this sense of extremity and allows Isaiah to paint a graphic and intimate picture of the vineyard's destruction. These verses leave no doubt about the state of the vineyard, nor do they suggest that the vineyard may survive if it changes its ways. The owner removes its support and abandons it. The verbs used in v. 5, "devour" (*ba'ar*) and "trample" (*mirmas*), connote particularly destructive activities. Isaiah uses very violent imagery to convey the thorough decimation of the vineyard.⁹

Isaiah waits until v. 7 to compare the vineyard with Judah and Israel not because the comparison comes as a surprise ending to trap his addressees. Again, addressees seem sophisticated enough to recognize when a parable applies to them elsewhere in prophetic literature. Rather, he waits until v. 7 so that he may compare them to an utterly destroyed and not just unproductive vineyard. Unlike Nathan in 2 Sam 12:7–12, Isaiah does not need to announce his addressee's punishment because he has already graphically conveyed that punishment in his narration of the vineyard's fate. Delaying the comparison until v. 7 intensifies the finality of the announcement of the people's fate. The rhetorical force of the comparison comes not from a surprise ending. Rather, it comes from a complete and utter ending.

This interpretation finds support in Isaiah's other uses of vintage imagery. Susan Ackerman has shown that Isaiah invokes vintage festivals and music in the context of laments over a people's fate elsewhere in the book.¹⁰ While lamenting Moab, Isaiah announces the cessation of the joyful shout in the vineyards (*kerem*) and the "vintage shout" (*hedad*) that typically accompany vintage festivals (16:10). Isaiah 32:10 contains the same image in a passage where Isaiah again announces judgment and destruction. Instead of singing joyful vintage festival songs, the prophet depicts people wailing for a fruitful vineyard (*gepen*) in 32:12. As in 5:6, the land will become overrun with "thorns and biers" according to 32:13. Throughout 32:9–14, Isaiah invokes images of vintage festivals to heighten the sense of sorrow when the harvest does not produce the expected results.¹¹ Instead of an occasion for celebration, Isaiah uses festival imagery to announce divine destruction. Given this use of imagery in

Isaiah 16 and 32, it appears that the prophet employs a similar rhetorical technique in 5:1–7.[12]

Ultimately, we do not know whose side the addressees would take in this dispute based on Isaiah's narration. Thus, contrary to the proposed function of a juridical parable, we should not conclude that v. 3 aims to trick its addressees into self-condemnation. In fact, the prophet does not seem concerned with the addressees' reactions. He does not even bother to record their reactions. Instead, the prophet is primarily concerned with announcing the destruction of Judah and Israel (vv. 5–7). The narration moves immediately to the vineyard's destruction without pausing for the addressees' judgment (unlike other supposed examples of juridical parables in 2 Samuel 12, 14; 1 Kings 20).[13]

In this sense, Isa 5:1–7 resembles Jotham's fable in Judges 9 more than other supposed examples of the juridical parable. As we saw in chapter 2, Jotham shows no concern for how the Shechemites interpret his fable involving the trees. He employs the fable to introduce and add rhetorical force to his curse on the relationship between the Shechemites, the house of Millo, and Abimelech. Jotham's curse against his addressees gains additional rhetorical intensity through its comparison with the bramble's curse, which serves as the culmination to Jotham's slowly narrated and detailed fable. Isaiah employs a similar rhetorical technique when he slowly narrates the song of the vineyard culminating in the vineyard's detailed destruction. He then compares Judah and Israel to this destroyed plant. Rather than set a trap for the addressees based on their (unrecorded) reaction, v. 3 allows for a transition from third-person to first-person narration. This move adds intimacy to the announcement of the vineyard's graphic destruction in vv. 5–6. In v. 7, Isaiah does not simply compare Judah and Israel to the poorly producing vineyard of vv. 1–2. Rather, he compares them to the vineyard already marked for utter destruction in vv. 5–6. As with other parables studied throughout this book, the comparison intensifies the announcement of hostile actions against Isaiah's addressees, regardless of whether they endorse this judgment prior to v. 7. We may label Isaiah 5:1–7 a parable because it creates a comparison out of a narrative, not because it belongs to the genre of juridical parable.

The previous paragraph's conclusion, however, does not resolve the issue of the narrative genre(s) invoked in vv. 1–6 that becomes a parable in v. 7. Throughout this book, we have argued that the genre invoked in the narrative that becomes a parable plays an important role in the forcefulness of the comparison's rhetoric. John T. Willis labels vv. 1–7 as "*a parabolic song of a disappointed husbandman.*"[14] Yet, as Willis notes, this label describes the text's content more than its genre. Isaiah may aim to convey deep disappointment through this song. Nonetheless, we must still examine how a particular genre invoked in this passage helps him convey such disappointment.

Building on the label of "love-song" in v. 1a (cf. Ps 45:1), Gary Roye Williams argues that the terms "beloved" (*yadid*) and "vineyard" (*kerem*) suggest that the love song aims to praise the beloved based on comparative biblical and other ancient Near Eastern love poetry (cf. Song 8:11–13).[15] The use of a love song to narrate how the owner's expectations for the vineyard dissolve into frustration after he "waits" or "hopes" (*qawah*) for fruitful grapes only to yield sour grapes from his vineyard (vv. 2, 4) contributes to the sense of deep disappointment. The harvest of only sour grapes dashes the high praise and careful cultivation of the vineyard in vv. 1–2a. The vintage imagery may further contribute to the sense of expectation on the owner's part since it employs imagery associated with bountiful harvests (e.g., the festival of booths; Lev 23:34–43; Deut 16:13–15).[16] According to Deut 16:13, people should celebrate the festival of booths by bringing in the harvest from their threshing floors and wine presses. As with Deut 16:13, the owner of the vineyard in Isa 5:1–7 prepares his wine press in anticipation of a bountiful harvest. Invoking imagery associated with a vintage festival builds up the love song's sense of expectation.

Isaiah builds his comparison (his parable) around this sense of waiting or hoping conveyed and heightened through a love song about a vineyard that employs vintage festival imagery. To justify his complete destruction of his vineyard, the owner reiterates how he waited or hoped (*qawah*) for a bountiful harvest (v. 4). In v. 7, the prophet compares this unrealized hope that provoked the vineyard's destruction to YHWH's unrealized hope that Judah and Israel will produce justice and righteousness. Isaiah depicts God as "waiting" or "hoping" (*qawah*) for justice and righteousness from Israel and Judah only to yield bloodshed and an outcry from them. The invoked love song genre that forms the basis of this comparison intensifies both the sense of hope and the emotional impact when this hope is subsequently dashed.

To conclude this brief study of Isa 5:1–7, the final verse (v. 7) compares the disappointed owner to a disappointed deity and the bleak fate of a vineyard to the bleak fate of the people. Invoking the love song genre with vintage festival imagery allows the prophet to heighten the emotional impact of his comparisons, which highlights the deity's disappointment and, more importantly, the announcement of the people's grim fate. This comparison intensifies the sense of hope and the emotional impact when this hope is subsequently dashed. For Isaiah, this dashed hope helps justify the hostile divine action announced against Israel and Judah in 5:5–6.

EZEKIEL 17:1–24

As with Isa 5:1–7 and other parables studied in the previous chapters, the parable in Ezek 17:1–24 announces and facilitates hostile actions and further conflict (vv. 16–21). Generally, the same conclusion holds true for Ezekiel's other uses of parables (cf. Ezek 15:1–28; 16:1–58; 19:2–14; 23:1–29; 24:3–14). Yet, in contrast to Isaiah's song of the vineyard, scholars have not spent as much time discussing matters of genre in relation to Ezek 17:1–10. When they do, their discussion generally focuses on why Ezekiel labels this passage as both a "comparison" (*mashal*) and a "riddle" (*hidah*) in 17:1.[17] As we noted in chapter 1, both labels describe the function of a text rather than its form or genre. As with *meshalim*, we encounter *hidot* in various forms, such as short story *hidot* (Ezek 17:2–10) or proverbial *hidot* (Judg 14:14). If the term *mashal* describes a text's function as a comparison, the term *hidah* describes its function as a riddle. Regarding the content rather than the function of Ezek 17:2–10, we may also label this text as a fable *mashal* since the narrative deals primarily with personified plants and animals. As a number of scholars observe, Ezekiel's use of personified plants and animals lends ambiguity to his message and contributes to its riddling quality.[18] For example, an addressee could interpret the image of the first "great eagle" as a reference to either the Babylonian king Nebuchadnezzar as Ezekiel does in v. 12 (cf. Jer 48:20; 49:22) or to YHWH since other biblical texts, including some from Ezekiel, associate this image with YHWH (Exod 19:4; Deut 32:11; Ezek 1:10; 10:14; 17:22–24).[19] In this section, we explore how Ezekiel's presentation of his fable as a riddle bolsters his authority as an interpreter of current political events. The riddle format implies that only Ezekiel can discern the true significance of the political situation.

As discussed in chapter 1, parabolic *meshalim* tend to have a riddling quality that challenges the addressee to give the proper interpretation of the comparison. Depending on how one handles a *mashal* or *hidah*, one may demonstrate his or her wisdom (Eccl 12:9; Prov 1:6; 1 Kgs 10:1; Dan 8:23; cf. *ANET*, 427–30) or his or her foolishness (Prov 26:7, 9; Sir 20:20). As seen throughout this book, when speakers challenge their addressees with a parable in prose sections of the Hebrew Bible, the addressees usually demonstrate a lack of interpretative skill in their response (2 Samuel 12, 14; 1 Kings 20). After the addressees display their inability to interpret, the speakers counter with the intended interpretation and announce how it applies to the addressees' situation. Such exchanges lend authority to the parable speakers' announcement concerning the addressees' circumstances. The use of parables could give credibility to their speakers, over against their addressees, as skilled and authoritative commentators on the current events that occasioned the parable.

This type of exchange between speaker and addressee does not accompany the parable in Ezek 17:2–10. As with Isa 5:1–7, this passage does not include a response or judgment from Ezekiel's addressees. Nevertheless, we may assume that the addressees would not have interpreted the parable as Ezekiel intends. After completing his narrative, Ezekiel asks his addressees, "Don't you know what these things mean?" (v. 12). With this rhetorical question, Ezekiel implies that he does not expect his addressees to understand his fable.[20] The prophet uses a similar technique in 12:9, when he depicts his audience as asking, "What are you doing?" after he performs a sign-act (cf. 24:19). Whereas we have no idea of the addressees' reaction in Isa 5:1–7, Ezekiel suggests that his addressees could not supply the correct interpretation in 17:12. Immediately after this rhetorical question, Ezekiel explains his fable. This immediate explanation suggests further that the addressees would not have understood Ezekiel's fable (cf. 12:10–15).[21]

That Ezekiel intends to challenge and puzzle his addressees with his fable finds further support in the fact that YHWH instructs Ezekiel to present his fable as a riddle. YHWH chooses to communicate with the house of Israel through a riddle instead of a more direct method. In Num 12:6–8, YHWH claims to use "riddles" (*hidot*) as one of the methods of communicating with people. YHWH contrasts this riddle method with the clearer method of communication YHWH uses with Moses in an effort to promote Moses' authority as a prophet over against others. Similarly, YHWH's choice to communicate with Israel through a riddle in Ezek 17:2 puts Ezekiel in a privileged interpretative position. This does not suggest that the text presents Ezekiel as a prophet like Moses but that a divine riddle the people cannot solve reinforces Ezekiel's superior standing as an interpreter.[22] As with his sign-act in 12:1–15, Ezekiel supplies a divinely inspired interpretation of his announcement in 17:11–21.

The importance of establishing Ezekiel's authority in this situation has to do in part with the interpretation of political events that his parable provides. Although specific images in the fable remain ambiguous, the general subject matter focuses on political events surrounding the Babylonian exiles and the fates of the last Judean kings, Jehoiachin and Zedekiah. These events represent a popular topic for Ezekiel, who had already addressed them in his earlier sign-acts (cf. 12:1–15). We may summarize the fable and Ezekiel's interpretation of it succinctly: The first eagle that comes to Lebanon and removes the head of the cedar and carries it to the land of trade (vv. 3–4) represents Nebuchadnezzar's deportation of Jehoiachin from Jerusalem to Babylon (v. 12).[23] The seed the eagle plants and cultivates in fertile soil so that it becomes a productive but low vine whose branches turn toward the eagle (vv. 5–6) represents Nebuchadnezzar's instillation of Zedekiah as a Judean vassal loyal to Babylon (vv. 13–14). When the vine turns its root to a second eagle for water (vv. 7–8), Ezekiel depicts Zedekiah's choice to turn to the Egyptian Pharaoh Psammetichus II for aid in Zedekiah's rebellion against Nebuchadnezzar (v. 15).[24] Ezekiel questions the wisdom of this rebellion with a series of rhetorical questions that follow both the fable (vv. 9–10) and its interpretation (v. 15b). Of all the parables studied in this book, this one comes closest to a pure allegory.

The mere recital of events that Ezekiel presents would not seem controversial to his addressees. They would know about Zedekiah's failed rebellion all too well. Rather, the controversy would arise from Ezekiel's *interpretation* of Zedekiah's rebellion. In the fable, the prophet depicts the eagle as treating the vine well. The eagle provides the seed with fertile soil and enough water for the seed to grow into a vine (vv. 5–6). Then, Ezekiel contends that Nebuchadnezzar and Zedekiah formed a vassal treaty, which Zedekiah subsequently broke (cf. 2 Chr 36:13). Ezekiel even suggests that YHWH will punish Zedekiah for breaking this oath (vv. 16–18).[25] The prophet views this act as infidelity against YHWH (v. 20). Ezekiel details how YHWH makes an oath of YHWH's own, swearing that Zedekiah will die in Babylon (vv. 16, 20). Ezekiel's interpretation of the political events involving Zedekiah imply that YHWH worked through the Babylonians against Zedekiah.

As Jon D. Levenson observes, Ezekiel 17 suggests that "the best hope of the exiles is that the king of Babylon will confirm the kingship of the Davidic claimant, who will then serve his liege in fidelity."[26] This assessment differs greatly from the promise of an eternal Davidic throne (2 Sam 7:12–16; cf. 1 Kgs 11:36; 15:4; 2 Kgs 8:19). In keeping with traditions reflected in portions of First Isaiah, some may have viewed Ezekiel's position as compromising this Davidic tradition (cf. Isaiah 7, 37; 2 Kings 19). Like Ezekiel, Jeremiah speaks against relying on Egypt and rebelling against Babylon (Jer 37:7–10; cf. 21:1–10; 27:1–29:24; 34:1–7).[27] Yet Jeremiah faced strong opposition to his messages (Jer 32:3–5). Some Jerusalem officials even arrest Jeremiah after accusing him of having Babylonian sympathies (Jer 37:13). These parties call for Jeremiah's execution because they believe his message hurts the morale of the Judean soldiers (38:4). In other words, the book of Jeremiah provides evidence that some parties would contest the political analysis that Ezekiel offers in Ezek 17:11–21.

Furthermore, other portions of Jeremiah record political viewpoints that may counter those of Ezekiel 17.[28] Although we cannot say for certain, Ezek 17:22–24 may present hope for the restoration of Jehoiachin's throne when it speaks of YHWH exulting a "twig" (*yoneqet*), which YHWH takes from the top of the cedars of Lebanon. When describing Jehoiachin's deportation by Nebuchadnezzar in his fable (v. 4), Ezekiel uses a similar image of a "twig" (*yeniqah*), which the great eagle removes from the top of the cedars of Lebanon. By contrast, Jeremiah makes an emphatic announcement that Jehoiachin marks the end of the Davidic dynasty and that he will not regain his throne (Jer 22:24–30).[29] Jeremiah even denounces other prophets who hold out hope for Jehoiachin's restoration (Jeremiah 28). In addition, the end of 2 Kings offers little hope of the restoration of the Davidic dynasty through either Zedekiah or Jehoiachin. Rather, it addresses issues of quality of life in exile.[30] As with Ezekiel's interpretation of Zedekiah's rebellion in vv. 11–21, if Ezekiel implies Jehoiachin's restoration in vv. 22–24, certain parties would have opposed this interpretation as well.

Considering the debatable nature of Ezekiel's messages throughout chapter 17, presenting his messages as the solutions to a riddle, which other parties could not solve (v. 12), imbues them with additional authority. Ezekiel comments on political events representing a matter of public record that most likely invited a number of opinions. Yet, rather than comment on these events directly, Ezekiel packages them as an enigma that baffles everyone except himself. Turning familiar events into a fable gives them a puzzling quality that allows Ezekiel to present them as a riddle. When the prophet unlocks this fable through his divinely inspired comparison (*mashal*) in vv. 11–21, his interpretation comes across as the definitive word on the matter. Regarding Ezekiel's use of a fable, Walther Zimmerli comments, "If, in the sphere of Wisdom, the fable could at first communicate timeless truth, in Ezek 17 it has fully entered into the service of the prophetic preaching of history."[31] We could develop this comment by suggesting that invoking a fable helps Ezekiel communicate his prophetic preaching of history as timeless (divinely inspired) truth.

Ezekiel uses *meshalim* in various forms (proverbial, parabolic, and so on) more frequently than any other biblical prophet (cf. Ezek 12:22; 17:2; 18:2; 24:3; and so on). This brief study suggests that he does so in Ezekiel 17 to give additional authority to his interpretation of a contentious subject. This idea finds support in the next chapter of Ezekiel. In Ezek 18:1–4, the prophet uses a *mashal* in a different form (proverbial) as a way to engage another contentious issue that engenders multiple perspectives throughout the Hebrew Bible. Bernard M. Levinson has shown how Ezek 18:1–4 contributes to a larger biblical discourse on transgenerational punishment, the principle of descendants being punished for the sins of their ancestors (Exod 20:5; 34:7; Num 14:18; Deut 5:9). Since some texts voice concerns about the justice of such a principle (e.g., Lam 5:7), Levinson argues that Ezekiel frames this principle, which the Pentateuch presents as divine law, as a proverbial *mashal*. In Ezek 18:2–4, YHWH asks, "Why do you all speak this folk saying (*mashal*) regarding the land of Israel saying, 'Parents are eating sour grapes and children's teeth are blunted'.... [Instead] the person that sins, that one will die" (cf. Jer 31:29–30; Deut 24:16). According to Levinson, approaching the concept of transgenerational punishment as a popular proverb or folk saying instead of divine law allows Ezekiel to repudiate it without directly overturning divine law.[32]

Levinson's argument draws attention to how Ezekiel uses the folk saying genre for rhetorical purposes. To build on Levinson's point, we should note that packaging transgenerational punishment as a *mashal* rather than divine law enables Ezekiel to offer an authoritative opinion on the matter because of his reputation as a speaker of *meshalim* (Ezek 21:5). Thus, his addressees would acknowledge his ability to evaluate whether a particular proverb provides an appropriate fit for the current situation. Ezekiel could say whether this proverb or folk saying still performs within the present exilic circumstances.[33] Framing his opinion as an evaluation of a folk saying or proverb concerning transgenerational punishment gives his opinion greater authority than if Ezekiel had simply presented it as a response to a law recorded in the Decalogue. As with Ezekiel 17, the prophet's comparison invokes a genre in 18:1–4 that positions his opinion on a contested issue as the definitive word.

CONCLUSIONS

These brief explorations of Isaiah 5 and Ezekiel 17 show that this book's studies of parables within the Hebrew Bible's prose portions shed light on the communicative situations that provoke parables in the Latter Prophets. As with their counterparts within biblical prose, these prophetic parables appear in situations of conflict and function to intensify announcements of judgment. Although it may result from coincidence, in general the prophets do not employ parables when delivering messages of comfort or restoration (e.g., Isaiah 40–41; Jeremiah 30–31).

Furthermore, the genres invoked in Isa 5:1–7 and Ezek 17:1–10 provide particular rhetorical orientations that add force to their prophetic announcements. Their respective uses of fables connect with at least two ways seen throughout the previous chapters in which parables help intensify a speaker's announcement. First, Isaiah emphasizes the sense of divine disappointment by building his comparison around a love song with vintage festival imagery. With this move, he heightens the emotional impact of the owner's disappointment. This helps justify what his addressees may otherwise view as the owner's overreaction against the vineyard when he destroys it. The song's intensification of emotions helps the parable justify the hostile actions it announces. Second, Ezekiel emphasizes the riddling quality of his fable and thus challenges his addressees' ability to discern the meaning behind recent political events. This allows him to suggest that his addressees do not understand the complex political circumstances that surround them. Since only Ezekiel can discern their meaning correctly, the parable helps to establish the prophet as the definitive voice on the matter. As seen throughout this book, speakers use parables to reveal their addressees' lack of discernment and thus justify their condemnation of these addressees.

Both Isaiah and Ezekiel's use of parables resonates with how parables function within Hebrew Bible prose. Unlike the parables within the prose sections, we do not have access to the specific exchanges between speakers and addressees or specific situations that provoke parables in prophetic literature. Nevertheless, this book's earlier chapters shed light on the types of communicative situations that the Latter Prophets' parables seem to address even without access to the exact historical development of these texts. It may seem odd to save discussion of prophetic literature until the last chapter in a book about parables. Yet, in doing so, this final chapter shows that the prose studies throughout this book have great implications for the study of parables throughout the Hebrew Bible.

Notes

1. BREAKING DOWN PARABLES: INTRODUCTORY ISSUES

1. Uriel Simon, "The Poor Man's Ewe-Lamb: An Example of a Juridical Parable," *Bib* 48 (1967): 207–42. Simon's notion of a juridical parable has had a significant impact on subsequent scholarship dealing with these passages. See, among others, Bruce C. Birch, "The First and Second Books of Samuel," *NIB* 2: 1292; Craig A. Evans, "On the Vineyard Parables of Isaiah 5 and Mark 12," *BZ* 28 (1984): 82–6; Jean Hoftijzer, "David and the Tekoite Woman," *VT* 20 (1970): 419–44; W. Schottroff, "Das Weinberglied Jesajas (Jes 5, 1–7): Ein Beitrag zur Geschichte der Parabel," *ZAW* 82 (1970): 68–91; Gerald T. Sheppard, "More on Isaiah 5:1–7 as a Juridical Parable," *CBQ* 44 (1982): 45–7; Meir Sternberg, *The Poetics of Biblical Narrative: Ideological Literature and the Drama of Reading* (Bloomington: Indiana University Press, 1987), 429–30; Gale A. Yee, "A Form-Critical Study of Isaiah 5:1–7 as a Song and a Juridical Parable," *CBQ* 43 (1981): 30–40.
2. George W. Coats, "Parable, Fable, and Anecdote: Storytelling in the Succession Narrative," *Int* 35 (1981): 370.
3. Allen Howard Godbey argues that, in addition to verbal comparisons, the label *mashal* applies to a number of the performances of symbolic actions, which he calls "an acted *mashal.*" See Allen Howard Godbey, "The Hebrew Mašal," *AJSL* 39 (1923): 89–108. Yet his overall argument remains unconvincing because his range of examples appears too broad and he tends to ignore the distinction between the definitions of *mashal* as "to compare" and "to rule."
4. George Landes, "Jonah: A *Māšāl*?," in *Israelite Wisdom: Theological and Literary Essays in Honor of Samuel Terrien* (eds. John G. Gammie et al.; New York: Union Theological Seminary, 1978), 139. For helpful reviews of scholarship on *meshalim* in the Hebrew Bible, see Lawrence Boadt, "Understanding the *Mashal* and Its Value for Jewish-Christian Dialogue in a Narrative Theology," in *Parable and Story in Judaism and Christianity* (eds. Clemens Thoma and Michael Wyschogrod; New York: Paulist, 1989), 172–6; Carole R. Fontaine, *Traditional Sayings in the Old Testament: A Contextual Study* (Bible and Literature Series 5; Sheffield: Almond, 1982), 2–27; David B. Gowler, *What Are They Saying About the Parables?* (New York: Paulist, 2000), 42–6; Susan Niditch, *Folklore and the Hebrew Bible* (Guides to Biblical Scholarship; Minneapolis: Fortress, 1993), 67–87.

5. For representative examples of this opinion, see Birger Gerhardsson, "The Narrative Meshalim in the Synoptic Gospels," *NTS* 34 (1988): 353, n. 3; Simon B. Parker, *Stories in Scripture and Inscriptions: Comparative Studies on Narratives in Northwest Semitic Inscriptions and the Hebrew Bible* (New York: Oxford University Press, 1997), 33; Stuart Lasine, "Melodrama as Parable: The Story of the Poor Man's Ewe-Lamb and the Unmasking of David's Topsy-Turvy Emotions," *HAR* 8 (1984): 111–12; Ann M. Vater Solomon, "Fable," in *Saga, Tale, Novella, Fable: Narrative Forms in Old Testament Literature* (JSOTSup 35; ed. George W. Coats; Sheffield: JSOT Press, 1985), 119. As with the present book, several older studies of parables organize their chapters around a series of close readings of individual parables. Although such studies pay close attention to the immediate literary context of the parables, they tend to show greater interest in deriving a set of (often Christian) theological and moral teachings from the parables aimed at the books' contemporary readers. For example, see Clarence Edward Macartney, *The Parables of the Old Testament* (New York: Fleming H. Revell, 1916); Mark Guy Pearse, *The Bramble King and Other Old Testament Parables* (London: Charles H. Kelly, 1900). The same holds true for other older studies that organize their chapters around themes or genres. See Alfred Barry, *The Parables of the Old Testament* (London: Society for Promoting Christian Knowledge, 1846); John MacDougall, *The Old Testament Parables* (London: James Clarke and Company, 1934).
6. For a helpful discussion of this shift, see Gary N. Knoppers, "The Vanishing Solomon: The Disappearance of the United Monarchy from Recent Histories of Ancient Israel," *JBL* 116.1 (1997): 19–44.
7. Fontaine, *Traditional Sayings in the Old Testament*, 74; cf. Niditch, *Folklore and the Hebrew Bible*, 67–87.
8. William McKane, *Proverbs: A New Approach* (OTL; Philadelphia: Westminster, 1970), 27.
9. For a helpful catalogue of such comparisons in Psalms, Job, and prophetic literature, see Claus Westermann, *The Parables of Jesus in the Light of the Old Testament* (trans. and eds. Friedemann W. Golka and Alastair H. B. Logan; Minneapolis: Fortress, 1990), 25–149.
10. Timothy Polk, "Paradigms, Parables, and *Mĕšālîm*: On Reading the *Māšāl* in Scripture," *CBQ* 45.4 (1983): 567. Here Polk follows David Winston Suter, "*Māšāl* in the Similitudes of Enoch," *JBL* 100.2 (1981): 199.
11. As Landes notes, one may infer that Ezek 21:1–4 carries this label since the prophet complains in v. 5 that people call him a speaker of *meshalim* (Landes, "Jonah: A *Māšāl?*," 145, n. 60).
12. On rabbinic parables, see especially Harvey K. McArthur and Robert M. Johnston, *They Also Taught in Parables* (Grand Rapids: Zondervan, 1990); David Stern, *Parables in Midrash: Narrative and Exegesis in Rabbinic Literature* (Cambridge: Harvard University Press, 1991).
13. See especially Landes, "Jonah: A *Māšāl?*" and the works that he references.
14. Along these lines, Gilles Fauconnier and Mark Turner argue that a narrative basis underlines all human thinking. Our thinking involves conceptual blending by which multiple narratives come together in complex relationships and patterned webs of meaning (*The Way We Think: Conceptual Blending and the*

Mind's Hidden Complexities [New York: Basic Books, 2003]). Elsewhere, Mark Turner employs the term parable to discuss the intersection of literary interpretation and human cognitive science (*The Literary Mind: Origins of Thought and Language* [New York: Oxford University Press, 1998]). These ideas remain helpful in understanding the reader's experience of the text in terms of the making of meaning and demonstrating the comparative potential of every narrative. Nevertheless, the present work remains concerned with narratives actualized as explicit comparisons by characters within the Hebrew Bible.

15. Technically, the dream texts in Judges 7, Genesis 37–41, and Daniel 2 and 6 would also qualify as parables by our definition. We will touch on these dream texts in our discussion of 2 Samuel 12 in chapter 3.
16. See Martin Buss, *Biblical Form Criticism in Its Context* (JSOTSup 274; Sheffield: Sheffield Academic Press, 1999), 259.
17. For a helpful discussion of "proverb performance" in the Hebrew Bible during this time period, see Roland E. Murphy, *The Tree of Life: An Exploration of Biblical Wisdom Literature* (Grand Rapids: Eerdmans, 1996), 10–11; cf. Fontaine, *Traditional Sayings in the Old Testament*, 57–60. For a similar focus on the correct application of proverbs in the New Testament, see Charles E. Carlston, "Proverbs, Maxims, and the Historical Jesus," *JBL* 99.1 (1980): 87–105.
18. Carol A. Newsom, "Spying Out the Land: A Report from Genology," in *Bakhtin and Genre Theory in Biblical Studies* (ed. Roland Boer; SemeiaSt 63; Atlanta: Society of Biblical Literature, 2007), 20; cf. Jacques Derrida "The Law of Genre," in *Modern Genre Theory* (ed. David Duff; Harlow, U.K.: Longman, 2000), 219–31; Alastair Fowler, *Kinds of Literature: An Introduction to the Theory of Genres and Modes* (Cambridge: Harvard University Press, 1982).
19. Newsom, "Spying Out the Land," 21. For more on the implications of this shift in our understanding of genre for biblical studies, see a number of the essays in Boer's volume, *Bakhtin and Genre Theory in Biblical Studies*.
20. Marvin Sweeney and Ehud Ben Zvi, introduction to *The Changing Face of Form Criticism for the Twenty-First Century* (eds. Marvin Sweeney and Ehud Ben Zvi; Grand Rapids: Eerdmans, 2003), 10.
21. Newsom, "Spying Out the Land," 21.
22. With the possible exception of 2 Samuel 12 (but see chapter 3 of this book).
23. As a representative example of this type of approach to Hebrew Bible parables, see the influential study by Otto Eissfeldt, *Der Maschal im Alten Testament: eine wortgeschichtliche Untersuchung nebst einer literargeschichtlichen Untersuchung der Maschal genannten Gattungen "Volkssprichwort" und "Spottlied"* (Giessen: A. Töpelmann, 1913).
24. On the Babylonian letter, see Leo Oppenheim, *Letters from Mesopotamia* (Chicago: University of Chicago Press, 1967), 170. On proverbs in the Mari letters, see Jack M. Sasson, "Water beneath Straw: Adventures of a Prophetic Phrase in the Mari Archives," in *Solving Riddles and Untying Knots: Biblical, Epigraphic, and Semitic Studies in Honor of Jonas C. Greenfield* (eds. Ziony Zevit et al.; Winona Lake, IN: Eisenbrauns), 599–608.
25. Jean Pirot, "'Le *māšāl*' dans l'Ancien Testament," *RSR* 37 (1950): 566, 572.
26. Eissfeldt, *Der Maschal im Alten Testament*, 52; Fontaine, *Traditional Sayings in the Old Testament*, 137.

27. Landes, "Jonah: A *Māšāl*," 140–42.
28. Carole Fontaine, "Proverb Performance in the Hebrew Bible," *JSOT* 32.1 (1985): 99; cf. Katheryn Pfisterer Darr, "Proverb Performance and Trans-generational Retribution in Ezekiel 18," in *Ezekiel's Hierarchical World: Wrestling with a Tiered Reality* (eds. Stephen L. Cook and Corrine L. Patton; Atlanta: Society of Biblical Literature, 2004), 207–8.
29. Fontaine, *Traditional Sayings in the Old Testament*, 85.
30. Polk, "Paradigms, Parables, and *Měšālîm*," 570–71; A. S. Herbert, "The 'Parable' (*Māšāl*) in the Old Testament," *SJT* 7 (1954): 183.
31. See, for example, Gerhardsson, "The Narrative Meshalim in the Synoptic Gospels," 345–6; R. Stewart, "The Parable Form in the Old Testament and Rabbinic Literature," *EvQ* 36 (1964): 133–47. Kevin J. Cathcart provides a helpful review of the discussion of these terms within Hebrew Bible scholarship. See Kevin J. Cathcart, "The Trees, the Beasts, and the Birds: Fable, Parables and Allegories in the Old Testament," in *Wisdom in Ancient Israel: Essays in Honour of J.A. Emerton* (eds. John Day, Robert P. Gordon, H. G. M. Williamson; Cambridge: Cambridge University Press, 1995), 214; cf. Coats, "Parable, Fable, and Anecdote," 368–82.
32. Technically, this distinction between fable and parable suggests the influence of the western literary canon and does not appear applicable to material in the Hebrew Bible or comparative literature. For example, when defining the term "fable" in relation to Isa 5:1–7, Marjo C. A. Korpel cites the definition found in M. H. Abrams, *A Glossary of Literary Terms* instead of providing evidence that the definition was a meaningful literary category in the ancient Near East ("The Literary Genre of the Song of the Vineyard (Isa. 5:1–7)," in *The Structural Analysis of Biblical and Canaanite Poetry* [JSOTSup 74; eds. Willem van der Meer and Johannes C. de Moor; Sheffield: JSOT Press, 1988]; cf. M. H. Abrams, *A Glossary of Literary Terms* [4th ed.; New York: Harcourt Brace, 1981], 6–7). Noting the anachronistic quality of the terms fable and parable, Larry L. Lyke uses the more accurate but cumbersome term *narrative meshalim* (*King David with the Wise Woman of Tekoa: The Resonance of Tradition in Parabolic Narrative* [JSOTSup 255; Sheffield: Sheffield Academic Press, 1997], 136 n. 12). Yet, with this qualification in mind, we use the labels parable and fable for the sake of convenience.
33. See Adolf Jülicher, *Die Gleichnisreden Jesu* (2 vols. Freiburg: Adademische Verlagsbuchhandlung von J. C. B. Mohr, 1888), 1: 317.
34. Cathcart, "The Trees, the Beasts, and the Birds," 214.
35. Arland J. Hultgren, *The Parables of Jesus: A Commentary* (Grand Rapids: William B. Eerdmans, 2000), 13; cf. Raymond E. Brown, "Parable and Allegory Reconsidered," *NT* 5 (1962): 36–45; John Dominaic Crossan, "Parables," *ABD* 5: 146–7; Joachim Jeremais, *The Parables of Jesus* (rev. ed.; New York: Scribner's, 1963), 20.
36. Our description of parables as "limited allegories" comes from Craig L. Blomberg. He argues that, as with many works of fiction, parables operate on "a sliding scale of more and less allegorical narratives." See Craig L. Blomberg, "Interpreting the Parables of Jesus: Where Are We and Where Do We Go from Here?" *CBQ* 53.1 (1991): 52.

37. Frank Kermode notes this problem in regards to the parables of Jesus. See Frank Kermode, *The Genesis of Secrecy: On the Interpretation of Narrative* (Cambridge: Harvard University Press, 1979), 24–5.
38. Polk, "Paradigms, Parables, and *Měšālîm*," 579–81.
39. Lyke, *King David with the Wise Woman of Tekoa*, 193.
40. For a discussion of this literature, see especially Suter, "*Māšāl* in the Similitudes of Enoch," 194–5.
41. According to Kimhi, "A *hida* [riddle] is an obscure saying from which something else is to be understood, while a *mašal* [here, fable] is a likening of one matter to another." Cited in Moshe Greenberg, *Ezekiel 1–20: A New Translation with Introduction and Commentary* (AB 22; Garden City, NY: Doubleday, 1983), 309.
42. Fontaine, *Traditional Sayings in the Old Testament*, 144–5.
43. See Jeremy Schipper, "Narrative Obscurity of Samson's Riddle in Judges 14.14 and 18," *JSOT* 27.1 (2003): 339–53.
44. Westermann, *The Parables of Jesus in the Light of the Old Testament*, 151.
45. Although only fragments of this text remain extant, the fragments present the parable as part of a larger judgment or at least an admonishment when read together. For detailed studies of these texts, see Bilhah Nitzan, "4Q302/302a (Sap. A): Pap. Praise of God and Parable of the Tree: A Preliminary Edition," *RevQ* 17/1–4 (1996): 151–173; Bilhah Nitzan, "Post-Biblical *Rib* Pattern Admonitions in 4Q302/302a and 4Q381 69, 76–77," in *Biblical Perspectives: Early Use and Interpretation of the Bible in Light of the Dead Sea Scrolls* (STDJ 28; eds. Michael E. Stone and Esther G. Chazon; Leiden: Brill, 1998), 159–74.
46. Oppenheim, *Letters from Mesopotamia*, 170.

2. DEVOURING PARABLES: JOTHAM'S PARABOLIC CURSE IN JUDGES 9

1. Dennis T. Olson, "The Book of Judges: Introduction, Commentary, and Reflections," *NIB* 2: 816.
2. Martin Buber, *Kingship of God* (London: Humanities, 1967), 75; cf. Volkmar Fritz, "Abimelech und Sichem in Jdc. ix," *VT* 32 (1982): 129–44; J. Alberto Soggin, *Judges: A Commentary* (OTL; Philadelphia: Westminster, 1981), 174; Susan Niditch, *Judges: A Commentary* (OTL; Louisville: Westminster John Knox, 2008), 114, 116. For a critique of Buber's interpretation, see Dennis T. Olson, "Buber, Kingship, and the Book of Judges: A Study of Judges 6–9 and 17–21," in *David and Zion: Biblical Studies in Honor of J. J. M. Roberts* (eds. Bernard F. Batto and Kathryn L. Roberts; Winona Lake: Eisenbrauns, 2004), 199–218.
3. Eugene H. Maly, "The Jotham Fable – Anti-Monarchical?" *CBQ* 22 (1960): 303; cf. Baruch Halpern, "The Rise of Abimelek Ben-Jerubbaal," *HAR* 2 (1978): 79–100; idem, *The Constitution of the Monarchy in Israel* (Chico: Scholars, 1981), 142–4; Barnabas Lindars, "Jotham's Fable – A New Form-Critical Analysis," *JTS* 24 (1973): 364–66; Jan De Waard, "Jotham's Fable: An Exercise in Clearing Away the Unclear," in *Wissenschaft und Kirche: Festschrift für Eduard Lohse* (eds. Kurt Aland and Siegfried Meurer; Bielefeld: Luther-Verlag, 1989), 364.

4. Larry L. Lyke, *King David with the Wise Woman of Tekoa: The Resonance of Tradition in Parabolic Narrative* (JSOTSup 255; Sheffield: Sheffield Academic Press, 1997), 138, n. 15.
5. For a review of scholarly positions on the genre of Jotham's speech, see De Waard, "Jotham's Fable: An Exercise in Clearing Away the Unclear," 362–3.
6. See, among others, Theodor Herze Gaster, *Myth, Legend, and Custom in the Old Testament: A Comparative Study with Chapters from Sir James G. Frazer's Folklore in the Old Testament* (New York: Harper & Row, 1969), 423–7; Victor H. Matthews, *Judges and Ruth* (Cambridge: Cambridge University Press, 2004), 104–5; Silviu Tatu, "Jotham's Fable and the *Crux Interpretum* in Judges IX," *VT* 56 (2006): 108–10; Ronald J. Williams, "The Fable in the Ancient Near East," in *A Stubborn Faith: Papers on the Old Testament and Related Subject Presented to Honor W. A. Irwin* (ed. Edward Craig Hobbs; Dallas: Southern Methodist University Press, 1956), 5; W. C. Van Wyk, "The Fable of Jotham in Its Ancient Near Eastern Context," in *Studies in Wisdom Literature* (Ou-Testamentiese Werkgemeenskap in Suider-Afrika, 15 and 16; ed. W. C. Van Wyk; Hercules, South Africa: N.H.W. Press, 1981), 89–95.
7. This translation comes from Victor H. Matthews and Don C. Benjamin, *Old Testament Parallels: Laws and Stories from the Ancient Near East* (New York: Paulist, 1997), 287; cf. *ANET*, 429–30. For a more detailed comparison of Ahiqar and Jotham's fable, see Ingo Kottsieper, "Die alttestamentliche Weisheit in Licht aramäischer Weisheitstraditionen," in *Die Weisheit hat ihr Haus gebaut: Studien zur Gestalt der Sophia in den biblischen Schriften* (ed. Silvia Schroer; Mainz: Matthias-Grünewald-Verlag, 1996), 128–62.
8. On pure allegories, see chapter 1 of this book.
9. Among modern scholars who cite Redaq's interpretation, see De Waard, "Jotham's Fable," 369; Lyke, *King David with the Wise Woman of Tekoa*, 139. For an accessible review of the history of interpretation of Judges 9, see David Gunn, *Judges* (Blackwell Bible Commentaries; Oxford: Blackwell, 2005), 121–35; cf. Christopher Begg, "Abimelech, King of Shechem according to Josephus," *Ephemerides Theologicae Lovanienses* 72 (1996): 146–64.
10. For scholars who cite this difference as evidence that Jotham's story is secondary, see, among others, Lyke, *King David with the Wise Woman of Tekoa*, 138; Maly, "The Jotham Fable – Anti-Monarchical?" 300; Soggin, *Judges: A Commentary*, 174.
11. By contrast, for arguments that the parable was composed for Judges 9, see Rüdiger Bartelmus, "Die sogenannte Jotamfabel- eine politisch-religiöse Parabeldichtung," *TZ* 41 (1985): 105; George F. Moore, *A Critical and Exegetical Commentary on Judges* (ICC; New York: C. Scribner's Sons, 1895), 245; Karin Schöpflin, "Jotham's Speech and Fable as Prophetic Comment on Abimelech's Fable: The Genesis of Judges 9," *SJOT* 18 (2004): 15. For a succinct review of scholarly theories on the origin of Jotham's parable, see Schöpflin, "Jotham's Speech and Fable as Prophetic Comment on Abimelech's Fable," 3–4.
12. Lindars, "Jotham's Fable – A New Form-Critical Analysis," 358–61.
13. Ibid., 366. For others who focus on the centrality of the curse to the narrative art of Judges 9, see Graham S. Ogden, "Jotham's Fable: Its Structure and Function

in Judges 9," *BT* 46 (1995): 301–8; Uriel Simon, "The Parable of Jotham (Judges ix. 8–15): The Parable, its Application and the Narrative Framework," *Tarbis* 34 (1964–65): 1–34.

14. See T. A. Boogart, "Stone for Stone: Retribution in the Story of Abimelech and Shechem," *JSOT* 32 (1985): 45–56; J. Gerald Janzen, "A Certain Woman in the Rhetoric of Judges 9," *JSOT* 38 (1987): 33–7; Ogden, "Jotham's Fable," 301–2.
15. Although we may dispute their conclusions, for helpful discussions of primary texts containing curses in the Hebrew Bible and comparative ancient Near Eastern literature and reviews of scholarship on these curses, see Paul A. Keim, "The Politics of Malice: Ancient Near Eastern Malediction as Metaphor," in *Exploring New Paradigms in Biblical and Cognate Studies* (ed. Hugh R. Page, Jr.; Lewiston: Mellen Biblical Press, 1996), 17–45; Hans Ulrich Steymans, *Deuteronomium 28 und die adê zur Thronfolgeregelung Asarhaddons: Segen und Fluch im Alten Orient und in Israel* (OBO 45; Freiburg: Universitätsverlag, 1996); Noel Weeks, *Admonition and Curse: The Ancient Near Eastern Treaty/Covenant Form as a Problem in Inter-Cultural Relationships* (JSOTSup 407; London: T and T Clark, 2004).
16. Matthews, *Judges and Ruth*, 105; Olson, "The Book of Judges," 816.
17. David Jobling, *The Sense of Biblical Narrative: Structural Analyses in the Hebrew Bible II* (JSOTSup. 39; Sheffield: JSOT Press, 1986), 71. Barry G. Webb notes that the blessing "has ceased to be a real alternative because the crime is irrevocable. The detailing of the curse in v. 20 is in effect a pronouncement of judgment" (*The Book of Judges: An Integrated Reading* [JSOTSup. 46; Sheffield: Sheffield Academic Press, 1987], 155). Tatu interprets the conditional statements of the bramble in v. 15 as setting up what he calls "the irony of dilemma" in which the Shechemites face a "no win" situation. According to Tatu, the conditions that the Shechemites face are "that any servant should come under [the bramble's] shade or else a fire should spring from it and quickly extend to Lebanon consuming everything in its path. The irony falls on the citizens of Shechem who were actually in a situation without exit. Death is all they can get out of their unfortunate covenant with Abimelech" (Tatu, "Jotham's Fable," 123–4; cf. Maly, "The Jotham Fable – Anti-Monarchical?" 304). According to this interpretation, even the conditional presentation of Jotham's curse does not offer any hope of escape for its addressees.
18. Jan P. Fokkelman, "Structural Remarks on Judges 9 and 19," in *"Sha'arei Talmon": Studies in the Bible, Qumran, and the Ancient Near East Presented to Shemaryahu Talmon* (eds. Michael Fishbane and Emanuel Tov; Winona Lake, IN: Eisenbrauns, 1992), 36.
19. Ogden, "Jotham's Fable," 306.
20. Lillian R. Klein observes, "The spirit does not come *upon* Abimelech – he is evil enough – but *between* him and the lords, punishing both sides for slaying Gideon's sons" (*The Triumph of Irony in the Book of Judges* [JSOTSup 68; Sheffield: Almond, 1988], 73 [italics original]).
21. In this regard, some scholars have suggested that Judges 9 presents Jotham as standing within the prophetic tradition. For example, Robert G. Boling connects Jotham's opening statements in v. 7b ("Listen to me, Lords of Shechem, so that God may listen to you!") to prophetic speech patterns (*Judges: Introduction, Translation, and Commentary* [AB 7; Garden City, NY: Doubleday, 1975], 172).

Schöpflin argues that Jotham's speech reflects a prophetic "oracle of doom" and that the parable "reinforces Jotham's function as a prophetic figure" since it employs personified plants as seen in other prophetic passages ("Jotham's Speech and Fable as Prophetic Comment on Abimelech's Fable," 19).

22. Tammi J. Schneider, *Judges* (Berit Olam; Collegeville, MN: Liturical, 2000), 144.
23. For a catalogue of the similarities between Abimelech and Gaal, see Boogart, "Stone for Stone," 50.
24. Lyke, *King David with the Wise Woman of Tekoa*, 142.
25. Robert G. Boling suggests that the "Tower of Shechem," which appears for the first time in v. 46, represents an alternative designation for the "House of Millo," presumably from another source (*Judges*, 180; cf. Schneider, *Judges*, 147).
26. Olson, "The Book of Judges," 817.
27. Interpreters have observed the poetic justice of Abimelech's fate since at least the time of the Talmud. See Louis Ginzberg, *The Legends of the Jews* (7 vols. Baltimore: The Johns Hopkins University Press, 1998), 4:41. Among modern scholars, see especially Boogart, "Stone for Stone," 51.
28. Janzen, "A Certain Woman in the Rhetoric of Judges 9," 34–5.
29. Ibid., 34–6.
30. Jobling observes that Judges 6–9 stresses family issues as much as individual characters (*The Sense of Biblical Narrative II*, 69). Noami Sternberg argues that Judges 9 does not condemn Abimelech's monarchical aspirations, but condemns his violation of societal kinship rules ("Social Scientific Criticism," in *Judges and Method: New Approaches in Biblical Studies* [ed. Gale Yee; Minneapolis: Fortress, 1995], 45–64).

3. OVERALLEGORIZING AND OTHER DAVIDIC MISINTERPRETATIONS IN 2 SAMUEL 11–12

1. In order to preserve the repetition of the root "to show pity" (*hamal*) in vv. 4 and 6 (see later), we have borrowed the translation "it seemed a pity to him to take..." from Robert Alter. See Robert Alter, *The David Story: A Translation with Commentary of 1 and 2 Samuel* (New York: W.W. Norton & Company, 1999), 258.
2. For examples of majority positions, see Walter Brueggemann, *First and Second Samuel* (IBC; Louisville: John Knox, 1990), 280; Hans Wilhelm Hertzberg, *I and II Samuel: A Commentary* (trans. J. S. Bowden; Philadelphia: Westminster, 1964), 312; Gwilym H. Jones, *The Nathan Narratives* (JSOTSup 80; Sheffield: Sheffield Academic Press, 1990), 96–101; P. Kyle McCarter, *2 Samuel: A New Translation with Introduction and Commentary* (AB 9; Garden City, NY: Doubleday, 1984), 304–5; Steven McKenzie, *King David: A Biography* (Oxford: Oxford University Press, 2000), 159. In contrast, Bernard C. Lategan suggests that the recognized parabolic quality of Nathan's speech puts David at ease (*Text and Reality: Aspects of Reference in Biblical Texts* [Philadelphia: Fortress; Atlanta: Scholars, 1985], 81). Hugh Pyper provides a helpful review of the vast scholarship on Nathan's parable (*David as Reader: 2 Samuel 12:1–15 and the Poetics of Fatherhood* [Leiden: Brill, 1996], 84–110); cf. Randall C. Bailey, *David in Love and War: The Pursuit of*

Power in 2 Samuel 10–12 (JSOTSup 75; Sheffield: Sheffield Academic Press, 1990), 101–10.
3. Uriel Simon, "The Poor Man's Ewe-Lamb: An Example of a Juridical Parable," *Bib* 48 (1967): 207–42.
4. Ibid., 221.
5. For example, see George W. Coats, "Parable, Fable, and Anecdote: Storytelling in the Succession Narrative," *Int* 35 (1981): 368–82; David Gunn, *The Story of King David: Genre and Interpretation* (JSOTSup 6; Sheffield: JSOT Press, 1978), 41.
6. For example, see Jean Hoftijzer, "David and the Tekoite Woman," *VT* 20 (1970): 419–44; W. Schottroff, "Das Weinberglied Jesajas (Jes 5,1–7): Ein Beitrag zur Geschichte der Parabel," *ZAW* 82 (1970): 68–91; Gerald T. Sheppard, "More on Isaiah 5:1–7 as a Juridical Parable," *CBQ* 44 (1982): 45–7; Meir Sternberg, *The Poetics of Biblical Narrative: Ideological Literature and the Drama of Reading* (Bloomington: Indiana University Press, 1987), 429–30; Gale A. Yee, "A Form-Critical Study of Isaiah 5:1–7 as a Song and a Juridical Parable," *CBQ* 43 (1981): 33–4. Hoftijzer, however, argues that the purpose of the parable is to induce "the king to give the ruling on the fictitious case that [Nathan] wants for the real one" (p. 421) rather than to induce him to pass judgment on himself.
7. Pyper, *David as Reader*, 102–3.
8. As Bruce Birch observes, "This scene [12:1–7a] does not seem like a customary session of royal judicial practice.... No names, places, witnesses or other petitioners are in evidence. Instead, we find an encounter between prophet and king in which Nathan has chosen the rhetorical device of a parable of injustice for his purpose of confronting David" ("The First and Second Books of Samuel," *NIB* 2:1292).
9. Simon also cites Isa 5:1–7 and Jer 3:1–5 as examples of juridical parables, but see Burke O. Long, "The Stylistic Components of Jeremiah 3, 1–5," *ZAW* 88 (1976): 387.
10. For a number of differences between 2 Sam 14:1–24 and other juridical parables, see Hoftijzer, "David and the Tekoite Woman," 442–44.
11. Jan P. Fokkelman, *Narrative Art and Poetry in the Books of Samuel: A Full Interpretation based on Stylistic and Structural Analysis* (4 vols.; Assen: van Gorcum, 1981), 1:74.
12. On Isa 5:1–7 as a parable as opposed to an allegory, see John T. Willis, "The Genre of Isaiah 5:1–7," *JBL* 96 (1977): 337–62. Birger Gerhardsson describes it as an "allegorizing parable" ("The Narrative Meshalim in the Synoptic Gospels: A Comparison with the Narrative Meshalim in the Old Testament," *NTS* 34 [1988]: 345).
13. Alter, *The David Story*, 257.
14. Simon B. Parker, *Stories in Scripture and Inscriptions: Comparative Studies on Narratives in Northwest Semitic Inscriptions and the Hebrew Bible* (New York: Oxford University Press, 1997), 33; cf. Stuart Lasine, "Melodrama as Parable: The Story of the Poor Man's Ewe-Lamb and the Unmasking of David's Topsy-Turvy Emotions," *HAR* 8 (1984): 111–12.
15. Parker, *Stories in Scripture and Inscriptions*, 34. We consider the "petitionary narrative" genre in more detail in the next chapter. Parker labels this petition

as "hypothetical" because Nathan delivers it in the third person and does not specify the parties involved.

16. For a detailed discussion of *hamal*, see George W. Coats, "II Samuel 12:1–7a," *Int* 40 (1986): 170–75.
17. Ezekiel 18:2 labels the fable in the following verses as both a "parable" and a "riddle" (see the discussion of "riddles" in chapter 1). Several scholars have observed that biblical texts such as Num 12:6–8 equate visions and dreams with riddles. See the sources cited in Scott B. Noegel, *Nocturnal Ciphers: The Allusive Language of Dreams in the Ancient Near East* (New Haven: American Oriental Society, 2007), 120–1.
18. Noegel, *Nocturnal Ciphers*, 52–3; Jean-Marie Husser observes a similar interpretative strategy in Egyptian literature: "This principle of interpretation was widespread, as is attested in a good number of dream books. Here is an example from the Chester Beatty III papyrus (18th–19th dynasty): 'If, in a dream, a man sees himself looking into a well of deep water, -bad: he will be out in prison' (recto 8.5). The protasis puts forward the idea of drawing water (*'ith*), which in turn calls up the image of a prison (*'ith*) by virtue of homonymy" (*Dreams and Dream Narratives in the Biblical World* [Biblical Seminar 63; trans. Jill M. Munro; Sheffield: Sheffield University Press, 1999], 118).
19. It is worth observing that the limited allegorizing of dreams by Joseph and Daniel tend to result in the announcement of condemnation or greater conflict rather than resolution. The same holds true for Samuel's dream in 1 Samuel 3. As seen below, a similar dynamic unfolds with Nathan's fable in 2 Samuel 12. Robert K. Gnuse has made a convincing case for understanding 1 Samuel 3 as an ancient Near Eastern dream report rather than a call narrative. See Robert K. Gnuse, "A Reconsideration of the Form-critical Structure of 1 Samuel 3: An ANE Dream Theophany," *ZAW* 94 (1982): 379–89; cf. idem, *The Dream Theophany of Samuel: Its Relation to Ancient Near Eastern Dreams and its Theological Significance* (Lanham: University Press of America, 1984).
20. Some scholars observe that while the David Story provides the reader with information about other Saulides' inner lives (Jonathan and Michal), it does not do the same for David. See, among others, Robert Alter, *The Art of Biblical Narrative* (New York: Basic Books, 1981), 118–19; Robert Polzin, *Samuel and the Deuteronomist: A Literary Study of the Deuteronomic History: Part Two: 1 Samuel* (San Francisco: Harper & Row, 1989), 191; Patricia Tull, "Jonathan's Gift of Friendship," *Int* 58 (2004): 132.
21. For example, see Brueggemann, *First and Second Samuel*, 280; cf. Tod Linafelt, "Taking Women in Samuel: Readers/Responses/Responsibility," in *Reading Between Texts: Intertextuality and the Bible* (ed. Danna Fewell; Louisville: WJKP, 1992), 99–113.
22. For a more detailed discussion of rabbinic interpretations of this passage, see Peter Coxon, "A Note on 'Bathsheba' in 2 Samuel 12, 1–6," *Bib* 62 (1981): 247–50; cf. Louis Ginzberg, *The Legends of the Jews* (7 vols. Baltimore: The John Hopkins University Press, 1998), 4:101–4; 6:261–6.
23. Larry L. Lyke, *King David with the Wise Woman of Tekoa: The Resonance of Tradition in Parabolic Narrative* (JSOTSup 255; Sheffield: Sheffield Academic Press, 1997), 148.

24. Ibid., 155; Robert Polzin, *David and the Deuteronomist: A Literary Study of the Deuteronomic History: Part Three: 2 Samuel* (Bloomington: Indiana University Press, 1993), 123–26. Leinhard Delekat argues that YHWH represents the rich man who eliminates the ewe-lamb for David, who represents the traveler ("Tendenz und Theologie der David-Salomo-Erzählung," in *Das Ferne und nahe Wort: Festschrift Leonhard Rost zur Vollendung seines 70. Lebensjahres am 30. November 1966* [ed. Fritz Maass; Berlin: A. Töpelmann, 1967], 33).
25. Hermann Gunkel, *The Folktale in the Old Testament* (trans. M. D. Rutter; Sheffield: Almond, 1987), 54–5.
26. P. Chibaudel, "David et Bethsabée; une Tragédie de l'Abstentin," *La Vie Spirituelle* 143 (1989): 79; Delekat, "Tendenz und Theologie der David-Salomo-Erzählung," 33; J. W. Wesselius, "Joab's Death and the Central Theme of the Succession Narrative" (2 Samuel 9–1 Kings 20)," *VT* 40 (1990): 346–7, n. 15.
27. Coxon, "A Note on 'Bathsheba' in 2 Samuel 12, 1–6," 249; Polzin, *David and the Deuteronomist*, 123. The narrator reinforces this connection between the sequence of these three roots and Uriah for the reader in v. 13, which reads, "David summoned Uriah. Uriah ate (*'okal*) before him and drank (*shatah*) and David made him drunk. Yet when it was evening, Uriah went out to lay (*shakab*) on his bed among the servants of his lord, but he did not go down to his own house."
28. YHWH does appear by name in 11:27b and 12:1a. Of course, David would not have known about YHWH's involvement in this episode. Thus, he would have no reason to identify YHWH with one of the actors in the parable.
29. On this point, see Jones, *The Nathan Narratives*, 98.
30. Baruch Halpern, *David's Secret Demons: Messiah, Murder, Traitor, King* (Grand Rapids: Eerdmans, 2001), 83–4; P. Kyle McCarter, "The Apology of David," *JBL* 99 (1980): 489–504; McKenzie, *King David: A Biography*, 32–4.
31. Of course, a major difference between Uriah's death and those of Abner and Amasa lies in the fact that the former dies in battle (cf. 1 Kgs 2:5). Unlike Abner and Amasa, Joab does not kill Uriah himself and does not have an obvious motive for doing so. Thus, David may not see the need to condemn Joab in 11:25a.
32. Regarding David's outburst in vv. 5–6, David Gunn writes, "We recognize once more the David who could so tellingly lend his emotions to a public occasion (e.g., at the deaths of Saul, Abner, and Ishbosheth, chap. 1–4)" ("2 Samuel," in *HarperCollins Bible Commentary* [revised ed.; James L. Mays, ed.; San Francisco: Harper San Francisco, 2000], 270).
33. Based on the LXX, we may restore the Hebrew text of v. 22a as follows: "[The messenger] told David all that [*panta* = *'et kol*] Joab sent him [to say], all of [*panta* = *'et kol*] the affairs of the war . . . " The MT's reading of v. 22 results from haplography involving *'et kol*. Thus, everything in v. 22 following the second use of *'et kol* dropped out of the MT.
34. Based on a parallel with 2 Sam 16:7, McCarter translates the phrase as "a fiend of hell." With this translation, he avoids having David contradict himself by recommending the death penalty only then to recommend that the man pay restitution for the lamb. See McCarter, *2 Samuel*, 299. We should note that in the parallel passage that McCarter cites, Shimei accuses David of murder (cf. 16:7–8).
35. In connection with the phrase "son of death" in 2 Sam 12:5, Pyper notes that in Num 17:25 the phrase "sons of rebellion" refers to the people responsible for the

rebellion and in Jer 48:45 the phrase "sons of uproar" refers to the people responsible for the uproar (Pyper, *David as Reader*, 159). The phrase "son(s) of death" (*ben-mawet/bene-mawet*) also occurs in 1 Sam 20:31 and 26:16, but does not necessarily mean "deserving to die" in either case. See Anthony Campbell, *2 Samuel* (FOTL 8; Grand Rapids: Eerdmans, 2005), 116–17; Pyper, *David as Reader*, 161–2.
36. Pyper, *David as Reader*, 159.
37. Most likely, the MT's reading attempts to bring David's reaction in line with the law preserved in Exod 21:37. Nevertheless, the "sevenfold" reading (*shib'atayim*) plays off of the name Bathsheba (*bat-sheba'*), which appears within the more immediate context of the verse (cf. 11:3; 12:24). See Coxon, "A Note on 'Bathsheba' in 2 Samuel 12, 1–6," 249; Samuel R. Driver, *Notes on the Hebrew Text of the Books of Samuel* (Oxford: Clarendon Press, 1890), 291; McCarter, *2 Samuel*, 294, 299; cf. Roland de Vaux, *Ancient Israel* (2 vols.; trans. J. McHugh; New York: McGraw-Hill, 1961), 1:160.
38. R. A. Carlson observes that Prov 6:31 demands a sevenfold restitution for stealing (*David, the Chosen King: A Traditio-Historical Approach to the Second Book of Samuel* [Stockholm: Almqvist & Wiksell, 1964], 152–57). Yet 6:31 discusses a crime performed in order to satisfy the thief's hunger (v. 30), which is clearly not the case in 2 Samuel 11–12.
39. Several scholars note that Joab does not execute David's battle plan exactly as written in 11:15. As McKenzie observes, Joab's changes to the plan result in the deaths of many other troops besides Uriah in 11:16–17 (McKenzie, *King David: A Biography*, 158–9). For a detailed study of this issue, see Keith Bodner, "Is Joab a Reader-Response Critic?" *JSOT* 27 (2002): 19–35.
40. Polzin reads this repositioning of David as the various "men" in the parable as pointing to David's entire career. He writes, "David *was* the wayfarer, 'the one who comes,' insofar as his past dealings with God are concerned (12:7–8); he *is* the rich man when his present crimes are brought into the picture (12:9–10); and he *will be* the poor man when God's punishing future for him and his house arrives (12:11–12)" (Polzin, *David and the Deuteronomist*, 126 [italics original]).
41. On the principle of correspondence between sin and judgment as it relates to 2 Samuel 12, see Patrick D. Miller, *Sin and Judgment in the Prophets: A Stylistic and Theological Analysis* (Society of Biblical Literature Monograph Series 27; Chico, CA: Scholars, 1982), 81–4. Noegel shows that some biblical punning and word plays reflect the principle of *lex talionis* when used to interpret enigmatic narratives (*Nocturnal Ciphers*, 129–40).
42. For other interpretations of Ahithopel's connection to David and Bathsheba, see especially, Bailey, *David in Love and War*, 87–8; Halpern, *David's Secret Demons*, 402–3; Wesselius, "Joab's Death and the Central Theme of the Succession Narrative," 349.

4. CHANGING FACE AND SAVING FACE: PARABOLIC PETITIONS IN 2 SAMUEL 14

1. For a more detailed discussion of this issue, see Robert Polzin, *David and the Deuteronomist: A Literary Study of the Deuteronomic History: Part Three: 2 Samuel* (Bloomington: Indiana University Press, 1993), 139–40.

2. Jan P. Fokkelman, *Narrative Art and Poetry in the Books of Samuel: A Full Interpretation based on Stylistic and Structural Analysis* (4 vols.; Assen: van Gorcum, 1981), 1:129.
3. Uriel Simon, "The Poor Man's Ewe-Lamb: An Example of a Juridical Parable," *Bib* 48 (1967): 225.
4. See, among others, Bruce C. Birch, "1 and 2 Samuel," *NIB* 2:1314; Walter Brueggemann, *First and Second Samuel* (IBC; Louisville: John Knox, 1990), 292–3.
5. George W. Coats, "Parable, Fable, and Anecdote: Storytelling in the Succession Narrative," *Int* 35 (1981): 377–82.
6. Jean Hoftijzer, "David and the Tekoite Woman," *VT* 20 (1970): 419–44; cf. Keith W. Whitelam, *The Just King: Monarchical Judicial Authority in Ancient Israel* (JSOTSup. 12; Sheffield: JSOT Press, 1979), 127–32.
7. Hugh Pyper, *David as Reader: 2 Samuel 12:1–15 and the Poetics of Fatherhood* (Leiden: Brill, 1996), 129. Pyper reads the story in 2 Samuel 14 as a parody of Nathan's parable in 2 Samuel 12 (ibid., 111–29). For a "parody on 2 Samuel 12" reading, see also Patricia K. Willey, "The Importunate Woman of Tekoa and How She Got Her Way," in *Reading Between Texts: Intertextuality and the Hebrew Bible* (ed. Danna Nolan Fewell; WJKP, 1992), 115–31.
8. Elizabeth Bellefontaine, "Customary Law and Chieftainship: Juridical Aspects of 2 Samuel 14:4–21," *JSOT* 38 (1987): 48; cf. Birch, "1 and 2 Samuel," 1314.
9. Larry L. Lyke, *King David with the Wise Woman of Tekoa: The Resonance of Tradition in Parabolic Narrative* (JSOTSup 255; Sheffield: Sheffield Academic Press, 1997), 176–82. For further arguments for the "kill Absalom" message, see William H. Propp, "Kinship in 2 Samuel 13," *CBQ* 55 (1993): 50–53.
10. Willey, "The Importunate Woman of Tekoa," 130.
11. David Gunn, *The Story of King David: Genre and Interpretation* (JSOTSup 6; Sheffield: JSOT Press, 1978), 40–3.
12. Coats, "Parable, Fable, and Anecdote," 379.
13. Lyke, *King David with the Wise Woman of Tekoa*, 92.
14. Miriam Lichtheim observes that the word for the herdsman's "cattle" plays off of the word for Osiris' "office," since the two words sound alike. See Miriam Lichtheim, *Ancient Egyptian Literature: A Book of Readings: Volume II: The New Kingdom* (Berkeley: University of California Press, 1976), 223 n. 10. This word play strengthens the comparison between Isis' story and Seth's conflict with Horus, which, like many biblical parables, does not represent a pure allegory. For a complete translation of the story of "Horus and Seth," see ibid., 214–3.
15. For example see, Andre Lemaire, "L'ostracon de Masad Hashavyahu (Yavneh-Yam) replacé dans son contexte," *Semetica* 21 (1971): 75; F. W. Dobbs-Allsopp, "The Genre of the Mesad Hashavyahu Ostracon," *BASOR* 295 (1994): 51; Victor Sasson, "An Unrecognized Juridical Term in the Yavneh-Yam Lawsuit and in an unnoticed Biblical Parallel," *BASOR* 232 (1978): 62 n. 13.
16. For the text of this inscription as well as a translation, commentary, and bibliography, see *Hebrew Inscriptions: Texts from the Biblical Period of the Monarchy with Concordance* (eds. F. W. Dobbs-Allsopp et al.; New Haven: Yale University Press, 2004), 358–70.
17. Dobbs-Allsopp, "The Genre of the Mesad Hashavyahu Ostracon," 51.

18. Simon B. Parker, *Stories in Scripture and Inscriptions: Comparative Studies on Narratives in Northwest Semitic Inscriptions and the Hebrew Bible* (New York: Oxford University Press, 1997), 18–34.
19. Dobbs-Allsopp, "The Genre of the Mesad Hashavyahu Ostracon," 49–55; cf. Raymond Westbrook, *Studies in Biblical and Cuneiform Law* (Cahiers de la Revue Biblique 16; Paris: Gabalda, 1988), 30–5.
20. Parker, *Stories in Scripture and Inscriptions*, 13.
21. Ibid., 28.
22. Ibid., 28; cf. Coats, "Parable, Fable, and Anecdote," 377–82.
23. Parker, *Stories in Scripture and Inscriptions*, 15–17.
24. Ibid., 29.
25. Although he argues along different lines than we do, Polzin also considers the possibility that Joab wants David to see through his ploy and to understand the actual topic of the wise woman of Tekoa's coded speech. Polzin writes, "Joab may want David to discover by himself that he, Joab, is speaking through the Tekoite's story. When the woman tells David about 'the man who would destroy me and my son together from the heritage of God' (v. 16), Joab may want David to suspect that this is precisely what he, Joab, is doing through the woman's words, namely, threatening David and his throne" (Polzin, *David and the Deuteronomist*, 142).
26. Willey makes a similar observation and comments further, "In fact, he has put the burden on this woman to drag her powerful adversary to the palace before he will consider her suit. Whether she can do this before her son is killed is, evidently, her problem" (Willey, "The Importunate Woman of Tekoa," 119).
27. See, among others, Brueggemann, *First and Second Samuel*, 293; Lyke, *King David with the Wise Woman of Tekoa*, 172–3; P. Kyle McCarter, *2 Samuel: A New Translation with Introduction and Commentary* (AB 9; Garden City, NY: Doubleday, 1984), 349; Propp, "Kinship in 2 Samuel 13," 50 n. 45.
28. In v. 14a, the wise woman of Tekoa tells David, "For we will surely die (*ki-mot namut*)." Hoftijzer cites every other case of the Qal infinite absolute form of *mwt* that appears in the Bible and concludes that, aside from Gen 2:17 and 3:4, the term does not address inevitable death. Rather, "in all other cases there is the question of untimely death, and/or (in most cases) a punishment for transgressions or sins" (Hoftijzer, "David and the Tekoite Woman," 432, n. 2).
29. See, among others, Peter Ackroyd, *The Second Book of Samuel* (Cambridge Bible Commentary; Cambridge: Cambridge University Press, 1977), 131–2; Birch, "The First and Second Books of Samuel," 1313; Karl Budde, *Die Bücher Samuel* (Tübingen: J. C. B. Mohr, 1902), 267; Lyke, *King David with the Wise Woman of Tekoa*, 182; John Mauchline, *1 and 2 Samuel* (London: Oliphants, 1971), 266–7; McCarter, *2 Samuel*, 345–6. For arguments against this emendation, see Anthony Campbell, *2 Samuel* (FOTL 8; Grand Rapids: Eerdmans, 2005), 134; Hans Joachim Stoebe, *Das zweite Buch Samuelis* (Gütersloh: Gütersloher Verlagshaus, 1994), 346–7.
30. My translation follows several major witnesses (LXX, Syr., Vulg.) against the MT, which reads, "I hereby authorize this matter." See McCarter, *2 Samuel*, 342.

5. GRASPING THE CONFLICT: AHAB'S NEGOTIATION OF
CONFLICTS AND PARABLES IN 1 KINGS 20

1. On the "petitionary narrative" genre, see chapter 4 of this book.
2. Although the word "bandage" (*'aper*) does not appear anywhere else in the Hebrew Bible, it has cognates in other Semitic languages. See Mordecai Cogan, *1 Kings: A New Translation with Introduction and Commentary* (AB 10; New York: Doubleday, 2000), 470. In addition, the LXX reads "strap," which seems to understand the Hebrew word *'aper* as meaning some sort of bandage.
3. We have translated the term *'ish-hermi* as "the man whom I trapped" in order to capture its multiple nuances. Considering the primary and secondary definitions of the root *hrm* as "devoted thing (involving destruction)" (cf. Isa 34:5; BDB, 356) and "net" (cf. Ezek 32:3; Hab 1:15; BDB, 357), one may translate the phrase as "the man whom I devoted to destruction" (cf. NRSV) or "the man of my net" (cf. Philip D. Stern, "The *herem* in 1 Kings 20,42 as an Exegetical Problem," *Bib* 71 [1990]: 43–7). The term may represent a multivalent way of hinting at both a means of Ben-Hadad's capture (a net) and a possible intended reason for his capture (destruction).
4. On the chiastic structure of vv. 1–34, see Burke O. Long, "Historical Narrative and the Fictionalizing Imagination," *VT* 35.4 (1985): 406; cf. Jerome T. Walsh, *1 Kings* (Berit Olam; Collegeville, Minn.: Liturgical, 1996), 294.
5. For example, see Walter Brueggemann, *Testimony to Otherwise: The Witness of Elijah and Elisha* (St. Louis: Chalice, 2001), 120; Simon J. Devries, *1 Kings* (WBC 12; Waco, TX: Word Books, 1985), 250; Burke O. Long, *1 Kings with an Introduction to Historical Literature* (FOTL 9; Grand Rapids: Eerdmans, 1984), 222; Richard Nelson, *First and Second Kings* (Interpretation; Louisville: John Knox, 1987), 134; C. L. Seow, "I and II Kings," *NIB* 3:152; Uriel Simon, "The Poor Man's Ewe Lamb: An Example of Juridical Parable," *Bib* 48 (1967): 207–42; Marvin A. Sweeney, *I and II Kings: A Commentary* (OTL; Louisville: Westminster John Knox, 2007), 244.
6. Larry L. Lyke, *King David with the Wise Woman of Tekoa: The Resonance of Tradition in Parabolic Narrative* (JSOTSup 255; Sheffield: Sheffield Academic Press, 1997), 133.
7. According to the LXX, Ahab replies, "Look! You have murdered the ambush [intended] for me!" (v. 40b). This response implies that he thinks the prisoner was brought into Israel's camp to ambush him, but that the wounded soldier foiled this ambush by letting the prisoner die. Most likely, the LXX's reading of Ahab's reply results from a metathesis of the Hebrew letters. See Sweeney, *I and II Kings*, 237.
8. James A. Montgomery, *A Critical and Exegetical Commentary on the Books of Kings* (ICC; Edinburgh: T. and T. Clark, 1976), 325.
9. Simon B. Parker, *Stories in Scripture and Inscriptions: Comparative Studies on Narratives in Northwest Semitic Inscriptions and the Hebrew Bible* (New York: Oxford University Press, 1997), 13.
10. Ibid., 30 (italics in the original).
11. Alternatively, for the translation of *malke hesed* as "kings who honor treaties," rather than "kings of mercy," see Simon J. Devries, "A Reply to G. Gerlemann on *Malkê Hesed* in 1 Kings XX 31," *VT* 29 (1979): 359–62.

12. For examples of such parallels, see Cogan, *1 Kings*, 468; John Gray, *I and II Kings: A Commentary* (OTL; Philadelphia: Westminster, 1963), 381–82; Montgomery, *A Critical and Exegetical Commentary on the Books of Kings*, 324.
13. On familial terms within ancient Near Eastern political rhetoric, see Paul Kalluveettil, *Declaration and Covenant: A Comprehensive Review of Covenant Formulae from the Old Testament and the Ancient Near East* (AnBib 88; Rome: Pontifical Biblical Institute, 1982), 99–101; 198–209; J. David Schloen, *The House of the Father as Fact and Symbol: Patrimonialism in Ugarit and the Ancient Near East* (Winona Lake: Eisenbrauns, 2001).
14. In a letter from Elba, the language of "brothers" describes the treaty relationship between two kings. See Dennis McCarthy, "Elba, *horkia temnein, tb, šlm*: Addenda to *Treaty and Covenant*," *Bib* 60 (1979): 248; cf. Long, *1 Kings with an Introduction to Historical Literature*, 215.
15. Walsh, *1 Kings*, 296.
16. For a review of interpretations, see Christopher Begg, "'This Thing I cannot Do": (1 Kgs 20, 9)" *SJOT* 2 (1989): 23–27.
17. Ibid., 25–27.
18. Cogan, *1 Kings*, 465.
19. For example, see Devries, *1 Kings*, 250; Nelson, *First and Second Kings*, 134, 137; Seow, "I and II Kings," 150–51.
20. For an argument against these parallels, see Cogan, *1 Kings*, 467.
21. For example, see Lyke, *King David with the Wise Woman of Tekoa*, 130–31; Montgomery, *A Critical and Exegetical Commentary on the Books of Kings*, 325; Nelson, *First and Second Kings*, 135; Walsh, *1 Kings*, 310–11.
22. Lyke, *King David with the Wise Woman of Tekoa*, 134.

6. INTELLECTUAL WEAPONS: THE PARABLE'S FUNCTION IN 2 KINGS 14 AND 2 CHRONICLES 25

1. For example, see, among others, Kevin J. Cathcart, "The Trees, the Beasts, and the Birds: Fable, Parables and Allegories in the Old Testament," in *Wisdom in Ancient Israel: Essays in Honour of J. A. Emerton* (eds. John Day, Robert P. Gordon, H. G. M. Williamson; Cambridge: Cambridge University Press, 1995), 217–8; James A. Montgomery, *A Critical and Exegetical Commentary on the Books of Kings* (ICC; Edinburgh: T. and T. Clark, 1976), 440–41; C. L. Seow, "The First and Second Books of Kings: Introduction, Commentary, and Reflections," *NIB* 3:242; Marvin A. Sweeney, *I and II Kings: A Commentary* (OTL; Louisville: Westminster John Knox, 2007), 365.
2. For more detailed reviews of the differences between 2 Kings 14 and 2 Chronicles 25, see M. Patrick Graham, "Aspects of the Structure and Rhetoric of 2 Chronicles 25," in *History and Interpretation: Essays in Honour of John H. Hayes* (JSOTSup 173; eds. M. Patrick Graham, William P. Brown, and Jeffrey K. Kuan; Sheffield: JSOT Press, 1993), 79–81; Sara Japhet, *I and II Chronicles: A Commentary* (Louisville: WJKP, 1993), 860–73.
3. See the examples given in Mordechai Cogan and Hayim Tadmor, *II Kings: A New Translation with Introduction and Commentary* (AB 9b; Garden City, NY:

Doubleday, 1988), 156; cf. Albrecht Götze, *Old Babylonian Omen Texts* (New Haven: Yale University Press, 1947).
4. Ann M. Vater Solomon, "Jehoash's Fable of the Thistle and the Cedar (2 Kings 14.8–14 and 2 Chronicles 25.17–24)," in *Saga, Legend, Novella, Fable: Narrative Forms in Old Testament Narrative* (ed. George W. Coats; JSOTSup 35; Sheffield: JSOT Press, 1985), 129.
5. Cogan and Tadmor, *II Kings*, 156.
6. Walter Brueggemann, *1 and 2 Kings* (Smyth and Helwys Bible Commentary; Macon, GA: Smyth and Helwys, 2000), 588.
7. Stephanie Page, "A Stele of Adad-Nirari III and Nergal Ereš from Tell al Rimah," *Iraq* 30 (1968): 139–53; cf. Sweeney, *I and II Kings*, 365 n. 3.
8. Sweeney, *I and II Kings*, 365 [italics added].
9. Japhet, *I and II Chronicles*, 868.
10. In fact, the parable's interpretative possibilities are so broad that Midrash Tanchuma connects it to the story of Dinah's rape in Genesis 34. Focusing on the marriage request, it reads the bramble as Shechem and the cedar as Jacob since Shechem asks for Jacob's daughter Dinah's hand in marriage (34:11–12). The animal of the field represents Dinah's brothers Simeon and Levi who kill Shechem (34:25) just as the animal tramples the bramble. Even if the story referred to the incident in Genesis 34, the implied comparison between Amaziah and Shechem would still be quite insulting.
11. Solomon, "Jehoash's Fable of the Thistle and the Cedar," 129, 130.
12. Ann M. Vater Solomon, "Fable," in *Saga, Legend, Novella, Fable: Narrative Forms in Old Testament Narrative* (ed. George W. Coats; JSOTSup 35; Sheffield: JSOT Press, 1985), 121.
13. Richard Nelson, *First and Second Kings* (Interpretation; Louisville: John Knox, 1987), 219.
14. Gina Hens-Piazza, *1–2 Kings* (Abingdon Old Testament Commentaries; Nashville: Abingdon, 2006), 328.
15. Brueggemann, *1 and 2 Kings*, 588.
16. This reading takes *ki 'im* as introducing an emphatic statement in the midst of direct speech (cf. 1 Sam 21:6; Ruth 3:12) and understands the suffix of the infinitive (*hesireka*) as objective rather than subjective (The KJV reads it subjectively: "Except thou take away the blind and the lame, thou shalt not come in hither"). For other possible readings and an extended discussion of these issues, see Edward D. Herbert, "2 Samuel V 6: An Interpretative Crux Reconsidered in the Light of 4QSam[a]," *VT* 44 (1994): 340–48; P. Kyle McCarter, *2 Samuel: A New Translation with Introduction and Commentary* (AB 9; Garden City, NY: Doubleday, 1984), 135–6.
17. Taunts or insults do not only appear in prebattle contexts within ancient Near Eastern literature. As noted in chapter 1, a number of taunts surface in the Sumerian "School Dialogues" (*COS* 1.184–85:588–92).
18. Burke O. Long, *2 Kings* (FOTL 10; Grand Rapids: Eerdmans, 1991), 168–9; cf. Solomon, "Jehoash's Fable of the Thistle and the Cedar," 115.
19. Wilfred G. Lambert, *Babylonian Wisdom Literature* (Oxford: Oxford University Press, 1960), 150.

20. Ibid.
21. For texts, translations, and introductions for these fables, see Lambert, *Babylonian Wisdom Literature*, 150–212.
22. Ibid., 151. Yet the contest between Nisaba and the wheat contains the phrase "Ereškigal answered," which may suggest a judgment scene since the deity Ereškigal serves in a judicial capacity elsewhere. In addition, the text contains a hymn that praises Nisaba, which suggests she won the contest (Ibid., 164).
23. Ibid., 189.
24. For an introduction, transition, and bibliography for Etana, see also Benjamin R. Foster, *Before the Muses: An Anthology of Akkadian Literature* (3rd edn. Bethesda: CDL Press, 2005), 533–54.
25. Graham notes that one should not understand the Chronicler's reference to Deut 24:16 as completely positive. He writes, "It illuminates and interprets the outcome of Amaziah's reign. Amaziah was assassinated at the end of the Chronicler's narrative 'for his own sin' [cf. 2 Chr 25:27–28]. It is ironic that the text in Deuteronomy, apparently cited to praise Amaziah, serves to underscore the justice of God's subsequent decision to destroy the king. Amaziah's text for dealing with his own subjects became God's text for dealing with him: Amaziah was not destroyed because of his father Joash's sin, but because of his own" ("Aspects of the Structure and Rhetoric of 2 Chronicles 25," 86).
26. Japhet comes to a similar conclusion regarding v. 19. She cites Pharaoh Neco's words to Josiah in 2 Chr 35:21–22 as a parallel in addition to material from Exodus. See Japhet, *I and II Chronicles*, 868–9.
27. Bruce C. Birch makes this type of suggestion regarding Nathan's parable in 2 Samuel 12 as does Carole Fontaine regarding 2 Samuel 14. See respectively, Bruce C. Birch, "The First and Second Books of Samuel: Introduction, Commentary, and Reflections," *NIB* 2.1292; Carole Fontaine, "Proverb Performance in the Hebrew Bible," *JSOT* 32 (1985): 96–7, 97 n. 40.

7. CONCLUSIONS AND IMPLICATIONS FOR THE STUDY OF HEBREW BIBLE PARABLES

1. For a detailed discussion of the absence of "epic" poetry in the biblical material, see Robert Alter, *The Art of Biblical Poetry* (New York: Basic Books, 1985), 27–61. We should also note that referring to Isa 5:1–7 as a "song *mashal*" does not mean that it does not qualify as a "fable *mashal*" as well. A fable refers to a narrative that primarily involves personified plants or animals and at times their interaction with humans. If such a narrative comes in the form of a song, as it does in Isa 5:1–7, then it qualifies as both a fable and a song.
2. See, among others, A. Graffy, "The Literary Genre of Isaiah 5:1–7," *Bib* 60 (1979): 400–09; Marjo C. A. Korpel, "The Literary Genre of the Song of the Vineyard (Isa. 5:1–7)," in *The Structural Analysis of Biblical and Canaanite Poetry* (JSOTSup 74; eds. W. van der Meer and J. C. de Moor; Sheffield: JSOT Press, 1988), 119–55; H. Niehr, "Zur Gattung von Jes 5, 1–7," *BZ* 30 (1986): 99–104; H. G. M. Williamson, *A Critical and Exegetical Commentary on Isaiah 1–27: Volume 1: Commentary on Isaiah 1–5* (3 vols.; ICC; New York: T. and T. Clark, 2006), 327–9; John T. Willis, "The Genre of Isaiah 5:1–7," *JBL* 96.3 (1977): 337–62.

3. Williamson, *A Critical and Exegetical Commentary on Isaiah 1–27*, 328. Unfortunately, we see this tendency to overallegorize Isa 5:1–7 in light of Israel and Judah's history in Gary Roye William's otherwise excellent article, "Frustrated Expectations in Isaiah V 1–7: A Literary Interpretation," *VT* 35.4 (1985): 459–65.
4. For example, see the comments and citations in W. Schottroff, "Das Weinberglied Jesajas (Jes 5, 1–7): Ein Beitrag zur Geschichte der Parabel," *ZAW* 82 (1970): 68–91; Gerald T. Sheppard, "More on Isaiah 5:1–7 as a Juridical Parable," *CBQ* 44 (1982): 45–47; Gene M. Tucker, "The Book of Isaiah 1–39: Introduction, Commentary, and Reflections," *NIB* 6.88; J. William Whedbee, *Isaiah and Wisdom* (Nashville: Abingdon, 1971), 47; Williams, "Frustrated Expectations in Isaiah V 1–7," 462; Williamson, *A Critical and Exegetical Commentary on Isaiah 1–27*, 327–28; Gale A. Yee, "A Form-Critical Study of Isaiah 5:1–7 as a Song and a Juridical Parable," *CBQ* 43 (1981): 30–40. On Simon's notion of the so-called "juridical parable" genre, see chapter 3 of this book.
5. Sheppard, "More on Isaiah 5:1–7 as a Juridical Parable," 45–7. On the hypothetical or ideal form of a juridical parable, see Yee, "A Form-Critical Study of Isaiah 5:1–7 as a Song and a Juridical Parable," 34–5.
6. Due to the lack of the addressee's reaction in Isa 5:1–7, we should not compare Nathan's "you are the man" statement in 2 Sam 12:7a to Isaiah's announcement that Judah and Israel are the vineyard. In contrast to Nathan, we do not know whether Isaiah uses this statement to correct his addressees' misunderstanding since we do not have access to their interpretation in the first place (contra, among others, Tucker, "The Book of Isaiah 1–39," 88; Williamson, *A Critical and Exegetical Commentary on Isaiah 1–27*, 328).
7. Peter D. Miscall connects a number of the images in 5:1–7, including the vineyard, with Isaiah's oracles against Judah as well as Israel in Isaiah 1–4 (*Isaiah* [Sheffield: JSOT Press, 1993], 31). Although Yee acknowledges that plant imagery appears in connection with Judah throughout Jeremiah (6:9; 12:2; 18:9; 24:6; 32:41; 42:10; 45:4) and in Isaiah's second song of the vineyard (27:2–7), she argues that since these texts come from a later period than First Isaiah, we have no textual evidence for the vineyard motif applied to Judah in the eighth century. Nonetheless, although Isa 27:2–7 reflects a much later date, Jeremiah's use of this image appears chronologically close enough to First Isaiah to serve as a source for textual comparison. We may make the same claim regarding Isa 1:5–7, even if it refers to the Assyrian ruler Sennacherib and therefore dates no earlier than 701 BCE.
8. Williamson, *A Critical and Exegetical Commentary on Isaiah 1–27*, 329. Other scholars note that it takes three to four years for vineyards to bear fruit. See Oded Borowski, *Agriculture in Ancient Israel* (Winona Lake, IN: Eisenbrauns, 1987), 110; Carey Ellen Walsh, *The Fruit of the Vine: Viticulture in Ancient Israel* (HSM 60; Winona Lake, IN: Eisenbrauns, 2000), 99. Elsewhere, Walsh writes, "Yahweh does not take the ruined harvest in stride, remaining hopeful that the next year's crop will fare better. Rather, he destroys the vineyard with the costly rashness of a spurned lover" ("God's Vineyard: Isaiah's Prophecy as Vintner's Textbook," *BRev* 14.4 [August 1998]: 53). Along these lines, Robert P. Carroll reads Isa 5:1–7 as, "YHWH going into a huff and wrecking his own vineyard and excusing himself

on the grounds that anyway the grapes were inedible... This reading of 5:1–7 belongs then to tales about the berserker god" ("YHWH's Sour Grapes: Images of Food and Drink in the Prophetic Discourses of the Hebrew Bible," *Semeia* 86 [1999]: 120).

9. Regarding these verbs in v. 5, J. Blake Couey writes, "The most common meanings [of *ba'ar*] are 'burn, consume' and, more generally, 'destroy,' all of which fit here.... The context of Isa 5:5 clearly demands the sense of 'destruction' for the verb [*mirmas*], but the wide semantic range leaves open a number of possibilities for the precise nature of the destruction, and we flatten the poetry by insisting upon only one of them, whether trampling or consumption by animals or burning by marauders" ("'The Most Perfect Model of Prophetic Poetry': Studies in the Poetry of First Isaiah" [Ph.D. diss., Princeton Theological Seminary, 2009], 94 n. 64).

10. Susan Ackerman, *Warrior, Dancer, Seductress, Queen: Women in Judges and Biblical Israel* (Anchor Bible Reference Library; New York: Doubleday, 1998), 264–7.

11. Although considerable debate exists among scholars over whether to attribute Isa 32:9–14 to First Isaiah, we see no compelling reason not to do so.

12. Unlike the use of vintage imagery in Isaiah 5, 16, and 32, the second song of the vineyard in Isa 27:2–7 employs vintage imagery very similar to Isa 5:1–7 to depict how YHWH will protect and defend the people rather than destroy them (compare 5:5–6 with 27:4). In addition, the plants representing Israel will produce fruit that fills the earth (27:6) instead of sour grapes (5:2). Nonetheless, as part of the so-called "Isaiah Apocalypse," Isa 27:2–7 comes from a period several centuries after First Isaiah and most likely serves as a response to 5:1–7. We should note that in another text from the Isaiah Apocalypse (24:7–13), various types of music and drinking will cease when YHWH brings the earth under judgment. The prophet declares that the vine (*gapen*) will become feeble (v. 7). This image probably refers to a failed harvest similar to 5:1–7. The passage concludes by comparing the earth's decimation to "the gleanings when the vintage is complete" (v. 13b). Nevertheless, we should not include these passages as textual evidence for First Isaiah's use of vintage festival imagery.

13. This book's previous chapters have questioned the existence of the juridical parable genre. Rather than juridical parables, we better understand 2 Sam 12:1–4 as a fable *mashal* and 2 Sam 14:1–20 and 1 Kgs 20:35–42 as petitionary narratives. Nor does Isaiah 5:1–7 fit the criteria for a juridical parable, in terms of either its form or function. Thus, although each of these texts becomes a parable when it serves as comparison, none of them provides compelling evidence for the existence of a juridical parable genre.

14. Willis, "The Genre of Isaiah 5:1–7," 359 (italics original).

15. See the comments and citations in Williams, "Frustrated Expectations in Isaiah V 1–7," 460.

16. See the comments and citations in Otto Kaiser, *Isaiah 1–12: A Commentary* (OTL; trans. R. A. Wilson; Philadelphia: Westminster, 1972), 59; Marvin A. Sweeney, *Isaiah 1–39, with an Introduction to Prophetic Literature* (FOTL XVI; Grand Rapids: Eerdmans, 1996), 129; Willis, "The Genre of Isaiah 5:1–7," 362 n. 116.

17. See, among others, Leslie C. Allen, *Ezekiel 1–19* (WBC 28; Dallas: Word Books, 1994), 254; Daniel I. Block, *The Book of Ezekiel: Chapters 1–24* (Grand Rapids: Eerdmans, 1997), 524–5; Katheryn Pfisterer Darr, "The Book of Ezekiel: Introduction, Commentary, and Reflections," *NIB* 6.1242–43; Moshe Greenberg, *Ezekiel 1–20: A New Translation with Introduction and Commentary* (AB 22; Garden City, NY: Doubleday, 1983), 309–10, 322–3; Walther Zimmerli, *Ezekiel 1: A Commentary on the Book of Ezekiel, Chapters 1–24* (Hermeneia; trans. Ronald E. Clements; Philadelphia: Fortress, 1979), 360.
18. See, among others, Block, *The Book of Ezekiel*, 525; Darr, "The Book of Ezekiel," 1245; Ellen F. Davis, *Swallowing the Scroll: Textuality and the Dynamics of Discourse in Ezekiel's Prophecy* (Bible and Literature 21; Sheffield: Almond, 1989), 96–104; Greenberg, *Ezekiel 1–20*, 321; Timothy Polk, "Paradigms, Parables, and *Měšālîm*: On Reading the *Māšāl* in Scripture," *CBQ* 45.4 (1983): 578–83; H. Simian-Yofre, "Ez 17, 1–10 como enigma y parabola," *Bib* 65 (1984): 27–43.
19. Following Greenberg, Darr notes, "The presence of the definite article on the noun 'eagle' [*hannesher*] indicates 'incomplete determination,' so should be translated 'a certain great eagle' [GKC § 126 q-t]. Ezekiel has a specific entity in mind, but he does not reveal its identity" (Darr, "The Book of Ezekiel," 1245). According to Greenberg, this use of "incomplete determination" also appears in the parable in 2 Kgs 14:9 (see chapter 6 of this book) and a proverb in Num 11:12 (Greenberg, *Ezekiel 1–20*, 309–10).
20. Block, *The Book of Ezekiel*, 524 n. 7; Greenberg, *Ezekiel 1–20*, 321.
21. For a treatment of the many lexical links and structural parallels between Ezekiel 12 and 17, see Block, *The Book of Ezekiel*, 522–3.
22. As my colleague Mark Leuchter observes in a private communication, Deuteronomy presents divine revelation as near and accessible (Deut 30:11–14) and Jeremiah and Deuteronomistic groups stand within this type of prophetic tradition. By contrast, Ezekiel presents divine revelation as opaque and accessible only to a Zadokite priest like himself (cf. Ezekiel 1). Rather than claiming to stand within the tradition of the Deuteronomic Moses, Ezekiel asserts his interpretative authority over against the Deuteronomists by claiming to have access to esoteric revelation. On Deuteronomistic responses to the rise of this Ezekiel tradition within the exilic period, see Mark Leuchter, *The Polemics of Exile in Jeremiah 26–45* (New York: Cambridge University Press, 2008).
23. Jeremiah 22:6, 23 seems to equate Judah with Lebanon as well (cf. 1 Kgs 7:2). See Darr, "The Book of Ezekiel," 1245; Greenberg, *Ezekiel 1–20*, 310.
24. For an influential discussion of Ezekiel 17 in light of Psammetichus II's foreign policy, see Moshe Greenberg, "Ezekiel 17 and the Policy of Psammetichus II," *JBL* 76.4 (1957): 304–9.
25. For many scholars, 2 Chr 36:13 provides evidence that Nebuchadnezzar forced Zedekiah to swear an oath by YHWH that he would remain loyal to the Babylonian king. In Babylonian treaties, vassals swore not only by Babylonian deities, but by their own deities as well. See Darr, "The Book of Ezekiel," 1250; Joseph A. Fitzmeyer, *The Aramaic Inscriptions of Sefîre* (Bibor 19; Rome: Pontifical Biblical Institute, 1967), 60–61; George E. Mendenhall, "Puppy and Lettuce in Northwest-Semitic Covenant Making," *BASOR* 133 (1954): 30 n.16; Zimmerli, *Ezekiel 1*, 365.

In addition, evidence of this practice exists in Hittite and Assyrian treaties as well as the Aramaic Sefire inscription (eighth-century BCE). See Mordechai Cogan, *Syria, Judah and Israel in the Eighth and Seventh Centuries B.C.E.* (SBLMS 19; Missoula: Scholars, 1974), 46–7; Matitiahu Tsevat, "The Neo-Assyrian and Neo-Babylonian Vassal Oaths and the Prophet Ezekiel," *JBL* 78 (1959): 199–204. If Ezekiel assumes that Zedekiah broke an oath that he swore in YHWH's name, then this may explain why YHWH appears so upset with Zedekiah in 17:18–21.

26. Jon D. Levenson, "The Last Four Verses of Kings," *JBL* 103.3 (1984): 359; idem, *Theology of the Program of Restoration of Ezekiel 40–48* (HSM 10; Missoula: Scholars, 1976), 77–84.

27. Some scholars view different redactional layers of Jeremiah as holding differing opinions of Zedekiah. For example, see John Applegate, "The Fate of Zedekiah: Redactional Debate in the Book of Jeremiah, Part I," *VT* 48 (1998): 137–60; idem, "The Fate of Zedekiah: Redactional Debate in the Book of Jeremiah, Part II," *VT* 48 (1998): 301–8; Herman-Josef Stipp, "Zedekiah in the Book of Jeremiah: On the Formation of a Biblical Character," *CBQ* 58 (1996): 627–48.

28. On responses within Jeremiah to the rise of the Ezekiel tradition during the exilic period, see Leuchter, *The Polemics of Exile in Jeremiah 26–45*, 156–65.

29. See Jeremy Schipper, "'Exile Atones for Everything': Coping with Jeremiah 22.24–30," *JSOT* 31.4 (2007): 481–92.

30. See Jeremy Schipper, *Disability Studies and the Hebrew Bible: Figuring Mephibosheth in the David Story* (LHBOTS 441; New York: T. and T. Clark, 2006), 116–22; idem, "'Significant Resonances' with Mephibosheth in 2 Kings 25:27–30: A Response to Donald F. Murray," *JBL* 124.3 (2005): 521–9. Juha Pakkala argues that the Deuteronomistic Historian wrote in support of Jehoiachin over Zedekiah, whereas Jeremiah favors Zedekiah ("Zedekiah's Fate and the Dynastic Succession," *JBL* 125.3 [2006]: 443–52).

31. Zimmerli, *Ezekiel 1*, 360.

32. Bernard M. Levinson, *Legal Revision and Religious Renewal in Ancient Israel* (New York: Cambridge University Press, 2008), 62–3.

33. On proverb performance, see chapter 1 of this book. For a detailed investigation that comes to different conclusions regarding how Ezek 18:1–4 performs, see Katheryn Pfisterer Darr, "Proverb Performance and Trans-generational Retribution in Ezekiel 18," in *Ezekiel's Hierarchical World: Wrestling with a Tiered Reality* (eds. Stephen L. Cook and Corrine L. Patton; Atlanta: Society of Biblical Literature, 2004), 199–223. The idea that Ezekiel evaluates whether the proverb of transgenerational punishment still "performs" in an exilic context may help to explain what Levinson observes when he writes, "Strikingly, while rejecting the proverb as offensive, the prophet never disputes that the moral economy it depicts has hitherto been valid! . . . [By contrast, Jeremiah] concedes that the proverb continues to be valid for the present and immediate future [Jer 31:27–33]. Only in the case of Ezekiel is the new principle immediately to replace the rejected one" (Levinson, *Legal Revision and Religious Renewal in Ancient Israel*, 61–2). In addition, Levinson shows that, unlike Ezekiel, the Deuteronomist uses the law of transgenerational punishment to "the third and fourth generation" (Exod 20:5; Deut 5:9) to explain the Babylonian exile since the deportation of

Jehoiachin in 2 Kgs 24:10–17 occurs four generations after the wicked reign of Manasseh in 2 Kgs 21:1–18 (ibid., 56 n. 57). By contrast, the author of Lam 5:7 complains about the justice of transgenerational punishment in regards to the exile (ibid., 57–60). All of these texts provide evidence that a consensus did not exist regarding transgenerational punishment and the exilic experience. Thus, some parties would have contested Ezekiel's opinion on this matter.

Works Cited

Abrams, M. H. *A Glossary of Literary Terms.* 4th ed. New York: Harcourt Brace, 1981.
Ackerman, Susan. *Warrior, Dancer, Seductress, Queen: Women in Judges and Biblical Israel.* Anchor Bible Reference Library. New York: Doubleday, 1998.
Ackroyd, Peter. *The Second Book of Samuel.* Cambridge Bible Commentary. Cambridge: Cambridge University Press, 1977.
Allen, Leslie C. *Ezekiel 1–19.* WBC 28. Dallas: Word Books, 1994.
Alter, Robert. *The Art of Biblical Narrative.* New York: Basic Books, 1981.
_____. *The Art of Biblical Poetry.* New York: Basic Books, 1985.
_____. *The David Story: A Translation with Commentary of 1 and 2 Samuel.* New York: W.W. Norton & Company, 1999.
Applegate, John. "The Fate of Zedekiah: Redactional Debate in the Book of Jeremiah, Part I." *VT* 48 (1998): 137–60.
_____. "The Fate of Zedekiah: Redactional Debate in the Book of Jeremiah, Part II." *VT* 48 (1998): 301–8.
Bailey, Randall C. *David in Love and War: The Pursuit of Power in 2 Samuel 10–12.* JSOT Supplement 75. Sheffield: Sheffield Academic Press, 1990.
Barry, Alfred. *The Parables of the Old Testament.* London: Society for Promoting Christian Knowledge, 1846.
Bartelmus, Rüdiger. "Die sogenannte Jotamfabel- eine politisch-religiöse Parabeldichtung." *TZ* 41 (1985): 97–120.
Begg, Christopher. "Abimelech, King of Shechem according to Josephus." *Ephemerides Theologicae Lovanienses* 72 (1996): 146–64.
_____. "'This Thing I cannot Do'": (1 Kgs 20, 9)." *SJOT* 2 (1989): 23–7.
Bellefontaine, Elizabeth. "Customary Law and Chieftainship: Juridical Aspects of 2 Samuel 14:4–21." *JSOT* 38 (1987): 47–72.
Birch, Bruce C. "The First and Second Books of Samuel: Introduction, Commentary and Reflections." *NIB* 2: 947–1383.
Block, Daniel I. *The Book of Ezekiel: Chapters 1–24.* Grand Rapids: Eerdmans, 1997.
Bloomberg, Craig L. "Interpreting the Parables of Jesus: Where Are We and Where Do We Go from Here?" *CBQ* 53.1 (1991): 50–78.
Boadt, Lawrence. "Understanding the *Mashal* and Its Value for Jewish-Christian Dialogue in a Narrative Theology." Pages 159–88 in *Parable and Story in Judaism*

and Christianity. Edited by Clemens Thoma and Michael Wyschogrod. New York: Paulist, 1989.

Bodner, Keith. "Is Joab a Reader-Response Critic?" *JSOT* 27 (2002): 19–35.

Boer, Roland, ed. *Bakhtin and Genre Theory in Biblical Studies*. Society for Biblical Literature Semeia Studies 63. Atlanta: Society of Biblical Literature, 2007.

Boling, Robert G. *Judges: Introduction, Translation, and Commentary*. AB 7. Garden City, NY: Doubleday, 1975.

Bonsignore, John J. "In Parables: Teaching through Parables." *Legal Studies Forum* 12.1 (1988): 191–209.

Boogart, T. A. "Stone for Stone: Retribution in the Story of Abimelech and Shechem." *JSOT* 32 (1985): 45–56.

Borowski, Oded. *Agriculture in Ancient Israel*. Winona Lake, IN: Eisenbrauns, 1987.

Brown, Raymond E. "Parable and Allegory Reconsidered." *NT* 5 (1962): 36–45.

Brueggemann, Walter. *First and Second Samuel*. IBC. Louisville: John Knox, 1990.

―――. *1 and 2 Kings*. Smyth and Helwys Bible Commentary. Volume 8. Macon, GA: Smyth and Helwys, 2000.

―――. *Testimony to Otherwise: The Witness of Elijah and Elisha*. St. Louis: Chalice, 2001.

Buber, Martin. *Kingship of God*. London: Humanities, 1967.

Buss, Martin. *Biblical Form Criticism in Its Context*. JSOT Supplement 274. Sheffield: Sheffield Academic Press, 1999.

Campbell, Anthony. *2 Samuel*. FOTL 8. Grand Rapids: Eerdmans, 2005.

Carlson, R. A. *David, the Chosen King: A Traditio-Historical Approach to the Second Book of Samuel*. Stockholm: Almqvist & Wiksell, 1964.

Carlston, Charles E. "Proverbs, Maxims, and the Historical Jesus." *JBL* 99.1 (1980): 87–105.

Carroll, Robert P. "YHWH's Sour Grapes: Images of Food and Drink in the Prophetic Discourses of the Hebrew Bible." *Semeia* 86 (1999): 113–310.

Cathcart, Kevin J. "The Trees, the Beasts, and the Birds: Fable, Parables and Allegories in the Old Testament." Pages 212–5 in *Wisdom in Ancient Israel: Essays in Honour of J.A. Emerton*. Edited by John Day, Robert P. Gordon, and H. G. M. Williamson. Cambridge: Cambridge University Press, 1995.

Chibaudel, P. "David et Bethsabée; une Tragédie de l'Abstentin." *La Vie Spirituelle* 143 (1989): 75–85.

Coats, George W. "Parable, Fable, and Anecdote: Storytelling in the Succession Narrative." *Int* 35 (1981): 368–82.

―――. "II Samuel 12:1–7a." *Int* 40 (1986): 170–75.

Cogan, Mordecai. *Syria, Judah and Israel in the Eighth and Seventh Centuries B.C.E.* SBLMS 19. Missoula: Scholars, 1974.

―――. *1 Kings: A New Translation with Introduction and Commentary*. AB 10. New York: Doubleday, 2000.

――― and Hayim Tadmor. *II Kings: A New Translation with Introduction and Commentary*. AB 9b. Garden City, NY: Doubleday, 1988.

Couey, J. Blake. "The Most Perfect Model of Prophetic Poetry: Studies in the Poetry of First Isaiah." Ph.D. diss., Princeton Theological Seminary, 2009.

Coxon, Peter. "A Note on 'Bathsheba' in 2 Samuel 12, 1–6." *Bib* 62 (1981): 247–50.

Crossan, John Dominaic. "Parables." Pages 146–7 in *ABD*. Edited by David Noel Freedman. 6 vols. New York: Random House, 1992.
Darr, Katheryn Pfisterer. "The Book of Ezekiel: Introduction, Commentary, and Reflections." *NIB* 6: 1037–1607.
———. "Proverb Performance and Trans-generational Retribution in Ezekiel 18." Pages 199–223 in *Ezekiel's Hierarchical World: Wrestling with a Tiered Reality*. Edited by Stephen L. Cook and Corrine L. Patton. Atlanta: Society of Biblical Literature, 2004.
Davis, Ellen F. *Swallowing the Scroll: Textuality and the Dynamics of Discourse in Ezekiel's Prophecy*. Bible and Literature 21. Sheffield: Almond, 1989.
Delekat, Leinhard. "Tendenz und Theologie der David-Salomo-Erzählung." Pages 26–36 in *Das Ferne und nahe Wort: Festschrift Leonhard Rost zur Vollendung seines 70. Lebenjahres am 30. November 1966*. Edited by Fritz Maass. Berlin: A. Töpelmann, 1967.
Derrida, Jacques. "The Law of Genre." Pages 219–31 in *Modern Genre Theory*. Edited by David Duff. Harlow, U.K.: Longman, 2000.
De Vaux, Roland. *Ancient Israel*. Vol. 1 of 2 vols. Translated by J. McHugh. New York: McGraw-Hill, 1961.
De Vries, Simon J. *1 Kings*. WBC 12. Waco, TX: Word Books, 1985.
De Waard, Jan. "Jotham's Fable: An Exercise in Clearing Away the Unclear." Pages 362–70 in *Wissenschaft und Kirche: Festschrift für Eduard Lohse*. Edited by Kurt Aland and Siegfried Meurer. Bielefeld: Luther-Verlag, 1989.
Dobbs-Allsopp, F. W. "The Genre of the Mesad Hashavyahu Ostracon." *BASOR* 295 (1994): 49–55.
———. Roberts J. J. M., Seow Leong, Richard E. Whitaker eds. *Hebrew Inscriptions: Texts from the Biblical Period of the Monarchy with Concordance*. New Haven: Yale University Press, 2004.
Driver, Samuel R. *Notes on the Hebrew Text of the Books of Samuel*. Oxford: Clarendon Press, 1890.
Eissfeldt, Otto. *Der Maschal im Alten Testament: eine wortgeschichtliche Untersuchung nebst einer literargeschichtlichen Untersuchung der Maschal genannten Gattungen "Volkssprichwort" und "Spottlied."* Giessen: A. Töpelmann, 1913.
Evans, Craig A. "On the Vineyard Parables of Isaiah 5 and Mark 12." *BZ* 28 (1984): 82–6.
Fauconnier, Gilles and Mark Turner. *The Way We Think: Conceptual Blending and the Mind's Hidden Complexities*. New York: Basic Books, 2003.
Fitzmeyer, Joseph A. *The Aramaic Inscriptions of Sefire*. BibOr 19. Rome: Pontifical Biblical Institute, 1967.
Fokkelman, Jan P. *Narrative Art and Poetry in the Books of Samuel: A Full Interpretation based on Stylistic and Structural Analysis*. Vol. 1 of 4 vols. Assen: van Gorcum, 1981.
———. "Structural Remarks on Judges 9 and 19." Pages 33–45 in *"Sha'arei Talmon": Studies in the Bible, Qumran, and the Ancient Near East Presented to Shemaryahu Talmon*. Edited by Michael Fishbane and Emanuel Tov. Winona Lake, IN: Eisenbrauns, 1992.
Fontaine, Carole R. *Traditional Sayings in the Old Testament: A Contextual Study*. Bible and Literature Series 5. Sheffield: Almond, 1982.
———. "Proverb Performance in the Hebrew Bible." *JSOT* 32.1 (1985): 87–103.

Foster, Benjamin R. *Before the Muses: An Anthology of Akkadian Literature.* 3rd edn. Bethesda: CDL Press, 2005.
Fowler, Alastair. *Kinds of Literature: An Introduction to the Theory of Genres and Modes.* Cambridge: Harvard University Press, 1982.
Fritz, Volkmar. "Abimelech und Sichem in Jdc. ix." *VT* 32 (1982): 129–44.
Gaster, Theodor Herze. *Myth, Legend, and Custom in the Old Testament: A Comparative Study with Chapters from Sir James G. Frazer's Folklore in the Old Testament.* New York: Harper & Row, 1969.
Gerhardsson, Birger. "The Narrative Meshalim in the Synoptic Gospels." *NTS* 34 (1988): 339–63.
Gerhard, von Rad. *Wisdom in Israel.* Translated by James D. Martin. Valley Forge: Trinity Press International, 1972.
Ginzberg, Louis. *The Legends of the Jews.* 7 vols. Baltimore: The John Hopkins University Press, 1998.
Gnuse, Robert K. *The Dream Theophany of Samuel: Its Relation to Ancient Near Eastern Dreams and its Theological Significance.* Lanham: University Press of America, 1984.
———. "A Reconsideration of the Form-critical Structure of 1 Samuel 3: An ANE Dream Theophany." *ZAW* 94 (1982): 379–89.
Godbey, Allen Howard. "The Hebrew Mašal." *AJSL* 39 (1923): 89–108.
Götze, Albrecht. *Old Babylonian Omen Texts.* New Haven: Yale University Press, 1947.
Goulder, M. D. *Midrash and Lection in Matthew.* London: SPCK, 1974.
Gowler, David B. *What Are They Saying About the Parables?* New York: Paulist, 2000.
Graffy, A. "The Literary Genre of Isaiah 5:1–7." *Bib* 60 (1979): 400–9.
Graham, M. Patrick. "Aspects of the Structure and Rhetoric of 2 Chronicles 25." Pages 78–89 in *History and Interpretation: Essays in Honour of John H. Hayes.* JSOT Supplement 173. Edited by M. Patrick Graham, William P. Brown, and Jeffrey K. Kuan. Sheffield: JSOT Press, 1993.
Greenberg, Moshe. *Ezekiel 1–20: A New Translation with Introduction and Commentary.* AB 22. Garden City, NY: Doubleday, 1983.
———. "Ezekiel 17 and the Policy of Psammetichus II." *Journal of Biblical Literature* 76.4 (1957): 304–9.
Gray, John. *I and II Kings: A Commentary.* OTL. Philadelphia: Westminster, 1963.
Gunkel, Hermann. *The Folktale in the Old Testament.* Translated by M. D. Rutter. Sheffield: Almond, 1987.
Gunn, David. *The Story of King David: Genre and Interpretation.* JSOT Supplement 6. Sheffield: JSOT Press, 1978.
———. *Judges.* Blackwell Bible Commentaries. Oxford: Blackwell, 2005.
———. "2 Samuel." Pages 262–78 in *HarperCollins Bible Commentary.* Revised edition. Edited by James L. Mays. San Francisco: Harper San Francisco, 2000.
Halpern, Baruch. *The Constitution of the Monarchy in Israel.* Chico: Scholars, 1981.
———. *David's Secret Demons: Messiah, Murder, Traitor, King.* Grand Rapids: Eerdmans, 2001.
———. "The Rise of Abimelek Ben-Jerubbaal," *HAR* 2 (1978): 79–100.
Hens-Piazza, Gina. *1–2 Kings.* Abingdon Old Testament Commentaries. Nashville: Abingdon, 2006.
Herbert, A. S. "The 'Parable' (*Māšāl*) in the Old Testament." *SJT* 7 (1954): 180–96.

Herbert, Edward D. "2 Samuel V 6: An Interpretative Crux Reconsidered in the Light of 4QSam^a." *VT* 44 (1994): 340–48.
Hertzberg, Hans Wilhelm. *I and II Samuel: A Commentary*. Translated by J. S. Bowden. Philadelphia: Westminster, 1964.
Hoftijzer, Jean. "David and the Tekoite Woman." *VT* 20 (1970): 419–44.
Hultgren, Arland J. *The Parables of Jesus: A Commentary*. Grand Rapids: William B. Eerdmans, 2000.
Husser, Jean-Marie. *Dreams and Dream Narratives in the Biblical World*. Biblical Seminar 63. Translated by Jill M. Munro. Sheffield: Sheffield University Press, 1999.
Janzen, J. Gerald. "A Certain Woman in the Rhetoric of Judges 9." *JSOT* 38 (1987): 33–7.
Japhet, Sara. *I and II Chronicles: A Commentary*. Louisville: Westminister John Knox Press, 1993.
Jeremais, Joachim. *The Parables of Jesus*. Revised edition. New York: Scribner's, 1963.
Jobling, David. *The Sense of Biblical Narrative: Structural Analyses in the Hebrew Bible II*. JSOT Supplement 39. Sheffield: JSOT Press, 1986.
Jones, Gwilym H. *The Nathan Narratives*. JSOT Supplement 80. Sheffield: Sheffield Academic Press, 1990.
Jülicher, Adolf. *Die Gleichnisreden Jesu*. 2 vols. Freiburg: Adademische Verlagsbuchhandlung von J. C. B. Mohr, 1888.
Kaiser, Otto. *Isaiah 1–12: A Commentary*. OTL. Translated by R. A. Wilson. Philadelphia: Westminster, 1972.
Kalluveettil, Paul. *Declaration and Covenant: A Comprehensive Review of Covenant Formulae from the Old Testament and the Ancient Near East*. AnBib 88. Rome: Pontifical Biblical Institute, 1982.
Keim, Paul A. "The Politics of Malice: Ancient Near Eastern Malediction as Metaphor." Pages 17–45 in *Exploring New Paradigms in Biblical and Cognate Studies*. Edited by Hugh R. Page, Jr. Lewiston: Mellen Biblical Press, 1996.
Kermode, Frank. *The Genesis of Secrecy: On the Interpretation of Narrative*. Cambridge: Harvard University Press, 1979.
Klein, Lillian R. *The Triumph of Irony in the Book of Judges*. JSOT Supplement 68. Sheffield: Almond, 1988.
Knoppers, Gary N. "The Vanishing Solomon: The Disappearance of the United Monarchy from Recent Histories of Ancient Israel." *JBL* 116.1 (1997): 19–44.
Korpel, Marjo C. A. "The Literary Genre of the Song of the Vineyard (Isa. 5:1–7)." Pages 119–55 in *The Structural Analysis of Biblical and Canaanite Poetry*. JSOT Supplement 74. Edited by Willem van der Meer and Johannes C. de Moor. Sheffield: JSOT Press, 1988.
Kottsieper, Ingo. "Die alttestamentliche Weisheit in Licht aramäischer Weisheitstraditionen." Pages 128–62 in *Die Weisheit hat ihr Haus gebaut: Studien zur Gestalt der Sophia in den biblischen Schriften*. Edited by Silvia Schroer. Mainz: Matthias-Grünewald-Verlag, 1996.
Lambert, Wilfred G. *Babylonian Wisdom Literature*. Oxford: Oxford University Press, 1960.

Landes, George. "Jonah: A *Māšāl?*" Pages 137–58 in *Israelite Wisdom: Theological and Literary Essays in Honor of Samuel Terrien.* Edited by John G. Gammie, Walter Brueggemann, Lee Humphreys, James Ward. New York: Union Theological Seminary, 1978.

Lasine, Stuart. "Melodrama as Parable: The Story of the Poor Man's Ewe-Lamb and the Unmasking of David's Topsy-Turvy Emotions." *HAR* 8 (1984): 101–24.

Lategan, Bernard C. *Text and Reality: Aspects of Reference in Biblical Texts.* Philadelphia: Fortress, Atlanta: Scholars, 1985.

Lemaire, Andre. "L'ostracon de Masad Hashavyahu (Yavneh-Yam) replacé dans son contexte." *Semetica* 21 (1971): 57–79.

Leuchter, Mark. *The Polemics of Exile in Jeremiah 26–45.* New York: Cambridge University Press, 2008.

Levenson, Jon D. *Theology of the Program of Restoration of Ezekiel 40–48.* HSM 10. Missoula: Scholars, 1976.

———. "The Last Four Verses of Kings." *JBL* 103.3 (1984): 353–61.

Levinson, Bernard M. *Legal Revision and Religious Renewal in Ancient Israel.* New York: Cambridge University Press, 2008.

Lichtheim, Miriam. *Ancient Egyptian Literature: A Book of Readings. Volume II: The New Kingdom.* Berkeley: University of California Press, 1976.

Linafelt, Tod. "Taking Women in Samuel: Readers/Responses/Responsibility." Pages 99–113 in *Reading Between Texts: Intertextuality and the Bible.* Edited by Danna Fewell. Louisville: WJKP, 1992.

Lindars, Barnabas. "Jotham's Fable – A New Form-Critical Analysis." *Journal of Theological Studies* 24 (1973): 355–66.

Long, Burke O. "The Stylistic Components of Jeremiah 3, 1–5." *ZAW* 88 (1976): 386–90.

———. *1 Kings with an Introduction to Historical Literature.* FOTL 9. Grand Rapids: Eerdmans, 1984.

———. "Historical Narrative and the Fictionalizing Imagination." *VT* 35.4 (1985): 405–16.

———. *2 Kings.* FOTL 10. Grand Rapids: Eerdmans, 1991.

Lyke, Larry L. *King David with the Wise Woman of Tekoa: The Resonance of Tradition in Parabolic Narrative.* JSOT Supplement 255. Sheffield: Sheffield Academic Press, 1997.

Macartney, Clarence Edward. *The Parables of the Old Testament.* New York: Fleming H. Revell, 1916.

MacDougall, John. *The Old Testament Parables.* London: James Clarke and Company, 1934.

Maly, Eugene H. "The Jotham Fable – Anti-Monarchical?" *CBQ* 22 (1960): 299–305.

Matthews, Victor H. *Judges and Ruth.* Cambridge: Cambridge University Press, 2004.

——— and Don C. Benjamin. *Old Testament Parallels: Laws and Stories from the Ancient Near East.* New York: Paulist, 1997.

Mauchline, John. *1 and 2 Samuel.* London: Oliphants, 1971.

McArthur, Harvey K. and Robert M. Johnston. *They Also Taught in Parables.* Grand Rapids: Zondervan, 1990.

McCarter, P. Kyle. "The Apology of David." *JBL* 99 (1980): 489–504.

———. *2 Samuel: A New Translation with Introduction and Commentary.* AB 9. Garden City, NY: Doubleday, 1984.

McCarthy, Dennis. "*Elba, horkia temnein, tb, šlm*: Addenda to *Treaty and Covenant*." *Bib* 60 (1979): 247–53.
McKane, William. *Proverbs: A New Approach*. OTL. Philadelphia: Westminster, 1970.
McKenzie, Steven. *King David: A Biography*. Oxford: Oxford University Press, 2000.
Mendenhall, George E. "Puppy and Lettuce in Northwest-Semitic Covenant Making." *BASOR* 133 (1954): 26–30.
Miller, Patrick D. *Sin and Judgment in the Prophets: A Stylistic and Theological Analysis*. Society of Biblical Literature Monograph Series 27. Chico, CA: Scholars, 1982.
Miscall, Peter D. *Isaiah*. Sheffield: JSOT Press, 1993.
Montgomery, James A. *A Critical and Exegetical Commentary on the Books of Kings*. ICC. Edinburgh: T. and T. Clark, 1976.
Moore, George F. *A Critical and Exegetical Commentary on Judges*. ICC. New York: C. Scribner's Sons, 1895.
Murphy, Roland E. *The Tree of Life: An Exploration of Biblical Wisdom Literature*. Grand Rapids: Eerdmans, 1996.
Nelson, Richard. *First and Second Kings*. IBC. Louisville: John Knox, 1987.
Newsom, Carol A. "Spying Out the Land: A Report from Genology." Pages 19–30 in *Bakhtin and Genre Theory in Biblical Studies*. Edited by Roland Boer. Semeia Studies 63. Atlanta: Society of Biblical Literature, 2007.
Niditch, Susan. *Folklore and the Hebrew Bible*. Guides to Biblical Scholarship. Minneapolis: Fortress, 1993.
———. *Judges: A Commentary*. OTL. Louisville: Westminster John Knox, 2008.
Niehr, H. "Zur Gattung von Jes 5, 1–7." *BZ* 30 (1986): 99–104.
Nitzan, Bilhah. "4Q302/302a (Sap. A): Pap. Praise of God and Parable of the Tree: A Preliminary Edition," *RevQ* 17/1–4 (1996): 151–73.
———. "Post-Biblical *Rib* Pattern Admonitions in 4Q302/302a and 4Q381 69, 77–77." Pages 159–74 in *Biblical Perspectives: Early Use and Interpretation of the Bible in Light of the Dead Sea Scrolls*. STDJ 28. Edited by Michael E. Stone and Esther G. Chazon. Leiden: Brill, 1998.
Noegel, Scott B. *Nocturnal Ciphers: The Allusive Language of Dreams in the Ancient Near East*. New Haven: American Oriental Society, 2007.
Ogden, Graham S. "Jotham's Fable: Its Structure and Function in Judges 9." *BT* 46 (1995): 301–8.
Olson, Dennis T. "The Book of Judges: Introduction, Commentary, and Reflections." *NIB* 2: 723–888.
———. "Buber, Kingship, and the Book of Judges: A Study of Judges 6–9 and 17–21." Pages 199–218 in *David and Zion: Biblical Studies in Honor of J. J. M. Roberts*. Edited by Bernard F. Batto and Kathryn L. Roberts. Winona Lake, IN: Eisenbrauns, 2004.
Oppenheim, Leo. *Letters from Mesopotamia*. Chicago: University of Chicago Press, 1967.
Page, Stephanie. "A Stele of Adad-Nirari III and Nergal Ereš from Tell al Rimah." *Iraq* 30 (1968): 139–53.
Pakkala, Juha. "Zedekiah's Fate and the Dynastic Succession." *JBL* 125.3 (2006): 443–52.
Parker, Simon B. *Stories in Scripture and Inscriptions: Comparative Studies on Narratives in Northwest Semitic Inscriptions and the Hebrew Bible*. New York: Oxford University Press, 1997.

Pearse, Mark Guy. *The Bramble King and Other Old Testament Parables.* London: Charles H. Kelly, 1900.
Pirot, Jean. "Le *māšāl* dans l'Ancien Testament." *RSR* 37 (1950): 565–80.
Polk, Timothy. "Paradigms, Parables, and *Mĕšālîm*: On Reading the *Māšāl* in Scripture." *CBQ* 45.4 (1983): 564–83.
Polzin, Robert. *David and the Deuteronomist: A Literary Study of the Deuteronomic History: Part Three: 2 Samuel.* Bloomington: Indiana University Press, 1993.
Propp, William H. "Kinship in 2 Samuel 13." *CBQ* 55 (1993): 39–53.
Pyper, Hugh. *David as Reader: 2 Samuel 12:1–15 and the Poetics of Fatherhood.* Leiden: Brill, 1996.
Sasson, Jack M. "Water beneath Straw: Adventures of a Prophetic Phrase in the Mari Archives." Pages 599–608 in *Solving Riddles and Untying Knots: Biblical, Epigraphic, and Semitic Studies in Honor of Jonas C. Greenfield.* Edited by Ziony Zevit, Seymour Gitin, Michael Sokoloff. Winona Lake, IN: Eisenbrauns.
Sasson, Victor. "An Unrecognized Juridical Term in the Yavneh-Yam Lawsuit and in an Unnoticed Biblical Parallel." *BASOR* 232 (1978): 57–63.
Schipper, Jeremy. "Narrative Obscurity of Samson's Riddle in Judges 14.14 and 18." *JSOT* 27.1 (2003): 339–53.
———. "'Significant Resonances' with Mephibosheth in 2 Kings 25:27–30: A Response to Donald F. Murray." *JBL* 124.3 (2005): 521–9.
———. *Disability Studies and the Hebrew Bible: Figuring Mephibosheth in the David Story.* LHBOTS 441. New York: T. and T. Clark, 2006.
———. "'Exile Atones for Everything': Coping with Jeremiah 22.24–30." *JSOT* 31.4 (2007): 481–92.
Schloen, J. David. *The House of the Father as Fact and Symbol: Patrimonialism in Ugarit and the Ancient Near East.* Winona Lake, IN: Eisenbrauns, 2001.
Schneider, Tammi J. *Judges.* Berit Olam. Collegeville, MN: Liturical, 2000.
Schöpflin, Karin. "Jotham's Speech and Fable as Prophetic Comment on Abimelech's Fable: The Genesis of Judges 9." *SJOT* 18 (2004): 3–22.
Schottroff, W. "Das Weinberglied Jesajas (Jes 5,1–7): Ein Beitrag zur Geschichte der Parabel." *ZAW* 82 (1970): 68–91.
Seow, C. L. "The First and Second Books of Kings: Introduction, Commentary, and Reflections." *NIB* 3: 1–295.
Sheppard, Gerald T. "More on Isaiah 5:1–7 as a Juridical Parable." *CBQ* 44 (1982): 45–7.
Simian-Yofre, H. "Ez 17, 1–10 como enigma y parabola." *Bib* 65 (1984): 27–43.
Simon, Uriel. "The Parable of Jotham (Judges ix. 8–15): The Parable, its Application and the Narrative Framework." *Tarbis* 34 (1964–65): 1–34.
———. "The Poor Man's Ewe-Lamb: An Example of a Juridical Parable." *Bib* 48 (1967): 207–42.
Soggin, J. Alberto. *Judges: A Commentary.* OTL. Philadelphia: Westminster, 1981.
Solomon, Ann M. Vater. "Fable." Pages 114–25 in *Saga, Tale, Novella, Fable: Narrative Forms in Old Testament Literature.* JSOT Supplement 35. Edited by George W. Coats. Sheffield: JSOT Press, 1985.
———. "Jehoash's Fable of the Thistle and the Cedar (2 Kings 14.8–14 and 2 Chronicles 25.17–24)." Pages 126–32 in *Saga, Tale, Novella, Fable: Narrative Forms in Old*

Testament Narrative. JSOT Supplement 35. Edited by George W. Coats. Sheffield: JSOT Press, 1985.

Stoebe, Hans Joachim. *Das zweite Buch Samuelis.* Gütersloh: Gütersloher Verlagshaus, 1994.

Stern, David. *Parables in Midrash: Narrative and Exegesis in Rabbinic Literature.* Cambridge: Harvard University Press, 1991.

Stern, Philip D. "The *herem* in 1 Kgs 20,42 as an Exegetical Problem." *Bib* 71 (1990): 43–7.

Sternberg, Meir. *The Poetics of Biblical Narrative: Ideological Literature and the Drama of Reading.* Bloomington: Indiana University Press, 1987.

Sternberg, Naomi. "Social Scientific Criticism." Pages 45–64 in *Judges and Method: New Approaches in Biblical Studies.* Edited by Gale Yee. Minneapolis: Fortress, 1995.

Stewart, R. "The Parable Form in the Old Testament and Rabbinic Literature." *EvQ* 36 (1964): 133–47.

Steymans, Hans Ulrich. *Deuteronomium 28 und die adê zur Thronfolgeregelung Asarhaddons: Segen und Fluch im Alten Orient und in Israel.* OBO 45. Freiburg: Universitätsverlag, 1996.

Stipp, Herman-Josef. "Zedekiah in the Book of Jeremiah: On the Formation of a Biblical Character." *CBQ* 58 (1996): 627–48.

Suter, David Winston. "*Mašāl* in the Similitudes of Enoch," *JBL* 100.2 (1981): 193–212.

Sweeney, Marvin A. *Isaiah 1–39, with an Introduction to Prophetic Literature.* FOTL XVI. Grand Rapids: Eerdmans, 1996.

———. *I and II Kings: A Commentary.* OTL. Louisville: Westminster John Knox, 2007.

——— and Ehud Ben Zvi. Introduction to *The Changing Face of Form Criticism for the Twenty-First Century.* Edited by Marvin Sweeney and Ehud Ben Zvi. Grand Rapids: Eerdmans, 2003.

Tatu, Silviu. "Jotham's Fable and the *Crux Interpretum* in Judges IX." *VT* 56 (2006): 105–24.

Tsevat, Matitiahu. "The Neo-Assyrian and Neo-Babylonian Vassal Oaths and the Prophet Ezekiel." *JBL* 78 (1959): 199–204.

Tucker, Gene M. "The Book of Isaiah 1–39: Introduction, Commentary, and Reflections." *NIB* 6: 25–305.

Tull, Patricia. "Jonathan's Gift of Friendship." *Int* 58 (2004): 130–43.

Turner, Mark. *The Literary Mind: Origins of Thought and Language.* New York: Oxford University Press, 1998.

Van Wyk, W. C. "The Fable of Jotham in Its Ancient Near Eastern Context." Pages 89–95 in *Studies in Wisdom Literature.* Ou-Testamentiese Werkgemeenskap in Suider-Afrika, 15 and 16. Edited by W. C. Van Wyk. Hercules, South Africa: N. H. W. Press, 1981.

Walsh, Carey Ellen. "God's Vineyard: Isaiah's Prophecy as Vintner's Textbook" *BRev* 14.4 (August 1998): 43–49, 52–53.

———. *The Fruit of the Vine: Viticulture in Ancient Israel.* HSM 60. Winona Lake, IN: Eisenbrauns, 2000.

Walsh, Jerome T. *1 Kings.* Berit Olam. Collegeville, MN: Liturgical, 1996.

Webb, Barry G. *The Book of Judges: An Integrated Reading*. JSOT Supplement 46. Sheffield: Sheffield Academic Press, 1987.

Weeks, Noel. *Admonition and Curse: The Ancient Near Eastern Treaty/Covenant Form as a Problem in Inter-Cultural Relationships*. JSOT Supplement 407. London: T. and T. Clark, 2004.

Wesselius, J. W. "Joab's Death and the Central Theme of the Succession Narrative, (2 Samuel 9 – 1 Kings 20)." *VT* 40 (1990): 346–7.

Westbrook, Raymond. *Studies in Biblical and Cuneiform Law*. Cahiers de la Revue Biblique 16. Paris: Gabalda, 1988.

Westermann, Claus. *The Parables of Jesus in the Light of the Old Testament*. Translated and edited by Friedemann W. Golka and Alastair H. B. Logan. Minneapolis, MN: Fortress, 1990.

Whedbee, J. William. *Isaiah and Wisdom*. Nashville: Abingdon Press, 1971.

Whitelam, Keith W. *The Just King: Monarchical Judicial Authority in Ancient Israel*. JSOT Supplement 12. Sheffield: JSOT Press, 1979.

Willey, Patricia K. "The Importunate Woman of Tekoa and How She Got Her Way." Pages 115–31 in *Reading Between Texts: Intertextuality and the Hebrew Bible*. Edited by Danna Nolan Fewell. Louisville: WJKP, 1992.

William, Gary Roye. "Frustrated Expectations in Isaiah V 1–7: A Literary Interpretation." *VT* 35.4 (1985): 459–65.

Williams, Ronald J. "The Fable in the Ancient Near East." Pages 89–95 in *A Stubborn Faith: Papers on the Old Testament and Related Subject Presented to Honor W. A. Irwin*. Edited by Edward Craig Hobbs. Dallas: Southern Methodist University Press, 1956.

Williamson, H. G. M. *A Critical and Exegetical Commentary on Isaiah 1–27: Volume 1: Commentary on Isaiah 1–5*. 3 vols. ICC. New York: T. and T. Clark, 2006.

Willis, John T. "The Genre of Isaiah 5:1–7." *JBL* 96 (1977): 337–62.

Yee, Gale A. "A Form-Critical Study of Isaiah 5:1–7 as a Song and a Juridical Parable." *CBQ* 43 (1981): 30–40.

Zimmerli, Walther. *Ezekiel 1: A Commentary on the Book of Ezekiel, Chapters 1–24*. Hermeneia. Translated by Ronald E. Clements. Philadelphia: Fortress, 1979.

Scriptural and Extra-Biblical Texts Index

Genesis
- 2:17 — 138
- 3:4 — 138
- 4:15 — 50
- 4:24 — 50
- 10:9 — 5
- 22 — 30
- 31:35 — 85
- 34 — 141
- 37–41 — 46
- 37:6–8 — 14
- 37:30 — 77
- 37–41 — 127
- 41 — 46
- 41:55 — 78
- 42:13 — 77
- 42:21–23 — 94
- 42:32 — 77
- 42:36 — 77
- 44:12 — 85

Exodus
- 5:2 — 88
- 5:15 — 78
- 6:7 — 88
- 7:5 — 88
- 8:11 — 107
- 8:28 — 107
- 9:34 — 107
- 10:1 — 107
- 10:2 — 88
- 14:4 — 88
- 14:18 — 88
- 14:25 — 88
- 19:4 — 118
- 20:5 — 121
- 21:12 — 65
- 21:32 — 78
- 21:37 — 50
- 22:23 — 78
- 22:26 — 78
- 34:7 — 121

Leviticus
- 23:34–43 — 116

Numbers
- 12:6–8 — 46, 119
- 14:18 — 121
- 21:27–30 — 12
- 21:34 — 86
- 35:21 — 68

Deuteronomy
- 2:5 — 98
- 2:9 — 98
- 2:19 — 98
- 2:24 — 98
- 5:9 — 121
- 11:19 — 29
- 16:13 — 116
- 16:13–15 — 116
- 17:17 — 84
- 24:16 — 105, 122
- 27:12 — 29
- 27–29 — 28
- 28:37 — 12, 100
- 29:22 — 34
- 32:11 — 118

Joshua
- 6:2 — 86
- 6:12–21 — 88

Joshua (cont.)

6:20	89
6	86
8:1	86
8:33	29
19:38	97

Judges

1:1–3	86
1:33	97
3:10	31
4:6–7	86
6:34	31
6:36–40	86
7:13–15	46
8:2	13
8:21	13
8:22	27
8:23	27
8:23–10:1	37
9	v, 2, 6, 7, 10, 19, 20, 23, 24, 26, 27, 28, 30, 31, 32, 33, 36, 37, 38, 39, 40, 43, 93, 103, 108, 109, 115, 129, 130, 131, 132, 151, 153, 155, 156
9:2	27
9:3	24, 25
9:4	36
9:5	23, 24, 32
9:6	33
9:7	31
9:7–15	24, 25, 93
9:7–21	14
9:8–13	27
9:8–14	28
9:8–15	27, 28, 77
9:14	27
9:15	24, 27, 28, 29, 33, 35
9:16	29
9:18	29, 30, 36
9:19	29, 31
9:20	29, 30, 31, 35
9:21	23
9:21–57	28
9:23–24	31
9:23–57	32, 37
9:25	32, 36
9:26	32
9:26–55	31
9:27	28
9:28	32
9:28–29	32
9:30–33	33
9:34	33, 36
9:34–49	25
9:35–39	33
9:36	33, 36
9:37	33, 36
9:38	34
9:39–41	34
9:43	36
9:43–44	34
9:44	36
9:48	34
9:49	35
9:51	35
9:52	35
9:53	35, 36, 37
9:54	37
9:56	37
9:56–57	30, 36
9:57	25, 28, 30, 31, 36
9	35
11:29	31
13–16	17
14:3–4	17
14:6	31
14:19	31
14:12–14	17
14:14	5, 117
14:18–19	17
15:9–11	17
15:14	31
15:19	31
16:9	31
20:18–28	86

1 Samuel

10:12	5
14:45	68
16:7	13
17:10	101
17:25	101
17:26	101
17:36	101
17:44	101
17:45	101
18–24	13
19:24	5
22:15	80

SCRIPTURAL AND EXTRA-BIBLICAL TEXTS INDEX

23:4	86	12:6	45, 50, 51
23:23	85	12:7	51, 79
24:13–14	13	12:7–12	41, 47, 48, 51, 114
24:14	5, 13	12:7–15	42, 52, 53
24:17–21	13	12:8	47
25	60, 61, 62	12:9	52
25:24	61, 66	12:9–10	52
26:1–2	13	12:10–11	54
		12:9–15	20
2 Samuel		12:11–12	53, 54
1:14–26	49	12:13	54
2:1	86	12:14	54
2:22–23	101	12:16–17	54, 55
3	55	12:20	55
3:6–39	71	12:24	55
3:27	49	12:26–31	72
3:28–29	49, 66, 67	13–14	71
3:28–35	49	13	56, 57, 58, 65, 70
3:35	55	13:21	65
3:38	49	13:39	65
3:39	67, 72	13:32–36	63
4:9	50	14	vi, 7, 9, 10, 15, 20, 23, 38, 39, 45, 56, 57, 58, 59, 61, 62, 65, 66, 72, 74, 83, 100, 108, 109, 118
4:9–11	49		
5	101		
5:6	101		
5:19	86		
7:12–16	120	14:1–24	43
11	20, 41, 42, 47, 48, 49, 52, 53, 54, 55, 60	14:1–11	61
		14:1	58, 63
11–12	20, 40, 83, 84	14:2	57, 63
11:3	52	14:3	63
11:4	47, 48, 54	14:5–7	1, 62, 63, 64, 67, 69
11:4–5	55	14:5–8	63
11:7	47	14:5–17	70
11:11	48, 52	14:8	66
11:11–13	55	14:9	61, 64, 66, 67, 68
11:22	37, 50	14:9–17	66
11:25	49, 51, 53	14:10	45, 67
11:25–27	51	14:11	64, 68
11:26	52	14:13–14	57, 66, 69
11:27	42, 49, 52	14:13	68, 69
12	7, 23, 39, 40, 42, 43, 45, 47, 54, 58, 63, 97, 108, 109, 115, 118	14:14	69
		14:15–17	69, 70
		14:17	60, 66, 70
12:1–4	1, 14, 41, 53, 77	14:18–23	70
12:1–6	51, 115	14:18–19	70
12:1–7	17, 64	14:19–20	64
12:3	47, 52	14:19	70, 71
12:4	45, 47, 48	14:20	71, 72
12:5	45, 49, 50	14:21–22	60
12:5–6	42, 49, 51, 55	14:21	71

2 Samuel (*cont.*)		20:15–21	75
14:22	71	20:15	78
14:23	71	20:16	87
14:24	59	20:17	79, 84
14:26	68	20:18	88, 89
14:28	59	20:20–29	88
14:32	59	20:20–21	86
15–18	53	20:20	88
16:21	53	20:22	87, 90
16:22	53	20:23–27	75
18:9	68	20:23	88, 91
18:14–15	63	20:27	78
19:27	80	20:28	75, 88, 91
19:29	80	20:29–30	75
20:10	49	20:29	88
21	101	20:30	89
23:34	54	20:31–34	80, 85, 87, 90, 91
		20:31–32	80
1 Kings		20:31	80, 81
3	61, 74	20:32–34	84
3:16–30	43, 83	20:32	80, 81, 84, 89
9:7	12	20:33	81
9:13	84	20:34	75, 79, 84, 91, 92
10:1	16, 64, 118	20:35–43	43, 83, 87
11:36	120	20:35–37	89, 90
13:20–26	90	20:35–36	90
15:4	120	20:35	75, 90
20–21	82, 91	20:36	90
20	vi, 2, 7, 9, 10, 13, 17, 21, 34, 38, 45, 69, 73, 74, 75, 76, 79, 80, 82, 83, 86, 88, 89, 90, 91, 92, 93, 100, 105, 108, 109, 115, 118	20:37	80, 90
		20:38–43	74–75, 85, 87
		20:39–42	1
		20:39–40	79, 83
		20:39	78, 81, 90
		20:40	77
20:1–34	79, 83	20:41	81
20:1–12	75	20:41 LXX	77
20:1	83	20:42	76, 79, 80, 81, 82, 84, 87, 90, 91
20:2	79, 84		
20:3–4	84, 91	20:43	77
20:5	79, 84	21	91
20:6–7	84	21:1–16	91
20:6	79, 84	21:4	77
20:7–8	81	21:8–16	82
20:7	79, 84, 87	21:17–19	82
20:9	79, 84, 85	21:17–29	77, 108
20:10	79, 84, 85	22	92
20:11	5, 6, 13, 85, 100		
		2 Kings	
20:13–14	75	1:1–17	77, 108
20:12	13, 88	2:5–6	49, 71
20:13	85, 88, 91	3	30
20:14	81, 86, 88	4:1	78

SCRIPTURAL AND EXTRA-BIBLICAL TEXTS INDEX

6	61, 74	7:23	113
6:24–30	83	14:4	12, 100
6:26	78	16	115
8:3	78	16:10	113, 114
8:19	120	17:14	77
8:26	96	28:23–29	5
10:24	78	32	115
12:21	105	32:9–14	114
14	vi, 2, 7, 8, 10, 21, 34, 93, 96, 98, 103, 105, 106, 107, 108, 109	32:10	114
		32:12	114
		32:13	114
14:3	105	37	120
14:7	93, 105	40	122
14:8	94, 96, 98	41	122
14:8–11	17		
14:8–14	14	Jeremiah	
14:8–15	94	3:1–5	1
14:9–10	77, 108	4:8	80
14:9	97, 98, 100, 102	19:1–15	89
14:10	97, 98, 99, 106, 108	21:1–10	108, 120
14:11–14	94	22:24–30	120
14:11	94, 96, 98, 99, 106	24:9	12, 28, 100
14:12–14	107	27:1–22	89
14:15	94, 95	27:1–29:24	89, 120
14:19–20	95	28	120
16:7	80	30	122
18:15	84	31	122
19	120	31:15	77
20:12–19	84	31:29–30	105, 122
		31:39	5, 11
Isaiah		32:3–5	120
1:8	113	34:1–5	108
3:13–15	113	34:1–7	120
5	20, 122	37:7–10	120
5:1–7	1, 5, 14, 22, 45, 77, 110, 111, 113, 115, 116, 117, 118, 122	37:13–14	120
		38:4	120
		48:20	117
5:1–6	43, 44	49:22	117
5:1–2	111, 112, 115, 116	50:24	98
5:1	116		
5:3–6	114	Ezekiel	
5:3–4	112	1:10	118
5:3	113, 115	5:15	12
5:4	116	6:7	88
5:5–7	115	7:4	88
5:5–6	112, 113, 114, 115, 117	10:14	118
		11:10	88
5:5	114	12:1–15	119
5:6	114	12:9	118
5:7	44, 111, 112, 113, 114, 115, 116, 117	12:10–15	118
		12:22	5, 11, 121
7	120	14:8	12

Ezekiel (*cont.*)		14:8	113
15:1–28	5, 44, 117		
16:1–58	5, 44, 117	Amos	
17	20, 120, 121, 122	5:18	5
		7:11	77, 108
17:1–10	5, 6, 44, 117, 122	9:3	85
17:1	117		
17:1–21	22	Micah	
17:1–24	110, 111, 117	2:4	12
17:2–10	14, 15, 17, 43, 44, 77, 117, 118	Habakkuk	
17:2	5, 16, 119, 121	2:6	12, 16
17:3–4	119		
17:3	15	Zephaniah	
17:4	120	1:12	85
17:5–6	119		
17:7–8	119	Psalms	
17:7	44	37:36	77
17:9–10	15, 119	44:15	12
17:11–21	15, 44, 119, 120, 121	45:1	116
		49	3, 10, 19
17:12	15, 111, 117, 118, 119, 121	49:5	16
		69:12	12
17:13–14	119	72:2	45
17:15	119	78	3, 10, 19
17:16–21	117	78:2	16
17:16–18	120	79:12	50
17:16	120	133:1	41, 52
17:20	120		
17:22–24	118, 120, 121	Proverbs	
18:1–4	121, 122	1:6	16, 118
18:2–4	121	9:1–6	5
18:2	5, 11, 121	10:4	43
18:4	105	13:7	43
18:20	105	13:8	43
19:1–14	77	14:20	43
19:2–14	5, 44, 117	18:23	43
20:42	88	22:2	43
21:1–4	44	24:30–32	5
21:5	44, 113, 122	26:7	16, 118
23:1–29	5, 44, 117	26:9	16, 118
24	90	28:6	43
24:3	5, 121		
24:3–5	17	Job	
24:3–14	5, 6, 44, 117	17:6	12
24:19	44, 113, 118	19:7	78
36:11	88	27	3, 10, 19
37:6	88	29–31	3, 10, 19
		33:15–33	5
Hosea			
9:8	113	Song of Songs	
10:1	113	8:11–13	116

SCRIPTURAL AND EXTRA-BIBLICAL TEXTS INDEX

Lamentations		25:13	96, 105
2:10	80	25:14–15	105
5:7	121	25:16	105
		25:17	96, 105
Ecclesiastes		25:18	94
8:1	111	25:19	99, 106, 107, 108
12:9	16, 46, 118	25:20–24	94
		25:20	106
Esther	61	25:21	96
		25:22–24	107
Daniel		35:21–22	101
2	46	36:13	120
6	46		
8:23	16, 118	Apocrypha	

Nehemiah		Sirach	
2:5	80	20:20	16, 118
6:13	12	39:3	16
		47:17	16

2 Chronicles		Wisdom	
9:1	16, 64	8:8	16
13:3	86		
22:2	96	Talmud and Midrash	
24:25	105	*b. B. Bat*, 15a	6
25	7, 10, 21, 93, 94, 96, 103, 105, 106, 107, 108, 109	*b. Sanh*, 20a	48
		b. Sukkah, 52b	47
		Song. Rab, 1:8	6
25:1–28	14		
25:2	105	Dead Sea Scrolls	
25:5–16	93	4Q302	19

General Index

Abimelech, 19, 23, 24, 25, 26, 27, 29, 30, 31, 32, 33, 34, 35, 36, 37, 108, 115, 129, 130, 131, 132, 149, 150, 152, 156
Abner, 49, 55, 66, 71, 135
Absalom, 20, 49, 53, 57, 58, 59, 60, 63, 67, 68, 69, 71, 72, 137
Ackerman, Susan, 114, 144, 149
Ahab, vi, 13, 21, 73, 74, 75, 76, 77, 78, 79, 80, 81, 82, 83, 84, 85, 86, 87, 88, 89, 90, 91, 100, 105, 108, 139
allegory, 15, 27, 28, 30, 46, 52, 64, 97, 112, 119, 133, 137
Alter, Robert, 44
Amaziah, 8, 93, 94, 95, 96, 97, 98, 99, 100, 101, 103, 104, 105, 106, 107, 108, 109, 141, 142
Amnon, 41, 58, 63

Bathsheba, 41, 47, 48, 52, 53, 54, 55, 134, 135, 136, 150
Bellefontaine, Elizabeth, 60
Ben-Hadad, 13, 21, 74, 75, 76, 77, 78, 79, 80, 81, 82, 83, 84, 85, 86, 87, 89, 90, 91, 100, 139
bramble, 19, 25, 27, 28, 29, 30, 33, 35, 37, 38, 94, 96, 97, 98, 100, 101, 103, 106, 115, 131, 141
Brueggemann, Walter, 98, 100, 132, 134, 137, 138, 139, 141, 150
Buber, Martin, 26

cedar, 94, 96, 97, 98, 99, 103, 119, 141
cedars, 25, 28, 29, 33, 35, 120
Coats, George, 1, 2, 59, 61, 125, 126, 128, 133, 134, 137, 138, 141, 150, 156
curse, 4, 10, 20, 23, 24, 28, 29, 30, 31, 32, 33, 34, 35, 36, 37, 38, 115, 130, 131

Daniel, 20, 46, 127, 134, 145, 149

David, v, 1, 13, 20, 37, 39, 40, 41, 42, 43, 44, 45, 46, 47, 48, 49, 50, 51, 52, 53, 54, 55, 56, 57, 58, 59, 60, 61, 62, 63, 64, 65, 66, 67, 68, 69, 70, 71, 72, 79, 83, 98, 101, 105, 108, 125, 126, 127, 128, 129, 130, 131, 132, 133, 134, 135, 136, 137, 138, 139, 140, 146, 149, 150, 151, 152, 153, 154, 155, 156, 157
Derrida, Jacques, 8, 127, 151
Deuteronomistic History, vi, 95, 107, 109, 110
diplomacy, 21, 85, 101
Disputation Texts, vi, 12, 100
Dobbs-Allsopp, F. W., 62, 137, 138, 151
Dream, 46, 134, 152, 153

eagle, 44, 104, 117, 119, 120, 145
Edom, 21, 93, 94, 97, 106
Egypt, 120
Etana, 104, 142
ewe lamb, 41, 47, 48, 50, 51, 52, 135
Ezekiel, 2, 7, 15, 20, 22, 44, 88, 90, 111, 117, 118, 119, 120, 121, 122, 123, 128, 129, 134, 145, 146, 149, 151, 152, 154, 157

fable, 14, 20, 23, 24, 25, 27, 28, 29, 30, 35, 37, 41, 42, 43, 44, 45, 46, 47, 48, 49, 52, 55, 56, 58, 77, 93, 94, 100, 101, 102, 103, 106, 108, 115, 117, 118, 119, 120, 121, 123, 128, 129, 130, 134, 142, 144
familial, 20, 42, 52, 53, 56, 60, 64, 65, 66, 67, 68, 70, 71, 84, 140
Fokkelman, Jan, 30, 43, 131, 133, 137, 151
Fontaine, Carole, 3, 13
Fowler, Alastair, 8

Gaal, 32, 33, 34, 36, 132

GENERAL INDEX

genre, i, 1, 2, 4, 7, 8, 9, 10, 12, 19, 20, 21, 24, 26, 27, 29, 30, 38, 42, 44, 55, 58, 60, 61, 62, 63, 65, 66, 68, 69, 73, 74, 76, 77, 78, 79, 80, 81, 95, 100, 101, 102, 104, 108, 112, 115, 116, 117, 122, 127, 130, 133, 139, 143, 144
Gideon, 24, 25, 27, 29, 30, 31, 36, 131
Goulder, M.D., 1, 152
Gunkel, Hermann, 7, 47, 135, 152

Hens-Piazza, Gina, 100, 141, 152
hidah, 16, 17, 117, 118
hidot, 16, 17, 117, 119
Hoftijzer, Jean, 59, 125, 133, 137, 138, 153
Horus, 11, 28, 61, 62, 137
hostile actions, i, 4, 12, 18, 21, 32, 95, 104, 107, 115, 117, 123
House of Millo, 23, 25, 26, 29, 31, 32, 33, 34, 35, 115

Isaiah, 1, 2, 7, 20, 22, 45, 111, 112, 113, 114, 115, 116, 117, 120, 122, 123, 125, 133, 142, 143, 144, 150, 151, 152, 153, 155, 156, 157
Isis, 11, 61, 62, 137

Japhet, Sara, 99, 103, 140, 141, 142, 153
Jehoash, vi, 8, 93, 94, 95, 96, 97, 98, 99, 100, 101, 102, 103, 104, 105, 106, 107, 108, 109, 141, 156
Jehoiachin, 119, 120, 146, 147
Jeremiah, 108, 120, 122, 133, 143, 145, 146, 149, 154, 156
Joab, vi, 21, 42, 48, 49, 50, 51, 57, 58, 59, 60, 63, 66, 67, 68, 69, 71, 72, 135, 136, 138, 150
Joseph, 46, 134, 145, 151
Jotham, v, 6, 19, 23, 24, 25, 26, 27, 28, 29, 30, 31, 32, 33, 34, 35, 36, 37, 38, 39, 40, 43, 93, 103, 108, 115, 129, 130, 131, 151, 154, 155, 156, 157
juridical parable, 1, 21, 42, 44, 45, 65, 112, 113, 115, 125, 143, 144

kinship, 23, 32, 38, 56, 132

Lambert, Wilfred, 102, 103, 141, 142, 153
Lebanon, 8, 25, 28, 29, 33, 35, 94, 119, 120, 131, 145
Levenson, Jon, 120, 146
Levinson, Bernard, 121, 122, 146, 154
Lindars, Barnabas, 27, 28, 29, 129, 130, 154
Long, Burke, 102
Lyke, Larry, 26, 35, 47, 57, 60, 61, 62, 91, 128, 129, 130, 132, 134, 137, 138, 139, 140, 154

Maly, Eugene, 26, 129, 130, 131, 154
mashal, 1, 2, 5, 6, 12, 13, 14, 15, 16, 17, 43, 46, 57, 85, 100, 111, 117, 118, 121, 122, 125, 142, 144
McCarter, P. Kyle, 50, 132, 135, 136, 138, 141, 154
mercy, 21, 43, 45, 51, 59, 62, 65, 66, 70, 74, 75, 76, 78, 80, 81, 82, 85, 86, 87, 139
Mesad Hashavyahu, 62, 66, 70, 83, 137, 138, 151
meshalim, 1, 2, 3, 5, 6, 7, 10, 11, 12, 13, 14, 16, 17, 18, 43, 46, 100, 101, 117, 118, 121, 122, 125, 126, 128

Nathan, v, 1, 20, 40, 41, 42, 43, 44, 45, 46, 47, 48, 49, 51, 52, 53, 54, 55, 56, 58, 63, 79, 97, 108, 114, 132, 133, 134, 135, 137, 142, 143, 153
Nelson, Richard, 100, 139, 140, 141, 155
Newsom, Carol, 8, 127, 155
Noegel, Scott, 46, 134, 136, 155

Ogden, Graham, 23, 31, 130, 131, 155
Olson, Dennis, 24, 35, 129, 131, 132, 155

parable, 1, 2, 3, 4, 6, 7, 8, 10, 11, 14, 15, 16, 17, 19, 20, 21, 23, 24, 25, 26, 27, 28, 29, 30, 31, 32, 33, 34, 35, 36, 37, 38, 39, 40, 41, 42, 43, 44, 45, 47, 48, 49, 50, 51, 52, 53, 54, 55, 56, 57, 58, 59, 60, 63, 70, 72, 74, 75, 76, 77, 78, 81, 82, 85, 90, 91, 92, 93, 94, 95, 96, 97, 98, 99, 100, 101, 102, 103, 104, 105, 106, 107, 108, 109, 112, 113, 114, 115, 116, 117, 118, 119, 123, 127, 128, 129, 130, 132, 133, 134, 135, 136, 137, 141, 142, 144, 145
Parker, Simon, 44, 45, 62, 64, 74, 79, 83, 126, 133, 138, 139, 155
petitionary narrative, 9, 10, 20, 21, 45, 46, 58, 63, 64, 65, 66, 68, 69, 70, 72, 74, 75, 76, 77, 78, 79, 80, 81, 82, 83, 87, 91, 133, 139
Polk, Timothy, 15, 126, 128, 129, 145, 156
Polzin, Robert, 47, 134, 135, 136, 138, 156
poor man, 41, 47, 48, 52, 98, 136
Pyper, Hugh, 42, 50, 59, 61, 132, 133, 135, 136, 137, 156

Rashi, 47, 89
Redaq, 27, 47, 130
rich man, 41, 44, 45, 47, 48, 49, 50, 51, 52, 98, 135, 136
riddle, 5, 16, 17, 18, 46, 117, 119, 121, 129, 134
riddling, 16, 17, 18, 117, 118, 123

Samson, 17, 129, 156
Saul, 5, 13, 47, 49, 135
Seth, 11, 28, 61, 62, 137

Shechem, 23, 25, 26, 29, 30, 31, 32, 33, 34, 35, 36, 108, 130, 131, 132, 141, 149, 150
Sheppard, Gerald, 113, 125, 133, 143, 156
Simon, Uriel, 1, 42, 43, 44, 45, 59, 62, 65, 74, 79, 112, 113, 125, 126, 131, 133, 137, 138, 139, 143, 151, 155, 156
Solomon, Ann M. Vater, 49, 83, 96, 100, 102, 126, 141, 153, 156
Sweeney, Marvin, 8
Syrian, vi, 21, 75, 77, 87, 88, 89, 91, 98

Tamar, 58
taunts, 4, 8, 10, 12, 13, 14, 34, 85, 100, 101, 104, 141
Tekoa, vi, 20, 43, 56, 57, 58, 59, 60, 61, 63, 64, 65, 66, 67, 68, 69, 70, 71, 72, 74, 75, 100, 108, 128, 129, 130, 132, 134, 137, 138, 139, 140, 154
traveler, 41, 45, 47, 48, 49, 51, 98, 135
twig, 120

Uriah, 41, 42, 47, 48, 49, 50, 51, 52, 53, 54, 98, 135, 136

vineyard, 1, 44, 45, 77, 91, 112, 113, 114, 115, 116, 117, 123, 143, 144
vintage, 114, 116, 117, 122, 144

Walsh, Jerome, 74, 139, 140, 143, 157
Webb, Barry, 23
Westermann, Claus, 18, 126, 129
Willey, Patricia, 57, 60, 137, 138
William, Gary Roye, 116
Williamson, H. G. M., 113, 128, 140, 142, 143, 150
Willis, John, 116
wise woman of Tekoa, 20, 43, 57, 58, 59, 60, 63, 64, 67, 68, 69, 70, 71
word plays, 45, 46, 136
wounded solider, 21, 43, 78

Yee, Gale, 113, 125, 132, 133, 143, 157

Zebul, 32, 33, 34
Zedekiah, 119, 121, 145, 146, 149, 155, 157
Zimmerli, Walther, 121